FLOWER GARDENS

PENELOPE HOBHOUSE

FLOWER GARDENS

FRANCES LINCOLN

Frances Lincoln Limited
Apollo Works, 5 Charlton Kings Road
LONDON NW5 2SB

Flower Gardens
Copyright © Frances Lincoln Limited 1991
Text copyright © Penelope Hobhouse 1991

British Library Cataloguing in Publication Data
    Hobhouse, Penelope
    Flower Gardens
        1. Gardening
        I. Title
        639.9

    ISBN 0-7112-0545-0

Set in Goudy Old Style by SX Composing,
Rayleigh, Essex
Printed and bound in Hong Kong by Kwong Fat
Offset Printing Co. Ltd

First Frances Lincoln Edition: October 1991

9 8 7 6 5 4 3 2 1

HALF TITLE PAGE *Leaf shapes, colours and textures are 'props' as important in a flower garden as flowers themselves. The prickly veined foliage of* Galactites tomentosa *and spiky iris leaves are in total contrast, but their flowers (and those of* Geranium malviflorum) *are in matching tones of mauvy pink.*

TITLE PAGE *In a late summer border at Powis Castle clumps of blue aconitum and the pink turtlehead (*Chelone obliqua) *are provided with a flowering backdrop by the rich velvety blooms of* Clematis × jackmanii *which has been trained on a tripod.*

RIGHT *Chilcombe in Dorset is a perfect flower garden, with a series of separate garden 'rooms' linked by arches and 'green' doorways revealing further vistas. Climbing roses and clematis clamber over old fruit trees and, at ground level, flowers are tightly packed into the beds and borders.*

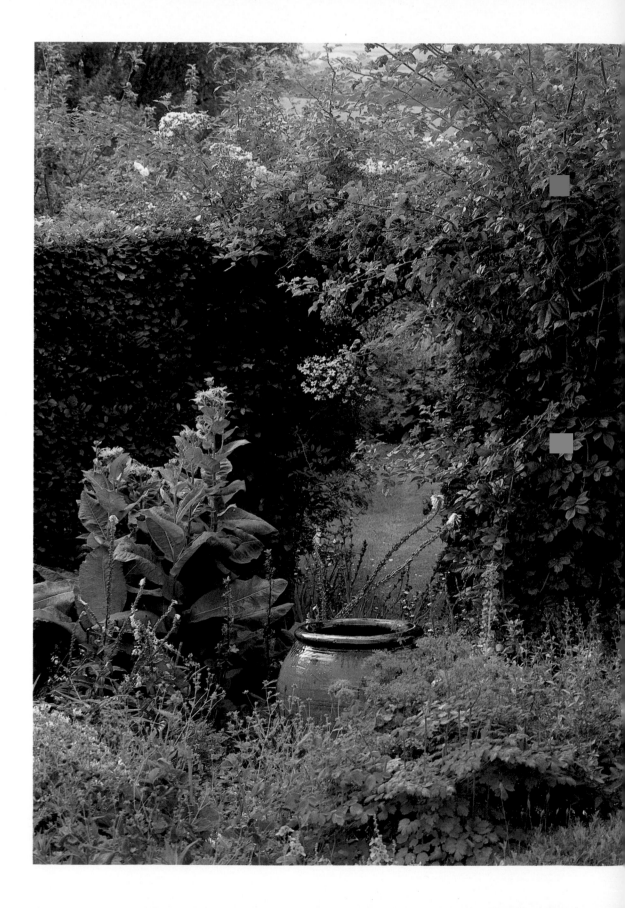

CONTENTS

Introduction   6

INTRODUCTION

When we begin to garden most of us notice individual plants. We fall in love with their beauty and grace before having any clear idea how we might arrange them in a garden. It is the flowers that we find most striking: their colour – often a subtle gradation of tints and shades; the texture of the petals – thick and solid in peonies, fragile and papery in poppies; and their intriguing variety of strange and beautiful shapes. I certainly started like this, wanting to grow certain flowers, rather than beginning with a garden plan and needing to find suitable plants to put in it. I soon extended my 'wants' to include those with wonderful leaves and plant forms as well as interesting blooms.

Even the most irresistible flowering plant, one that I call a 'key' performer, is part of a whole cast; it has to be considered as a component in an overall look as well as for its individual charms. It forms part of the garden. And this is a book about flower gardens rather than simply about flowers as such. In some ways the book's shape follows the broadening perspective I have just described, starting by focusing on flowers in some detail, going on to consider the attributes of a plant as a whole and its potential role in a planting scheme, and then looking at some garden styles where flowers hold the key to the whole effect.

By writing about flowers and how to use them in gardens I feel I am closely involved with the most practical aspects of gardening: not only with the 'hands-on' day-to-day decisions of management, but also with all the design considerations that dictate initial plant and flower choices. My concern in this book is with *flower* gardens as opposed to general principles of garden style and design, although these remain part of a broader philosophy that lies behind all the detail. While considering the more solid virtues of structure, foliage and growing possibilities, I always remember that it is the flowers themselves that in their fleeting and elusive radiance give one the greatest moments of gardening satisfaction.

I feel I am very fortunate to live at Tintinhull, which always seems to me a living, growing example of a true flower garden. It is quite inward-looking, an enclosed oasis, the layout owing little to its setting and more to the trees, walls and hedges that frame it and keep it separate from the surrounding Somerset countryside. Tintinhull's garden is its own world; the flowers have to contribute only to its beauty. It was brilliantly designed and laid out by someone else – we are only guardians for the National Trust – but the garden 'rooms', each with a separate plant or colour theme, provide me with a chance to experiment with all sorts of flowers in different situations. We do have sections in the garden corresponding roughly with the chapter headings in the 'gardens' section of this book. We have different types of border planting – including quite self-conscious colour coordinations – and beds framed by hedges, as well as more natural areas where plants are encouraged to break out of any preconceived role.

Gardening, unlike many other art forms, involves a time scale. Plants change and grow through a season and over the years. By living in a garden and watching plant and flowering performances over a period, one gains some extra sense of what plants can achieve, even allowing for disappointing years of freezing in winter and drought in summer. In fact these trials all give a wider perspective to flower-garden management, and are part of the learning process. I hope this book conveys both the essential joy I find in the beauty of flowers and the pleasures of using flowering plants to make a truly inspirational garden.

Frank Cabot's garden in Canada is eighty miles north of Montreal, near the St Lawrence River. The growing season is short and winters hard, although perennials often lie happily under a protective blanket of snow. The main double borders sloping below the house are planned around an axial grass path which stretches to the tall poplars above. The levels are adjusted by shallow stone risers. Trees and shrubs protect the beds and keep the borders visually separate from the other garden schemes to give more impact. Flower borders are 'made' not only by flowers; attractively coloured and textured leaves are almost as important, providing a frame to set off more fleeting flowers. In July delphiniums, which grow superbly here, back thickly growing clumps of flowering astilbes, cimicifugas and ligularias – all plants chosen for their good foliage as well as for flowering effects.

FLOWERS
IN DETAIL

The attraction of flowers
Plant breeding and selection
Growing healthy flowers

By happy coincidence many of the flowering mechanisms developed by plants to set seed and reproduce also find favour with humans, putting such plants firmly on the list of desirable garden plants. Some wind-pollinated flowers such as catkins and the plumes of grasses possess a subdued beauty. Brightly coloured seeds and berries intended to attract the birds or insects that will ensure their dispersal are also choice plant material for garden display. However, it is with 'flowers proper' that this book is chiefly concerned.

The arrangements developed by flowering plants seeking to attract specific active pollinators, usually from the insect world, offer most excitement for the gardener, with their extraordinary repertoire of alluring colour, pattern and scent. Sometimes form and colour make the flower overwhelmingly conspicuous; at other times the floral parts, while visually subtler, are framed with foliage that gives the plant as a whole some decorative value.

Understanding the botanical technicalities of the flowering process may increase a gardener's awareness and satisfaction in the same way that a familiarity with plant names may sharpen his or her enjoyment. Some knowledge of how these reproductive mechanisms operate may actually be useful – a reminder, perhaps, of the values and disadvantages of double flowers. Other gardeners may deliberately choose flowers for their attractiveness to bees or butterflies. Sometimes such information is simply of interest, deepening our appreciation of a flower's beauty with the knowledge that such-and-such a flower emits its scent in the evening to attract night-flying moths, or that some colour change occurs after fertilization. It may also encourage others to look closely into the hidden centre of a tubular flower to find the patterned pathway that guides the bee to its target.

Here we explore in close-up some aspects of flower form and colour – the 'anatomy' of flowers – before looking in a broader perspective at the garden roles these plants may be called upon to play.

Astrantias have dome-shaped flower-heads composed of tiny florets surrounded by a decorative collar of narrow segmented bracts, giving a charming star-like effect. This arrangement is typical of the Umbelliferae or carrot family; the clusters of small flowers in umbrella-shaped umbels offer an abundance of nectar and convenient landing platforms, making umbellifers popular both with insect pollinators and with the wildlife that preys on insects.

THE ATTRACTION OF FLOWERS

Most of our flowering garden plants are angiosperms, with a decorative flower structure composed of a modified leaf shoot having two functions: to protect the reproductive organs and to assure appropriate pollination.

Flowers pollinated by wind tend to be relatively small and inconspicuous; they produce neither scent nor nectar, and their colouring is incidental rather than being attuned to the vision of some bird or insect. Some are nevertheless valued by gardeners, among them hazel catkins, dierama with slender dangling bells and many ornamental grasses. The more elaborate structures we admire in countless flower species have infinite complexities of colour, form and scent, which evolved over millions of years, closely paralleled by the evolution of living pollinators of various kinds.

These active participators are very often insects, but also include birds, snails and bats. As these creatures travel and visit flowers (usually in search of food), they bring about fertilization by transferring pollen from the flower's male organs to receptive female organs, which then form seed. The male and female organs may be in the same flower, in a separate flower of the same plant, or even (as with most hollies) on separate plants of the same species. In very many instances the flowers whose appearance people find most intriguing have their floral parts organized in such a way as to avoid self-pollination and instead assure cross-fertilization by means of these visiting agents.

There are fascinating evolutionary links between the development of various flower adaptations such as form, colour, nectar and scent and the sensory perception of the different classes of insect pollinator available. The earliest of these were probably wingless insects, succeeded by various forms of beetle. Such insects crawled into primitive flowers to eat the pollen grains, some of which would be distributed over the short distances necessary to assure self-pollination. Certain more evolved flowers developed nectar-secreting glands to attract flies (and later the more intelligent

BELOW LEFT *The Lenten rose* (Helleborus orientalis) *has basin-shaped flowers with distinctive protruding stigmas rising above the golden pollen-covered stamens.*

BELOW *The tightly clustered double flowers of this delphinium cultivar have powerful garden impact. The conspicuous spurs, which in unimproved species provided nectar for pollinators, have become modified into the extra ring of decorative petals.*

bees, moths and butterflies). These would accidentally brush against the pollen en route to the food store of nectar and so transport pollen to fertilize other flowers or other plants. Flower forms of tubular shape, or with specially adapted nectary structures (such as the conspicuous spurs of aquilegia and delphinium), first developed hand-in-hand with the evolution of insects and birds equipped with an elongated sucking proboscis capable of reaching their nectar.

In order to assure cross-pollination, some species possess special flower shapes, or allow their male and female organs to mature at different moments. The shape of the flower is sometimes designed to attract and admit the intended pollinator while excluding undesirables. Some complicated flowers such as the snapdragon-shapes of antirrhinum and linaria will only 'open' when an insect pollinator of the appropriate size and weight lands on the lower lip. The higher insects such as bees are able to follow sophisticated visual signals marking the path to the nectary, and often have to force their way through the folds of the flower to reach it. In the specialized pollinating mechanism of salvia, the visiting insect gains access to the nectar by knocking against the lower part of the stamen, which causes the top end to swing down and deposit pollen on the creature's back. The individual blooms on a flower-spike of *Lobelia cardinalis* pass through the pollen-producing male phase before the female organs become receptive, and it is possible to compare the older lower flowers, which have reached their female stage, with the upper ones, which function as males on opening.

Scent is another adaptation, aimed to attract from a distance pollinating insects that possess a well-developed sense of smell. Flower scents are often extremely pleasing to human tastes, but the smell of rotting meat that lures carrion-flies to pollinate arum flowers demonstrates that this is not invariably so. Some flowers such as night-scented stock, tobacco plants and the Chilean *Cestrum parqui* emit their fragrance only at evening, when colours fade. Others only open as dusk falls. In the case of evening primroses, the flowers open as daylight fails and do not close until dawn. Many attract night-flying moths, which have a keen sense of smell: the evolutionary appearance of honeysuckle in the Eocene era is known to have coincided with the emergence of the long-tongued moths. A particularly specialized relationship in North America is the interdependence between night-scented yucca and the moth *Pronuba yuccasella*, in which the female moth fertilizes the yucca flower while laying its eggs: moth larvae and flower seeds develop together.

The decorative structure of flowers

The parts of the flower surrounding and protecting the reproductive organs are known as the perianth, and normally consist of a corolla (often divided into petals) and calyx (an outer layer, sometimes divided into sepals). The petals, coloured and often scented, are usually the showiest part of the flower. Sometimes they are separate and arranged to form simple saucer-shaped blooms, such as those of mallow and cranesbill geraniums. At other times they are more elaborately shaped, or fused together into a tube or some more highly specialized shape such as that of pea-flowers. Calyces may be green or brownish, and in some flowers such as clematis and anemone they resemble and actually replace the petals. In flowers such as water-lilies, and in many cacti, the sepals on the other hand

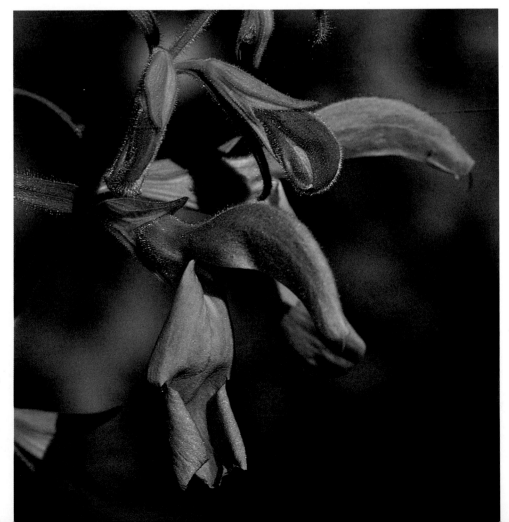

Salvia flowers have the distinctive protruding lips of the Labiatae which offer a platform for visiting pollinators such as hummingbirds or bees with long proboscises. When pollinators touch the lower part of the stamen while seeking nectar at the base of the corolla tube, they release a lever which deposits pollen grains on their backs for distribution to the next flower they visit. The bright blue Salvia patens from Mexico is receptive to any suitable pollinator and, like most American and European salvias, readily produces viable seed in many gardens.

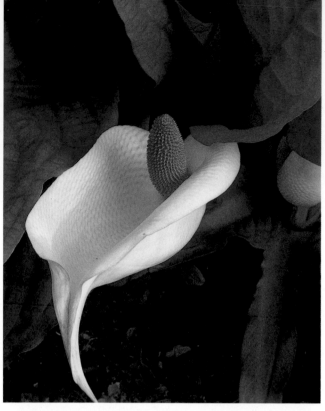

TOP LEFT *The waterlily is one of the earliest known plants to have developed flowers which produced pollen that attracted beetles. Primitive species had a simple arrangement of inner petals merging with stamens and outer petals fusing with sepals. The modern* Nymphaea tuberosa *'Richardsonii' has green-tinged outer sepals.*

TOP RIGHT *In the bog arum or skunk cabbage, as in other aroids, a showy bract or spathe encloses a single spike of tiny male and female flowers which has a heavy scent that attracts pollinating insects. Yellow* Lysichiton americanus *has a disagreeable odour, while* L. camtschatcensis *flowers, with white outer bracts, are more pleasingly scented.*

Cape figworts (Phygelius) *and foxgloves* (Digitalis) *are both members of the Scrophulariaceae, with tubular flower-trumpets into which pollinating insects must crawl. In some species the human eye can see 'bee-markings' which guide pollinators to their target. Flowers of the garden cultivar* Phygelius aequalis *'Yellow Trumpet'* (FAR LEFT) *are without distinctive markings, although the parent species and other cultivars with soft red or coral outer colourings have a lemon throat and mahogany lip which attracts insects in their native South Africa. The markings of the species foxglove* Digitalis ferruginea (LEFT) *are easily distinguished.*

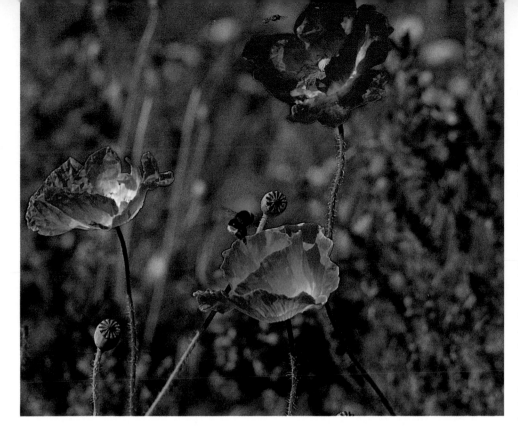

In the single form of the wild field poppy Papaver rhoeas, *the wonderfully translucent papery petals frame a ring of almost equally decorative stamens surrounding a central stigma. The stamens, the male organs, consist of filaments topped with pollen-carrying anthers and attract insects which transfer pollen to the stigma. Later the green seed-capsules split to scatter seed. These poppies hybridize easily and produce different colour forms which can germinate on site in the following spring, although the seeds can remain viable for years in uncultivated soil.*

resemble petals. Occasionally, as in a narcissus, there is no clear distinction between petals and sepals.

The stamens – the male organs consisting of filaments topped with pollen-carrying anthers – are also often decorative features. In winter-flowering shrubs such as hamamelis, wintersweet (*Chimonanthus praecox*) and sarcococcas the flowers are little more than bundles of scented stamens, less susceptible than soft petals to frost and rain damage. Australian trees and shrubs including acacias and callistemons also have flowers in which stamens are most prominent.

Stamens are modified into petals in some plants, resulting in 'double' flowers. These are less likely to produce fertile seed; in the wild they would not reproduce, and in the garden they generally have to be propagated from vegetative cuttings. (For the gardener this is a mixed blessing. A double-flowered Rugosa rose is less likely than a single one to produce the autumn bonus of attractive hips; on the other hand double flowers usually last many more days than single ones, since they are not hurrying to form seed.)

In other flowers it is the female organs that have evolved into a particularly decorative form. In the bearded iris, for example, the true petals are the three 'falls' and the three standards. Each of the three innermost 'petals', however, is actually a female style modified into a flattened petal-like form, with the frilly

'crest' arching outwards to protect its fertile stigmatic surface.

Bracts are a form of modified leaf at the base of a flower stalk or on the stem of a cluster of flowers. When the bracts are bright and decorative they are generally grouped around clusters of very small flowers that have no petals. The pocket handkerchief tree (forms of davidia), all euphorbias (including the exotic-looking poinsettia) and many dogwoods as well as the tropical bougainvilleas have sterile bracts instead of petals. The small flowers are fertile, but the sterile bracts provide an insect- or bird-attracting display. With lace-cap hydrangeas what are loosely identified as decorative flowers are in fact large flattened corymbs of fertile flowers surrounded by a ring of more conspicuous infertile ray florets. In the familiar mop-headed hortensia hydrangeas all the florets are sterile.

The 'flower' of members of the arum family is really a showy bract or spathe, with an interesting role in the pollination mechanism. The actual flowers are enfolded in the swollen base of the spathe, clustered around the central spadix, the lower female ones maturing earlier than the male ones higher up. The spathe's inner surface is lined with minute downward-slanting hairs: these trap flies that have crawled or fallen in, lured by the nectar, for long enough to fertilize the receptive females with pollen brought from a previously visited flower. Gradually the hairs wither and allow the flies to crawl upwards and escape – on their way passing the now-mature male flowers, and so becoming dusted with the pollen, which they may transport to a new flower.

In some species colouring and patterning such as spots or lines, as in horse chestnut, mimulus and eyebright, are designed to provide insects with a route to the nectar. Not all these signals are perceived by the human eye. Bees, wasps, beetles and birds have slightly different vision. Bees, for instance, perceive short wavelengths of light in the ultraviolet range invisible to humans (stamens are often 'lit up' in this way) but cannot distinguish longer-wavelength reds. Birds possess excellent colour awareness, though they lack a sense of smell. Despite their poor sight, beetles can locate large white plants and strong scents.

Having achieved their role in attracting a pollinator, petals normally start to wither, but some, such as those on double flowers, being sterile, are not transformed by fertilization. Those flowers with fragile petals are very transient: rock roses and cistus, day-lilies and giant waterlilies last only for a day, while morning glory flowers shrivel by afternoon. Many flowers that open at specific times perform only for their pollinators: marvel of Peru is called the four o'clock plant for this reason. Most of these plants produce a succession of short-lived flowers, and this quality assures them a place in the garden.

Some of the longer-lasting flowers change appearance dramatically during the flowering period. Buds about to open are often very different in colour from open petals; fading blossoms are tinged with a new range of tones. Some flowers actually change colour once effectively pollinated, usually becoming less rich and vivid as the need to attract passes; leaves also, especially those of crisp grey or silver plants, fade after the flowers have been fertilized.

Colour in flower and leaf

The amazing colour gradations and markings in flower petals are due to the distribution of pigments, most of them soluble in cell sap, and their chemical interaction. Perceived colour is also affected by the molecular structure of the surface texture, which can reflect light differently depending on whether it is smooth and glossy, waxy, matt or velvety. These visual qualities affect our preferences for flowers and the way we plant them, and this more subjective side of flower colour is considered as part of the 'palette' of flowering plants in the following chapter. The chemicals essential to plant growth and development affect the quality of both flower and leaf growth and are indicators of general plant health and of any deficiencies.

Anthocyanins and anthoxanthins are the main flower pigments. Anthocyanins give reddish tints to flowers and leaves, making pelargoniums scarlet, roses red and magenta, and delphiniums mauve, purple and blue. Being water-soluble, these pigments are affected by soil acidity; flowers tend to become redder in acid soil and bluer in alkaline (although *Hydrangea macrophylla* is a noted exception to this rule: a soil with high acidity and high iron content will make its flower bluer). Anthoxanthins produce a range of yellows from ivory to deepest primrose. Sometimes both sets of soluble pigments are present, and colours range through browns, reds and blues. The colour of white petals is sometimes caused by air spaces in the plant tissue, which cause light to be refracted and reflected to make the surface appear white.

Plastid pigments are found in the wall lining of plant cells, and they do not dissolve. The most important plastid is green chlorophyll, which exists principally in leaf and stem cells (and is responsible for their 'greenness'). It also often tinges sepals and flower petals. Chlorophyll is essential for photosynthesis; to achieve this many plants hold their leaves horizontally in order to obtain maximum exposure to light. Thus the leaves of trees present a mosaic pattern when viewed from below, while humbler plants establish a firm upright stance with stiff stalks holding leaves up on a similar horizontal plane. In both cases functional requirements become a decorative asset.

Although much of the time masked by chlorophyll, soluble pigments – which reflect other colours – are also present in leaf cells. In some plants, however, these pigments override the green effects, and leaves

ABOVE LEFT *Some flowers can be pollinated only by night-flying moths. New buds of evening primrose snap open at dusk and the flowers gently close again at dawn. Flowers and stems of* Oenothera speciosa *are pink-flushed, but the pale gleaming upper surfaces of the petals are clearly visible to moths in the darkness.*

Red-toned foliage is not only a feature of autumn, when cold breaks down the chlorophyll in leaves and sugar activates pigments in the sap which turn leaves yellow, red and bronze. In evergreens such as Pieris formosa forrestii *'Jermyns'* (ABOVE CENTRE) *and* Photinia × fraseri *'Birmingham'* (ABOVE RIGHT) *the emergent young leaves are distinctly red-tinged and translucent in spring. Leaf texture is often more significant than colour; the shiny, waxy leaf surface of many evergreens protects against winter dehydration – though the young foliage is vulnerable to late frosts.*

become various shades of bronze, purple, red and pink. In deciduous plants these colours last the whole season, although they generally become darker and less start-ling towards the end of summer, and purple foliage becomes dark and heavy. In evergreen plants it is the young foliage that displays attractive flushed-tone colours.

In late summer chlorophyll breaks down, producing droplets of carotenoid pigment, which turns the leaf yellow. As nights get colder the sugars build up in the plant tissue (causing the leaves of trees such as cerci-diphyllums to exude a strong fragrance of crushed strawberries, and sugar maples to smell strongly of maple syrup). The sugar build-up activates the 'colour-ing' pigments – the anthocyanins and anthoxanthins – in the sap, and the leaves turn red and golden. In areas of high acidity, such as the east coast of America, autumn colours are startling with fiery and high-toned 'reds'. In more alkaline areas colours are less garish – duller purples and crimsons being commoner than the brighter tones. Similarly in regions with early sharp frosts, leaves produce more vivid autumn colours; a long gradual decline in temperatures, as often ex-perienced in British autumns, allows leaf textures to deteriorate and spoil before the sugars build up.

Variegated or marbled leaves, attractive and useful in gardening schemes, are often a sign of ill-health showing that there are imperfect chloroplasts in the leaf cells. White or yellow edges to a leaf indicate a lack of chloroplasts in the outer layer of leaf cells; leaves with green edges around a central splash or mark of white or gold possess a defective inner layer of cells. Leaves of plants such as hollies, euonymus and elaeag-nus with central splashes of pale colour are more likely to revert to plain green, while those edged with white or yellow – including other hollies and elaeagnus as well as many other very decorative hostas and grasses – usually retain this characteristic throughout the summer. In the variegated forms of members of the lily family, including lilies, Solomon's seal, day-lilies, phormiums and hostas, as well as grasses and bamboos, the longitudinal stripes of cream or yellow are formed by the imperfect chloroplasts. Most plants with these markings are technically 'sick' and seldom thrive as well as those with the 'perfect' green foliage; they are always less vigorous and more likely to suffer from drought or disease. In some forms of variegation com-pensatory feeding may turn the leaves green.

LEFT *Lily flowers are very showy and are colour-coded for insect attraction. Lilium pardalinum from California has attractive upswept spotted 'tepals', which are equal perianth segments rather than true petals, and pronounced stigmas and stamens.*

BELOW *Witch hazels (forms of Hamamelis) have a quite different garden appeal. Flowering in winter, their bundles of spidery stamens resist the rains and frosts that would damage larger, more extravagant petals. Instead of conspicuous patterning designed to lure pollinators equipped with a well-developed visual sense, the flowers of witch hazel are relatively modest-looking, though some species are also sweetly scented.*

PLANT BREEDING AND SELECTION

Surprisingly few of the palette of plants available in nurseries and garden centres are original species. Most have been 'improved' by special breeding programmes in search of more desirable and robust qualities in flower, leaf or form. Sometimes these changes are just to obtain shorter or longer flower-stems, but all are aimed at enhancing the gardening possibilities. This breeding for improvement is a sexual process, not a vegetative one whereby cuttings are taken or grafts made to reproduce a particular plant such as one that has attractive gold and silver foliage. To be certain of obtaining the same 'freak' appearance, it is not possible to use a sexual process.

In breeding, the main objective is to exaggerate features considered useful or decorative and to lose others less obviously desirable. The results of breeding and hybridizing are complicated. In the past breeders would spend years looking for one desirable seedling that demonstrated a noticeable improvement in quality. Today, in theory, the selector or hybridizer chooses two good wild or garden forms (species or cultivars) of a genus and breeds from them, deliberately hoping to produce a strain that inherits the best characteristics of both 'parents'. Of course it may still take time to find the desired combinations, and breeding is aimed not only at producing plants that look good but also at producing those that are disease-resistant, have extra hardiness or some such other more 'hidden' qualities. For final marketing of new hybrids a crucial discovery has been made: that first generation hybrids (called F_1 hybrids on the nurseryman's seed packet) are both uniformly reliable and possess the benefit of hybrid vigour. Such a discovery has transformed the horticultural trade and means that, once a strain is chosen, garden perennials and annuals may be produced by annual cross-breeding from two chosen parents. An additional marketing 'plus' is that the amateur does not find the same uniformity in saved seed but has to buy fresh F_1 hybrid seed each year.

Sometimes scientific breeding alters an harmonious natural balance, and highly bred 'improved' plants, selected for certain exaggerated characteristics such as flowering potential, lack the simple grace of their wild parents. Personally the more I garden, the more I prefer the elegant natural proportions of true species, even though I know that their performance is muted. With

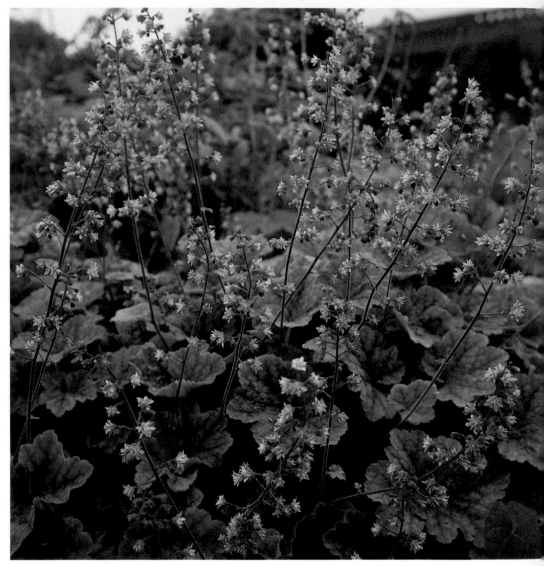

trees and shrubs such reticence would cause no problem, but in the flower garden my choice of perennials and annuals would be more limited and less satisfactory without 'improved' plants. However I do think it would be interesting to lay out a whole scheme using true species alone. I would certainly do this if I had a woodland garden in parts of the United States, where nature's 'produce' can hardly be bettered. But in general we use and are grateful for the thousand and one 'possibilities' provided by the dedicated breeders; from amongst their products we can choose plants exactly suited to any garden scheme. In 'natural'-type gardening, true species often look appropriate; in the formal border we need plants that give precise effects, and those specially bred for longer flowering periods,

ABOVE *Bigeneric hybrids, the product of crosses between two distinct genera, often inherit some desirable qualities from both parents.*
× Heucherella tiarelloides *has the wonderful marbled leaves of* Heuchera brizoides *and the floriferousness of* Tiarella cordifolia, *but with pale pink clouds instead of the foam flower's creamy bells.*

shorter stems and general robustness are a great asset.

The commercial hybridizer and nurseryman exist to satisfy a demand, and the practice of developing and manipulating plants to improve their potential for the ornamental garden is one that goes very much hand-in-hand with garden fashion. Centuries ago in China, chrysanthemums and peonies were hybridized by cross-fertilization, and the Turks improved their native tulips for ornament and use as earnestly as any Dutch nurseryman during the period of Tulipomania in the seventeenth century. The perfectionists who in late seventeenth-century England formed themselves into florists' societies concentrated only on eight specific flowers: anemone, auricula primula, carnation, hyacinth, pinks, polyanthus, ranunculus and tulip. They largely ignored the new flowering plants that were already pouring in from the New World and South Africa. Without understanding the sexuality of flowers (Linnaeus did not publish until the mid-eighteenth century), the florists selected fine or unusual seedlings from a batch, and then propagated them by vegetative means; among them would be some chance natural hybrids. Thomas Fairchild (author of *The City Gardener* published in 1722) crossed a carnation with a sweet William to produce *Dianthus caryophyllus × barbatus* – the first scientific hybrid, known as *D.* 'Fairchild's Mule' – but commercial hybridization had to wait until the mechanics of heredity were more fully understood.

Less than two hundred years ago a chance mating of China roses with Damask roses on the island of Réunion gave rise to repeat-flowering Bourbons,

RIGHT *When the seeds of the annual sweet pea* (Lathyrus odoratus) *were first brought from Sicily in 1699, the flowers were purplish-red and white, held on graceful upright stems and very sweetly fragrant. By the mid-nineteenth century some self-coloured strains had been developed through natural selection of seedlings. From then on intensive crossing produced ever larger flowers, such as Spencer sweet peas, developed by 1900.*

Unhappily, the more highly bred flowers had almost no scent. Today breeders, while aiming to produce single colours, are redirecting their interest towards older fragrant varieties.

ABOVE Rosa 'Charles de Mills', *with dark crimson cupped double flowers composed of deeply folded velvety petals, inherits its scent and its single flowering period in summer from* R. gallica. *The Gallica rose is one of the ancestors of all our garden hybrid roses, including the Bourbons, although many of its descendants bear little resemblance to the original.*

LEFT *In their native Peru annual nasturtiums* (Tropaeoleum majus) *flower in near drought conditions, but when planted in rich, moist garden soil they often produce more foliage than flowers. By cutting back the leaves and withholding water, the gardener can sometimes induce the plant to produce a new crop of flower-buds.*

inheriting characteristics from both parents; since then rose breeding has become a fine art. Spencer sweet peas with flat rather than undulating upper petals, Russell lupins with denser spikes than the original Californian *Lupinus douglasii*, Shirley poppies and Excelsior strain foxgloves with better, denser flower-spikes than *Digitalis purpurea* all began as spontaneous seedlings.

Scientific knowledge of plants' sexual reproduction systems, with an appreciation of the genetic material of which chromosomes are made, has now led to geneticists being able to predict and control breeding lines towards certain qualities. Cross-fertilization between families, very rare in nature, is now possible, while hybridizing species between plants in any one genus is almost commonplace. These new skills are exploited to extend flowering seasons, to produce plants with larger flower-heads, and to invent dwarf strains of well-known favourites as well as to extend the range of possible colours. Red delphiniums already exist and in the foreseeable future roses will be blue and tulips black.

Of course, plants and their flowers may also be altered by giving them artificial cultural conditions. In gardening as opposed to the wild, the rigours of nature can be mitigated. Cultivated plants have artificial living quarters where they are watered in times of drought and protected against cold and heat, and where pests and diseases are controlled and weed competition eliminated. It is often noticeable how plants grow bigger and better – sometimes too vigorously – when introduced to these 'softer' conditions. Indeed, native plants grown in 'native' gardens will often become too large or too woody for ordinary garden use, while foreign introductions may well achieve larger flowers and leaves when in a new garden environment than in their own habitats. 'Wild' flowers introduced into a garden may perform much more splendidly than they can do in a competitive native environment; given fertilizers and space, plants respond by growing ever better. A good example is the Burnet rose, which on Scottish shorelines only reaches a few centimetres high but once in good soil will achieve head height.

GROWING HEALTHY FLOWERS

Encouraging plants to flower well is not quite the same as getting them to grow and look healthy. Flowering plants only reach their potential if they are looked after and provided with suitable sites and growing conditions. Their cultural needs have to be correctly balanced. Much of the technical skill of gardening lies in supplying essential elements such as light, water and soil, so that plants may convert carbon dioxide into sugar and starches and absorb certain essential chemicals through their root systems.

But other skills are required to determine the relative proportions of plant foods which are needed at different times of year to obtain good flowers as well as healthy plants. The main elements are nitrogen (N), phosphorus (P) and potassium (K). Magnesium (Mg), calcium (Ca) and sulphur (S) are also essential, and there are another six minor elements (iron, manganese, boron, copper, zinc and molybdenum), besides some trace elements that plants can use. These foods are supplied by putting back plant material taken from the garden – composts of fallen leaves, flower petals, stems and lawn mowings usually spread on the ground as a mulch – or by means of soluble chemicals: the soil must be capable of retaining these nutrient salts until the plants require them (they may be 'leached' away by rain), and each plant should be supplied with each chemical according to its particular needs.

This skilled balancing act between plant food and soil also depends on the nature of the soil itself in each garden, its texture and its fertility. The extent of a garden's alkalinity or acidity, often called sweetness or sourness, is measured by a pH scale. Ericaceous rhododendrons, heathers and camellias and many other plants (often from acid woodlands in America or Japan) will not thrive in alkaline soils. This is because they cannot tolerate lime, since it prevents plants absorbing elements such as iron and manganese which are essential to these calcifuge plants. Peonies and clematis, on the other hand, prefer an alkaline soil. In general the limitation imposed by the existing pH in the garden soil should be accepted, although it is possible to raise a low pH by adding lime. It is difficult, however, to lower the pH with any lasting effects. In the short term, acid-loving shallow-rooted plants may flourish in naturally alkaline soil if top-dressings of peat

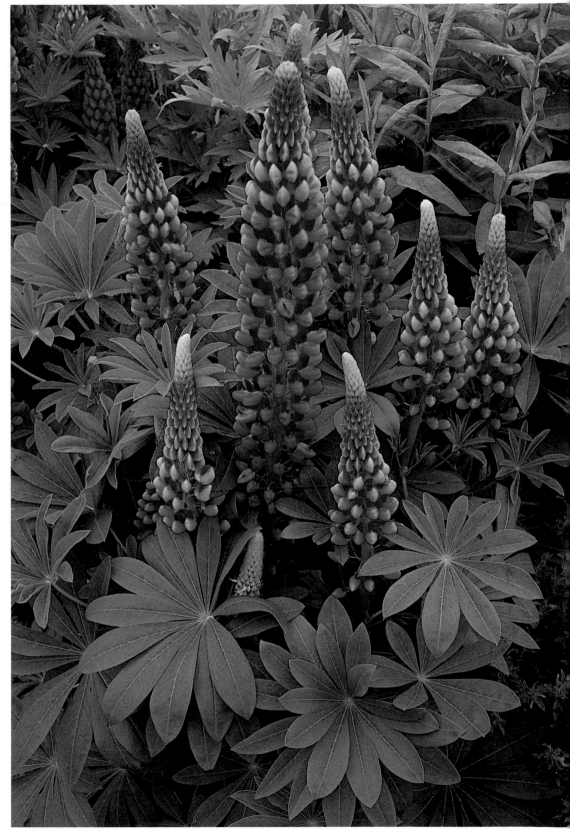

Russell lupins, descendants of Lupinus polyphyllus *from California, have been bred for denser flower-spikes and predictable colours for the garden. Plant breeding for visual qualities like these, as well as for greater yield, is increasingly dependent on science rather than on selecting likely seedlings.*

are used regularly and a dressing of flowers of sulphur is given when planting.

Most plants do their best and flower in what might be called their optimum circumstances, producing good blooms seen against a refreshing background of healthy foliage. Most thrive if the soil is regularly mulched with humus-making organic composts, and a balanced complete chemical fertilizer (supplying nitrogen, phosphorus and potassium in one mixture) is used to correct deficiencies and promote growth in spring. But too much rich nitrogen feeding may sometimes be counterproductive, especially for soft-stemmed plants that make extensive growth in one season, encouraging them to put all their energies into leaf and stem production and 'forget' to flower. Their stalks may fail to remain upright, and they may become prone to fungus disease. These plants need a more balanced diet, incorporating the nitrogen essential to all growth but with an increased proportion of phosphorus and potassium. Phosphates (given organically as bonemeal or inorganically as superphosphate) are particularly important for vigorous plants such as annuals and summer-flowering perennials. Potassium (most easily available as sulphate of potash, obtained by grinding up rocks rich in natural potash) helps shrubs to ripen their wood and form next year's flower-buds as well as being quick-acting to improve colour intensity in flowers.

Other plants, especially those that bear grey or 'silver' leaves to protect them against hot sun, thrive in well-drained stony soils approximating to those of their native habitat, and thus do not need rich feeding. Often they only flower as the leaf colour and texture starts to deteriorate. Some plants actually flower best under stress; when threatened with extinction through drought or disease plants hurry to produce the flowers and the seeds which make regeneration possible. In extreme circumstances a cure for woody plants that consistently refuse to flower is to cut around the outer roots in order to put pressure on the plant.

In hot climates, or in unusually hot and dry summers, perennials flower earlier and for much shorter periods. If the soil is well mulched and water-retentive, lack of rain has less ill-effect. In the southern states of America hot days and nights and high humidity reduce the length of flowering time considerably. Farther north in New England or on the west coast of North America the summers are hotter than an average British summer, so the flowering period is also more

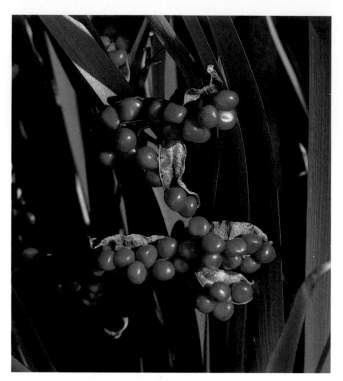

limited. On the other hand many sun-loving plants (especially those from South Africa such as phygelius, agapanthus and nerines) flower best and longest during a hot summer or in hot countries. Even in the British Isles there is a marked difference between the sun-lovers' performance in East Anglia and their flowering potential in wetter western coastal districts.

The gardener must therefore be concerned with finding suitable situations and providing the correct soil for individual plants as well as considering appropriate plant associations. It may be worse than useless to put plants that require moisture next to those that need a dry well-drained site, or acid-loving plants close to those requiring alkaline conditions, and so on. The art of gardening lies not only in designing with shapes and colours; in a successful composition plants should look and be happy growing together because they require similar conditions. Some garden design is common sense but is easily overlooked by the flower-gardener who may initially think of colour and leaf association rather than considering these fundamentals. Lavenders do not really thrive in the rich soil demanded by roses; most German-type irises dislike rich soil and do not thrive in well-mulched borders. The gardener must also bear in mind that the foliage of silver and grey plants becomes increasingly green if the

LEFT *The leaves of* Iris foetidissima *are aromatic when bruised – hence its popular name of roast beef plant. Thriving in the shade of deciduous shrubs or trees, this iris has insignificant flowers in summer, but comes into its own in autumn and winter with its decorative orange seed-pods.*

ABOVE RIGHT Pennisetum villosum *is a grass with rather ordinary leaves but worth growing for its lax arching stems carrying long white fluffy flower-heads followed by bronze seeds. Grasses' graceful way of growth, with stems moving gently in a breeze, contrasts well with the more upright habits of tall stiff perennials. Many ornamental grasses look most beautiful in late summer and autumn when other herbaceous plants have lost their glow.*

BELOW RIGHT *Some plants, such as this yellow-flowered* Geum montanum, *are as attractive when carrying seed-heads as they are when in flower. The geum's beautiful wispy seed-heads tinged with pink and buff give the plant an extended season of value in the garden. Many other flowers and grasses are equally decorative at the seeding stage, but some flowers are weakened if left to set seed regularly, and some plants look better for longer if every seed-head is scrupulously removed.*

plants are grown in rich soil, making lax woody growth and being more easily killed in a cold winter.

In order to grow plants successfully, dead-heading and pruning must be undertaken according to the needs of the individual plant – and to its garden role. Flowers are sometimes succeeded by handsome seed-pods or colourful berries that are part of the plant's attraction for gardeners, and so these are treasured for a later-season display: grass-plumes, for instance, may be as beautiful when faded to buff as when they first emerge in summer. In North America autumns are crisp and deterioration of grassy foliage and many other leaves is delayed to give beautiful effects through the months up to Christmas; in Britain, where damp weather probably follows wetter, cooler summers, the 'fall' display is much more limited.

Dead-heading encourages further flowering as well as improving the colour impact of the remaining blooms on the plant. Many perennials and most annuals and repeat-flowering roses will continue to flower well during the summer season if dead flowers are removed regularly. Gardeners who want to save seed can leave a few flower-heads to mature in relatively inconspicuous places.

Some shrubs (and in particular the repeat-flowering bush roses) also respond to dead-heading, but more generally their summer pruning consists of removing flowering shoots in order to promote the growth of the young wood which will bear next season's flower display. Other woody plants – usually those that bloom late in the season – are pruned back in winter to encourage the growth of new flowering wood.

It is up to the gardener to decide what maintenance is wanted and – with plants that possess the appropriate versatility – to enhance the characteristics that best suit the site. Some plants grown for their foliage may be prevented from flowering in order to preserve the integrity of a colour scheme. Sometimes, as with flowering hedges, later blossom or fruit will be sacrificed to decorative shaping. Shrubs may be either clipped into formal shapes or allowed to grow more naturally. Some climbers, too, do equally well when formally trained as when allowed to grow unrestricted: pillars of standard wisteria, for example, can earn a place in a formal border. The challenge for the gardener is not only in choosing pleasing plants from the wide palette available but also in using horticultural skills to grow them well and as an integral part of the garden style.

THE
PALETTE OF
FLOWERING
PLANTS

Key plants
Companion plants
Massing plants
Plants to use as backdrops
The colour question

Like painters, gardeners seize on the different characteristics of plants to build garden compositions – individual statements or expressions, sometimes within discernible styles or schools, every one unique because of its particular location, and every one changing gradually or dramatically to present a succession of images through time.

Plants, and particularly flowers, are peculiarly unstable building blocks. Flower and leaf colours and forms do not remain static, even for a short period. In a garden picture most flowers have to be considered with their background foliage rather than as isolated colour spots. During a season the behaviour of the plant as a whole has to be taken into account: the transformation effected by flowering may be a radical one, altering the whole colour balance of an area, but the plant's longer-term performance will influence the picture before and after it flowers. Some plants linger, fading gracefully after flowering or assuming new interest in colour or seed, while others rapidly disappear or – perhaps worse – discolour, shrivel and generally become unsightly. Nor do plants retain their size and shape: even the slowest-growing subjects gradually increase in bulk, while some fast-growing annuals and bulbs make measurable growth from day to day.

There is no substitute for knowledge of plants when building successful garden pictures. Every aspect of a plant's appearance contributes something to the effectiveness of the current display. And to achieve the right timing, the cultivation needs of perennials, biennials, annuals, bulbs, shrubs and climbers must all be orchestrated and their behaviour managed.

Plants may be classified by colour or performance, so that each is cast in the role that suits it best. They can be allocated broad categories: key plants, good companion plants, plants for massing, and plants to use as backdrops. Inevitably many plants will not be typecast: they may be capable of many guises – depending on how they are grouped and presented, and on whose ideas are behind the garden design. There is always room for originality.

As finely tuned as paintings, garden pictures use flowers and leaves as the artist's tools, composing them to give delight for an entire season. In this Dutch garden, repeat-flowering catmint, pink clary, erigeron and astilbes are backed by annual cosmos, heliotrope and cleomes, and perennial Campanula lactiflora *'Loddon Anna', purple eupatorium and* Lysimachia clethroides.

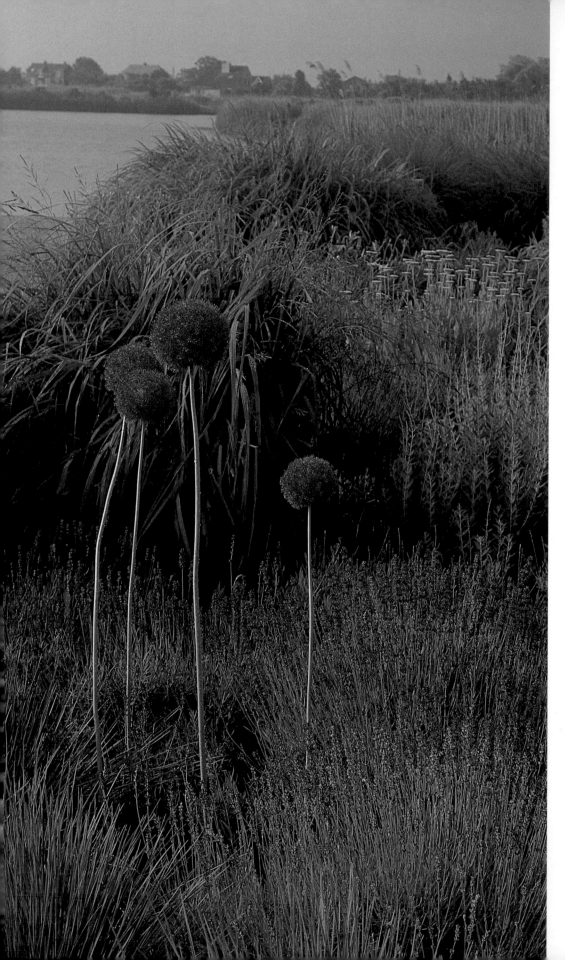

KEY PLANTS

The qualities that make a plant stand out from its neighbours or against its background include sheer stature as well as eye-catching colour and striking architectural form. Such accent, or climax, plants sustain a real presence whether they are set in isolation or combined in a graceful group. Inclusion of some of these key plants gives a lift to all garden schemes by punctuating a formal design, emphasizing its structure; they also provide focal points and underpin the seemingly artless compositions of more natural planting styles by giving textual depth and definition to an area of planting.

Unusual plants that attract attention because they are rarities may also be considered as key plants. On a garden tour such specimens will literally stop plantspeople in their tracks. Sometimes scorned by design buffs as collectors' plants, they add spice and provide talking points in a garden (even if they incidentally introduce an element of plant one-upmanship). Many unusual plants are distinguished in less conspicuous and rather more refined ways than the everyday accent plants, so that the plantsman-gardener's task is to allow the light of these subtler stars to shine without being eclipsed by brasher neighbours.

This process of controlled presentation in fact underlies the successful use of all key planting. Using too many accent plants turns a garden picture into a babble of confusion. For a climax to be truly climactic, neighbouring plants must play parts appropriate to the scene. This is demonstrated when foliage acts as a foil to shapely flowering specimens that star in containers used as dramatic focal points. The more extreme the contrast, the more dramatic the climax. A silvery-white thistle spreadeagled against a dark yew hedge represents almost positive/negative white/black contrast; a shining yellow flower-head silhouetted against a murky Venetian smoke bush also exploits extremes of colour contrast. Gentler effects are created when some

In this seaside garden globe-shaped heads of Allium giganteum on tall stems rise above a sea of massed lavender to make a dramatic keynote in a composition which is given substance by elegant rustling grasses.

These alliums, flowering in early summer, provide a link between spring bulbs and flowering perennials, but many other species and forms can extend the season to cover summer flowering periods.

other linking ingredients mediate between these extremes – a haze of white gypsophila softens dark foliage, for example.

The effectiveness of a key plant also depends on situation and presentation: a small pot planted with tulips becomes a clear focal point seen against a yew-hedge backdrop. However, when expanded into a bed, the same tulips might in their turn become the background carpet against which yew, clipped into an emphatic topiary shape, could act as climax.

Focus on bulbs

Bulbous plants provide good examples of striking form and flower through the seasons as many of them have the elegant clear-cut lines and definite shape that 'read' well among a group of different textures. In spring, crown imperials with their conspicuous clusters of red, orange or yellow bell-like flowers on statuesque leafy stems stand out against clustered leaves of emerging perennials. The grey-leaved *Fritillaria persica* 'Adiya-man' with dusty blackish-purple dangling bells might be the subtler equivalent for the plantsman.

Taller alliums with multi-flowered spherical heads command attention in early summer. Try growing *Allium christophii*, with its pale amethyst-coloured flowers and grassy leaves that die down gracefully after flowering, or *Nectaroscordum siculum bulgaricum*, which carries drooping greeny-white flower-heads on tall willowy stems. Interplanted among low-growing herbaceous plants – or even among the architectural leaves and elaborate flowers of irises, as at Tintinhull – the shapely allium flower-heads add a texture that lifts what would otherwise be merely pretty.

When in flower, some lilies are key plants through sheer size. Foxtail lilies are both valuable and statuesque: *Eremurus robustus* is the most spectacular in summer borders, with starry lily-like pink flowers on immensely tall stems. The giant lily *Cardiocrinum giganteum* – which takes several years to reach maturity and flower – provides a dramatic centrepiece in a woodland setting.

Lilies proper – *Lilium* species – are incomparably showy for later-season displays. A single-stemmed lily is statuesque, and groups look well as part of border schemes, their crisply outlined flower-heads giving definition to adjacent planting of fuzzier textures. This quality is valuable in more natural situations, too. Groups of golden-rayed imperial lilies are startlingly

vivid in woodland gardens in the late season, just as orange-flowered *L. lancifolium* make splendid clumps to contribute midsummer colour in open borders. Lilies are also excellent in containers. We plant Wilson's regal lilies (*Lilium regale*) in stone pots to flank the west door of the house at Tintinhull; as well as their role in emphasizing the entrance, they fill the garden with delicious fragrance and glow white and ghostly at dusk. As pot plants their emphatic role in design is already strong. Moreover it is possible to bring pot-grown plants into play in prime condition, and avoid the business of managing plants in important sites during their off-season phases.

Elements of architecture

Some key plants have handsome foliage and perhaps flower interest that provide good-quality furnishing throughout the year and are thus stars even in the off-season. Two of the shrubby spurges, *Euphorbia characias* and *E.c. wulfenii* (and cultivars of the latter), are among evergreen perennials that remain handsome in all seasons. Gertrude Jekyll grew these in her spring garden to create architectural features above drifts of small bulbs and above the unfolding pleated leaves

Two key plants are part of the bog garden composition in a moist area of Mrs Goossenaert's garden in Holland. The Japanese Iris laevigata *poses in front of a clump of the umbrella plant* (Darmera peltata), *with large, roughly heart-shaped leaves. Many moisture-loving plants have good decorative foliage which gives them individual eye-catching importance; the darmera also has attractive pink spring flowers which appear before the leaves on long stalks. The stately sun-loving iris, with rich red-purple velvet-textured flowers, revels in humus-rich soil; a 'quality' plant, it could be the main focal point in a garden scheme.*

In a coastal garden in Zeeland, strong clumps of evergreen Salvia officinalis *with a bluish-purple flower make statements between the more delicate* Knautia macedonica, *with yarrow glimpsed in the background. Emphatic planting in repetitive blocks can hold a design together.*

of veratrums. The brilliant red-flowered *E. griffithii* 'Fireglow' becomes a colourful focal point in early summer: a single plant will rapidly increase to produce a dense clump of vibrant flower-heads to glow in light shade or under deciduous trees and shrubs.

Hellebores, with elegant foliage and sumptuous white, cream, dusky-mauve and purple-splashed petals, may be grown as single specimens or in groups. Christmas roses (*Helleborus niger*), lenten roses (*H. orientalis*) and other species and hybrids with green and creamy flower-saucers extend the hellebore season

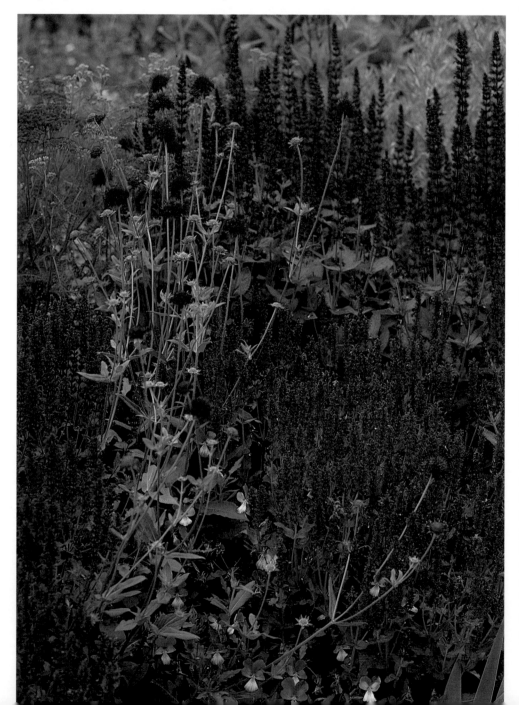

from early to late spring. *H. foetidus* has deeply divided dark evergreen leaves to contrast with neighbouring glossy bergenias and veined hostas; each bell-like pale green flower is edged with maroon, and the plant grows to make a fine individual clump.

There are many different types of Solomon's seal, some with interesting decorative variegated leaves, but none merits more attention than the old-fashioned cottage-garden *Polygonatum* × *hybridum*, with its dangling lily-of-the-valley greeny-white bells held on tall arching stems. Trilliums from America likewise attract the eye in shady borders or light woodland.

Irises with sword-like leaves are also valuable architectural plants, their shapes contrasting with softer textures and more rounded outlines and their flowers, in subtle colours, beautiful for a short season. They are effective on either side of a pathway or in clumps of three or more to give structure to perennial borders. Bearded irises used to be massed in specially designated beds, but such schemes are too extravagant in space and labour to be practical today, so they are teamed with suitable companions that will distract the eye from fading iris leaves.

Bearded irises thrive in well-drained soil and full sun but other garden-worthy irises, such as *I. sibirica* and the common yellow flag (*I. pseudacorus*), need or tolerate moisture around their rhizomes during the growing season, and will even bear some shade. *I. p.* 'Variegata' has eye-catching leaves early in the season although they turn plain green later. Most irises reach their flowering peak in early summer, but the foliage is already decorative much earlier.

Hostas, which produce undulating green, glaucous and golden or creamy variegated leaves, are strong bulky features when set beside delicate flowers such as Himalayan blue poppies. Peltiphyllums, rheums and rodgersias are moisture-loving plants with broad sculptured leaves; and astilbes and meadowsweet have deeply divided or fretted green and bronze-tinted foliage. When massed on a large scale their leaves merge into textured drifts, but these handsome plants retain key status in smaller groupings. All of them also have spectacular flowers: those of hostas are lavender-mauve or white, lily-like and fragrant; peltiphyllums carry pink clustered flowers on tall stalks before the leaves appear in spring; and rheums and rodgersias bear rhubarb-like fluffy panicles. Astilbes and meadowsweet produce flower-plumes in red, pink or white.

Some rules of punctuation

Key plants include some perennials whose architectural quality will, in season, contribute something towards the 'bones' of a garden layout. Sometimes a plant's profile stands out in the crowd so that it can become a valuable pivot of the garden layout, emphasizing a formal design. Repetition of such plants sets up useful rhythms – perhaps the compelling regularity of an avenue, or simply a firm baseline to hold together a more relaxed mixture of border plants.

Kniphofias and yuccas have dramatic punctuating shapes, making them useful features or accent plants for positions in full sun. Kniphofias are more appropriate in small gardens, the clusters of strap-like leaves are a foil for flower-spikes in tones of lemon-yellow through to hotter reds. Some yuccas may be specimens in lawns in larger-scale layouts, or form ideal corner plants framing the end of a border or flanking a gateway. Although less spectacular, I prefer to use those with soft flaccid leaves (such as *Yucca filamentosa* and

Y. recurvifolia) rather than those with dangerous stiff spiked leaf-tips. Yucca foliage alone is striking, but in a hot summer these desert plants produce statuesque flower-spikes of creamy-white bells.

A graceful grass, *Stipa gigantea*, can earn an important place in any scheme: a pair positioned on either side of a path acts as emphasis, perhaps creating a gateway to a new garden area. The large flower-heads, opening purple-tinged and turning to glistening tawny-yellow, look beautiful when seen with the sun's rays glowing through them.

The emerging leaves of silvery artichokes – and the related cardoons (forms of *Cynara*) – also make wonderful corner plants: we use them at Tintinhull to mark the ends of beds, where they contrast in spring with an informal planting of self-seeding small black-flowered violas and sweet rocket, and the pink flowers of *Geranium striatum* 'Glenluce'. Later, the artichokes' tall flower-stems bearing immense thistle-heads become a foil to pink roses, catmint and *Verbena patagonica*. (At

In this very grand garden composition, many of the participants have starring roles. False cypresses, trained into lollipop shapes, with topiary box in the foreground, are framed by a pair of silver-leaved cotton lavender bushes (Santolina pinnata neapolitana). These provide a structured background for good foliage plants and their seasonal flowers. Hostas, violas and opium poppies combine to complete the picture.

Mulleins with large grey (or sometimes green) leaves are statuesque in both foliage and flower. Here in Beth Chatto's garden at White Barn House in Essex a fine group of the biennial Verbascum olympicum *(or of the almost indistinguishable* V. bombyciferum*), whose branching stems give a candelabra effect, take up an important front-of-border position to make a show for the whole summer.*

Tintinhull this distinguished verbena self-seeds each year to flower by midsummer, its purplish-lilac flowers on tall stems rising like a hazy mist out of the catmint.) The artichokes, incidentally, also look spectacular when massed in a broad bed, to contrast with the green leaves of rosemaries and sages, which like the same sunny position.

Another excellent plant for corners is *Salvia sclarea turkestanica*, with large furry musk-smelling leaves and an architectural spreading habit. Like many of the best salvias, it is biennial. *S. argentea* is architectural in a lower key, usually grown for the wide leaf-rosettes of silvery velvet during its first season. The leaves turn green in the second year, and tall stalks bear typical whitish-green sage-flowers of great charm.

Some perennials are important eye-catchers for their foliage alone, with flowers a fleeting incident. Sun-loving *Melianthus major* bears large silvery-green almost glaucous pinnate leaves. In mild areas brownish-maroon flowers on tall stalks appear in spring, but it is the sculptural quality of the foliage that makes this plant the 'star' of a sunny bed and also spectacular planted in a decorative pot to mark a focal point.

Stars of stature

Some plants become stars through their sheer size. Giant *Ferula communis* does not flower every year, but the towering stems topped with greenish-yellow cow-parsley umbels are worth waiting for, and in the mean-time the finely cut midgreen foliage makes handsome furnishing through summer months. Giant kales – with cloudy small white flowers above dark heart-shaped leaves – are climax plants for borders, and especially useful on corners.

Although biennials take two seasons to reach their peak, they can play key roles in a flower garden. Angel-ica, for example, has large architectural divided leaves during the first season and, in the following year, tall distinguished yellowish-green umbels. I use angelica to give 'body' to kitchen-garden schemes or to fill gaps in first-year border plans. Soaring verbascums, grown as perennials or biennials, have stems to 2.4m/8ft or more above a rosette of green leaves. The yellow flower-spikes, described by Graham Stuart Thomas as 'like a great paint brush in the garden landscape', are borne for almost eight weeks in summer. Metallic-leaved eryngiums, such as the ghostly *Eryngium giganteum*, and silvery *Onopordum acanthium*, may frame pathways or doors. Cottage-garden hollyhocks in warm pinks and reds are deservedly back in favour; today yellow- and black-flowered species add spice to colour schemes. In a warm site the soaring stems of *Campanula pyramidalis* starred with blue or white bell-shaped flowers make an exciting focus in bed or flower pot.

Where there is space to accommodate its invasive roots, allow one of the stately plume poppies (*Macleaya microcarpa*) to tower over neighbouring perennials. It bears striking bronzy-green lobed leaves and panicles of fluffy pinkish flowers in summer. For the really wild gar-den, the giant hogweed (*Heracleum mantegazzianum*) has huge divided leaves that give a tropical effect in a damp corner; tall stems bear white giant cow-parsley-like flower-umbels. By water or at the edge of a wood these plants look fantastic, but cut stems exude juice that brings up painful blisters. The giant bristly leaves make *Gunnera manicata* an important landscape plant in any waterlogged setting, but floral conical spikes of dull green give it an extra edge.

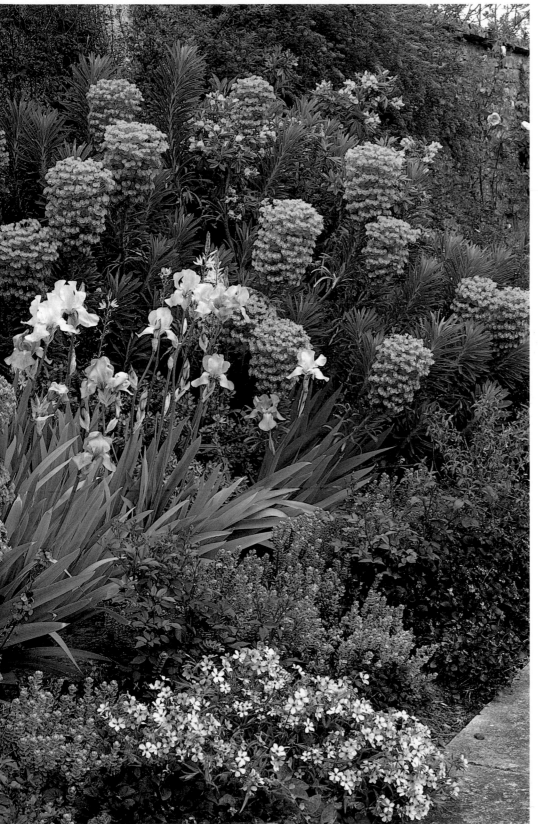

Small and beautiful

Smaller plants may also be important accents, giving emphasis at ground level; they are quality plants in their own right rather than associates of neighbouring groups. Among these are the spring-flowering pasque flower with its feathery leaves and open petals in tones and tints of mauve and purple with bright yellow centres; later the seed-heads are decorative and airy. Also of distinction are creeping phlox such as *Phlox* 'Chattahoochee' with pink-flushed starry blue flowers, *Viola* 'Irish Molly' with greenish-bronzy-yellow petals, diascias studded all summer with pink flowers above trailing stems, and *Sedum* 'Vera Jameson' with glaucous purple leaves and dusky pink flower-heads. Another good small key plant is *Saxifraga cortusifolia fortunei* 'Wada', which produces wax-like green leaves with startling red undersides and delicate white flowers in late summer.

An edge of quality

Certain perennials add depth of interest to border planting. One of the bluestars (*Amsonia tabernaemontana*), for example, has willowy stems and narrow leaves that are modest yet eye-catching in the early border, and in autumn its foliage and stems turn a tawny-gold. Another good perennial is *Baptisia australis* with its blue-green leaves and blue lupin-like flowers followed by dark seed-pods. Peonies of all types have interesting divided leaves and many are valuable border classics; particularly worth planting are the distinguished herbaceous species such as *Paeonia mlokosewitschii* with its clear lemon-yellow globular flowers and the small *P. cambessedesii* with its exotic red-tinted stalks and leaves. Garden peonies will hybridize to produce some interesting seedlings, probably taking four years to flower.

Gypsophila paniculata 'Bristol Fairy', although often temperamental and short-lived, is worth growing for the cloud of misty white flower-panicles carried in summer, and *Parahebe perfoliata* with its blue-green perfoliate leaves and delicate lavender-blue flowers on arching stems always attracts attention. *Gillenia trifoliata*, a perennial resembling an arching spiraea, carries

Irises and shrubby spurges such as Euphorbia characias wulfenii *are key plants in their own right. Here in full flower at Tintinhull they make a partnership behind edging mats of* Viola riviniana purpurea, Phlox 'Chattahoochee' *and grey-leaved* Hebe pinguifolia 'Pagei', *this last not yet in flower.*

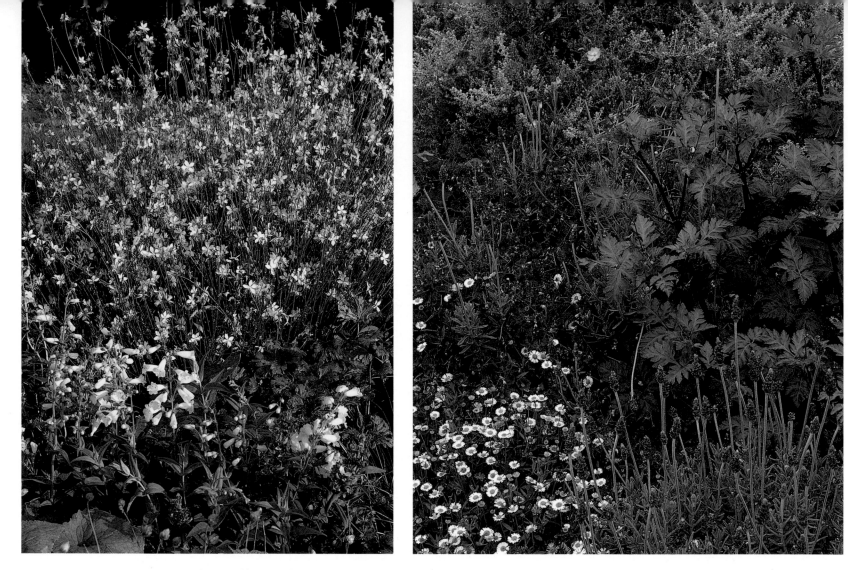

ABOVE Gaura lindheimeri *tolerates both drought and humidity, and in well-drained soil and full sun produces erect slender stems bearing subdued but charming white flowers that darken to pink as they age. The petals merit close observation.*

ABOVE RIGHT *A bright pink geranium from Madeira with dark stems and fresh green leaves adds distinction to a mass of grey foliage and little companion flowers. Tender in many areas, it self-seeds each season in this Californian garden.*

what William Robinson described as a 'loose panicle of white flowers, distinct and graceful'. These combined with attractive habit and foliage, make it a valued specimen plant. The white-flowering form of *Epilobium angustifolium* is a superlative perennial. Its ethereal flower-spikes enhance a white border and will draw the eye whether the plant is in sun or shade.

Drifts of Himalayan poppies with sculpted hairy leaves and blue or yellow flowers are focal points in woodland glades in early summer. They thrive in west coast gardens in the British Isles and the north-west American states and are matched in splendour by groups of summer-flowering lilies that prefer the same situation in shade. Flowering late in the season and revelling in moist acid loam and half shade, *Kirengeshoma palmata* has dangling yellow bells and distinguished vine-like leaves all season. Toad lilies also like shade and moisture, and their little exotic orchid-like flowers are intriguing at the end of summer.

Other late-summer flowerers need to be baked in full sun. The delicate *Gaura lindheimeri*, with small pinkish-white flowers and willow-like leaves, is modest in size, but a clump is always an eye-catcher in a hot dry border. Most salvia species, of which some are tender sub-shrubs, are valuable towards the end of summer; they revel in hot sun, but do need plenty of moisture. Branching woody plants with dark red or crimson flowers, such as forms of *Salvia microphylla neurepia* and *S. fulgens*, and some species with intense blue flowers, such as *S. guarantica*, deserve important sites.

The tender perennial swamp rose mallow (*Hibiscus moscheutos*) carries wide-open red, pink or white mallow-like flowers of satiny texture, and is one of the most startlingly beautiful late-flowerers in regions with strong summer sun. In a favoured climate the shrub-like French honeysuckle (*Hedysarum coronarium*), also known as sukka sweetvetch, will survive outside; it has glaucous leaves and deep rosy-red pea-like flowers.

Presented in pots

Simply growing plants in a container to some extent signals that they are out of the ordinary, but key plants framed in this way create a lasting impression of beauty and elegance.

Many plants that are perennials in their native habitat are counted as annuals in colder regions. These are best massed, since most put so much energy into their summer flower display that they have little left for developing good leaves or a fine stance. I think of annuals as having specimen potential if they look impressive when grown in pots: *Hibiscus trionum*, with papery cream-coloured petals and a central purplish-brown smudge, is an outstanding example. *Datura meteloides* (now *D. inoxia*) with greyish leaves and wide trumpet-shaped flowers is exotic in an urn; it is a prolific seeder in hot-summer countries (I have seen it spreading in fields in the American Midwest).

Tender woody plants may be grown outside in ornamental pots in the summer and overwintered in a greenhouse – a practice that puts a number of desirable plants within reach of many more gardeners. I use both the marguerite-like *Argyranthemum foeniculaceum*, with its fretwork glaucous leaves and white daisy-flowers, and *Anisodontea capensis*, with its pink flowers, as centrepieces in stone or terracotta jars. These and green- or bronze-leaved cabbage trees (*Cordyline australis* and *C. a. purpurea*) with bunches of sword-like leaves all need full sun. For shade orange-, red- and yellow-flowered mimulus such as *Mimulus aurantiacus* give a late-summer display.

Some of the most interesting plants that do well in containers are woody-based sub-shrubs, which die down each winter in cold or temperate climates and shoot from the base in spring like any hardy herbaceous perennial. Especially good are some of the richly exotic-looking fuchsias, which flower with vigour into the autumn months. I also plant the dahlia-like dark purple-red *Cosmos atrosanguineus* in containers. I find I can get it to flower earlier in summer if I keep specimens in pots over winter, otherwise it performs only from midsummer onwards, occupying valuable flower-bed space during the other months of the year.

In the warmer regions, seedlings of the more tender biennials may survive mild winters outside or be given winter protection: experiment with these rather than following any rule book or zoning formulae. Two geraniums from Madeira, both superlative plants for foliage, form and flower, are monocarpic (dying after flowering and seeding). *Geranium palmatum* is the hardier, and it and *G. maderense* have pink-flushed stems and dark-eyed purplish flowers. They make superb pot plants.

Some of the bulbous plants from hot climates also grow excellently in pots. If thickly mulched in winter, ginger lilies (*Hedychium*) create tropical effects in late borders with their canna-like leaves and heavy fragrance. With generous watering, they may also be grown in pots. Equally exotic in appearance, but hardier, is *Cautleya spicata* 'Robusta', with erect stems and two-ranked leaf-blades; the flower-spikes are dark yellow, each clasped with maroon bracts. Eucomis bulbs (pineapple flowers) come late into leaf when grown in the open, so are easily forgotten; their fleshy basal leaf-rosettes and dense spikes of starry flowers look well in pots, and plants are easy to overwinter.

In her garden at the Old Rectory, Burghfield in Berkshire, Mrs Ralph Merton fills ornamental pots with plants that flow over the edges. Good foliage shapes provide a base for flowers. An American agave with variegated leaves, a clump of hostas, Helichrysum petiolare 'Limelight' and Euphorbia mellifera give bulk to Argyranthemum 'Jamaica Primrose' and deeper yellow Bidens ferulifolia, with purple-flowered Tibouchina semidecandra lurking in the background.

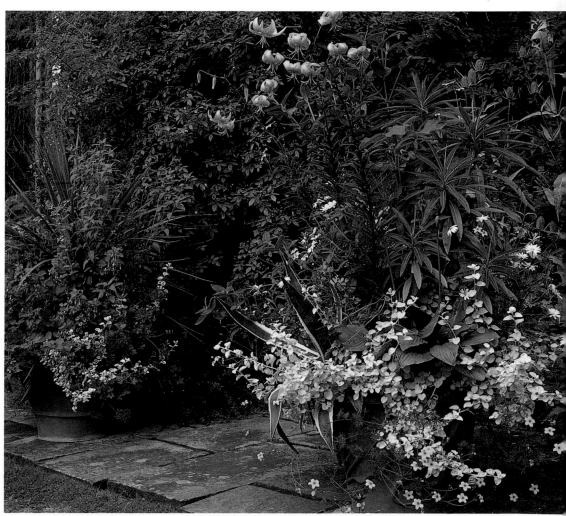

COMPANION PLANTS

These are the essential 'furniture' of garden planting, complementing the framework provided by the architectural key plants and the basic garden structure of walls, grass and so on. Their decorative value is more intimate, less easily registered. Even when grown in a fine group, they do not make a very definite statement on their own; their contribution to the garden scene depends on association. Using them correctly and to best advantage calls for a strong pictorial sense, employed so that neighbouring shapes and colours contribute to the overall garden picture at any given moment.

Most of the hardy herbaceous perennials are companion plants as they are not sufficiently impressive individually to merit key status. When grouped together they are the fundamental components of border schemes. Such plants are important for their flowers and foliage over a long period. While the permutations of perennials seem inexhaustible, especially during summer months, the judicious use of bulbs and specially grown annuals – together with plants that are self-seeders – increases still further the possibility of creating a succession of pleasing associations.

A well-planted garden should have no patches of bare earth. Seeders are especially valuable in the early part of summer before the main perennial groups get into their stride, and drifts of plants grown as annuals are sometimes brought in to complete the colour balance of a section of border planting.

Seeding companions

These come in many guises and include: true biennials flowering and making seed before dying; perennials treated as biennials; and annuals that self-seed and flower next year *in situ* – or are sown by the gardener as local infill. A degree of unpredictability in this kind of companionship creates a relaxed naturalness sympathetic to all but the most manicured layouts. Self-sown plants cropping up in unauthorized spots also rapidly foster an air of mellowness and maturity in newly laid-out garden areas. Allow self-sown seedlings to mature and only weed out those that are indisputably in the wrong place.

Some companion plants make charming informal carpets around and between other more special plants. Low-growing viola species and hybrids seed themselves beneath deciduous shrubs and roses and through paving cracks. They are particularly valuable under delicate-foliaged shrubs such as caryopteris, which come late into leaf. Treat them as biennials and pull them out once flowering is over, unless seedlings are desired for the coming year. Forget-me-nots also flower early; the F_1 hybrids, which look best planted as a mass, come in strong blues. Their seeds produce paler-flowered tints thereafter.

Tall self-seeders may form loose clusters of flowers to weave a colourful infill between permanent plants. In early summer self-seeding aquilegias make graceful clumps at midheight with their muted blue to pinkish-red flowers. Both sweet rocket, in washed-out mauves and whites, and valerian – preferably the white or deeper pink forms – seed in rich border soils and neglected stony ground. Valerian may form natural-looking drifts in gravel or drystone walls. Grey-leaved bright-flowered horned poppies love similarly well-drained garden sites. The Welsh poppy (*Meconopsis*

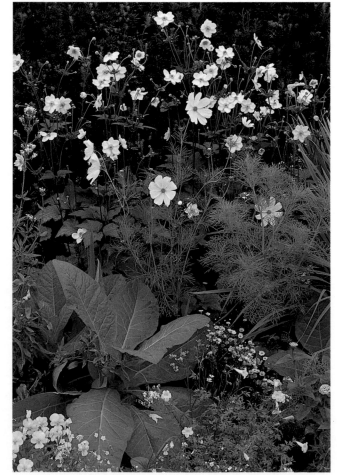

The most effective schemes for beds and borders use combinations of plants that seem to blend together in harmony. In this Dutch garden a white theme is sustained by a companionable group of the perennial Anemone × hybrida 'Honorine Jobert', with distinguished vine-like foliage, and annual Cosmos bipinnatus, with more lacy leaves. The leaves of a later-flowering tobacco plant underpin the group, and flowers of violas, zinnias and daisies fill in gaps of bare soil.

In Phoebe Noble's garden on Vancouver Island, white- and pink-flowered forms of biennial sweet rocket (Hesperis matronalis) and valerian (Centranthus ruber) perform in early summer in front of a large pink Weigela florida – through the branches of which clambers Clematis 'Nelly Moser' with its wide pink and white striped flowers. In this sort of companion planting, promiscuous self-seeders like sweet rocket and valerian are allowed to blend together in happy unison. Any seedlings that stray too far out of line and encroach on a colour scheme where they are less welcome can easily be removed.

cambrica) seeds very freely and will thrive in any soil in sun or shade, adding spots of clear yellow to the background green. The British native woad (Isatis tinctoria), with its brilliant lime-yellow panicles above glaucous leaves, self-seeds in full sun; an interesting alternative for shade is the similarly coloured Smyrnium perfoliatum, which produces less striking flower-umbels but attractive heart-shaped leaves.

Among the self-seeding biennials that are suitable for companion planting are some with more arresting profiles, such as the tall flower-spikes of purple and white foxgloves (Digitalis purpurea and D. p. alba), which look at home in woodland but also thrive in sun. The young green leaves of Miss Willmott's ghost become metallic silver before flowering in their second season, and the burnished flower-heads glisten between low-toned campanulas and brighter-flowered phlox. Mulleins and biennial evening primroses give a pleasingly unplanned air when, with towering flower-stems, they glow above neighbouring plants – their pale petals opening widest as dusk falls.

Annuals grown from seed sown in spring may be planted in groups among border perennials. The glowing pinks and reds of annual cosmos (Cosmos bipinnatus) make wonderful cut flowers, but are also graceful in a conventional border provided the soil is not too rich. Low-growing grey-leaved gazanias are perennials usually grown as annuals: their wide mainly orange daisy-flowers give colour in the front of borders. Interplanted clumps of violet, pink or white forms of spider flower make pretty dappled patches of blending pastel tones. Alonsoas, however, are straggly growers, whose orange-scarlet twisted flowers do not make distinctive blocks of solid colour; instead they convey a hint of bright tapestry hues to enrich 'hot' border schemes.

The annual delphiniums or larkspurs (Consolida ambigua) are fast-growing upright annuals; giant forms flower at head height, making them almost as valuable in border schemes as true perennial delphiniums – and less trouble. Lower-growing delphiniums are short-lived perennials that flower from seed in the first season, and I prefer them in small drifts complementing taller plants rather than massed in beds.

Tobacco plants, with their sweet scents in evening, are attractive in companionable drifts. Invaluable grouped behind late-summer flowerers is *Nicotiana sylvestris*, which carries soaring spikes of white tubular flowers. Lower-growing *N. langsdorfii* bears sulphur-yellow tubular flowers that fit into any colour scheme.

Fine tuning with tender plants

Some important companion plants are treated as annuals for seasonal garden purposes. These include woody penstemons, felicias and silver-leaved artemisias and helichrysums – sub-shrubs or tender woody plants that often have more presence than annuals but serve a similar purpose, contributing an edge of quality to borders and furnishing containers with interesting colours and textures. Plants may be overwintered or grown from cuttings.

Daisy-flowered felicias, with yellow centres amid blue ray florets, will sprawl like miniature marguerites in the front of sunny flower beds or grow happily in pots, flowering for many weeks if regularly dead-headed. Osteospermums have wide white or pink daisy-flowers and may be grown in the same situations. Penstemons are indispensable border plants with subtly rich colouring; in good soil they flower over a long season. Many are hardy but become rather battered by the end of winter, so it is best to treat them as annuals and take cuttings each autumn. Verbenas are among the most valuable seasonable companion plants. Dark

In Helen Dillon's town garden in Dublin, carefully selected strong colours are combined in the beds near the front door. Spikes of orange-yellow kniphofia and soaring plume poppies (Macleaya cordata) dominate lower-growing plants, among them yellow lilies, heuchera and penstemon, while the tender Dahlia 'Bishop of Llandaff gives the colour scheme continuity through the summer. Verbena patagonica, with airy flower-heads on a mesh of tall stems, makes a mauve haze in the background.

green deeply cut leaves make a background for dif-
ferent-coloured clusters of bloom – dark mauve, icy
pink and white and many others. Grow them from
easily rooted cuttings each year, planted out in drifts at
the edge of a bed.

Dahlias, grown from tubers, are valuable for their
consistent flowering and are especially useful where
colour-scheme continuity is important. Although tall
dahlias are stiff, with brittle stalks, few other annuals
contribute such height, bulk and floriferousness.
(Modern dwarf varieties, on the other hand, seem
superfluous, since plenty of other annuals can do their
job at the lower level.) All except the graceful airy
species *Dahlia merckii* with divided leaves and single
pale daisy-flowers need to be planted in blocks that can
be easily staked and tied. In return for dead-heading,
good rich soil and winter cosseting with a thick mulch
to protect them from damage, they flower consistently
for many months. A colour enthusiast might well experiment with some of the wide range of flower colours
and shapes that exists among the innumerable hybrid
strains. Marvels of Peru (*Mirabilis jalapa*) have dahlia-
like tubers and may be treated similarly. Fresh blooms
of white, yellow or crimson open every afternoon.

Stalwart companions

A handful of good perennials provide long-term under-
pinning in border schemes, partnering a series of
less enduring plant stars. Leathery-leaved bergenias
with creeping rhizomes flower as winter turns to
spring. Most are an undistinguished purplish-pink, but
B. 'Silberlicht' bears white flowers tinged with pink as
they age. Mainly evergreen, with the leaves of some
forms suffused with purple tones after frost, bergenias
give good winter ground cover and may be planted in
drifts or even as edging, formally setting off neighbouring flower groups of hellebores, *Brunnera macrophylla*, perennial or biennial honesties and overhead
canopies of flowering cherries. Gertrude Jekyll used
bergenias in many of her planting schemes. In the
Great Plat at Hestercombe, B. × *schmidtii* lines flower
beds set in the mown grass where roses, lilies and delphiniums flower later in the season. For early-autumn
effects Miss Jekyll allowed *Aster divaricatus* with starry
white daisy-flowers on floppy black stems to cascade
over bergenias along the edge of a north-facing bed.

Many perennials grown for beautiful flowers contribute foliage interest over a much longer period. The

LEFT *In a border at Powis Castle, Peruvian lilies (Alstroemeria* Ligtu Hybrids*) and scented lemon day-lilies (Hemerocallis lilio-asphodelus) weave together blending tones of orange, pink and yellow. The grassy foliage of the day-lilies will disguise the fading leaves of the alstroemerias, which begin to look untidy when flowering is over.*

BELOW *In George Radford's garden in Vancouver, large leaves of ligularia make a background foil to the deep red flowers and handsome green foliage of* Paeonia officinalis *'Rubra Plena' and a more delicate-looking* lactiflora *peony not yet in flower. The fleshy-leaved* Sedum telephium *is in the foreground.*

grass-like leaves of day-lilies make a good foil to neigh-bouring plants: those of the old favourite *Hemerocallis fulva* 'Flore Pleno' emerge golden-yellow in spring. Such leaf colours look wonderful against sweeps of blue-flowered bulbs or forget-me-nots. Earliest to flower is *H. lilio-asphodelus* (until recently more familiar as *H. flava*) with clear yellow flowers: although each flower lasts only a day, a succession of blooms ensures a long flowering period. Mid- to late-summer species and cultivars produce coarser leaves and lemon-yellow, bronze or orange flowers, which are attractive with neighbouring blues or more startling in 'hot' red and yellow schemes.

Herbaceous peonies flower at the same time as the first roses, to give a border early summer colour and interest, and also look good under the skirts of gracefully arching deciduous shrubs. Both the old-fashioned *Paeonia officinalis*, with its blowzy heads of cottage-garden luxuriance, and the more aristocratic *P. lacti-flora* hybrids have valuable foliage that remains decorative – especially if sprayed at intervals against botrytis – through the summer months.

Some of the hardy cranesbill geraniums are more suitable for massing, but the less vigorous associate well with shrub roses and may be planted to make front-of-border drifts in sun and shade. Cutting back after early flowering produces new leafy growth that remains attractive all summer and sometimes colours with the

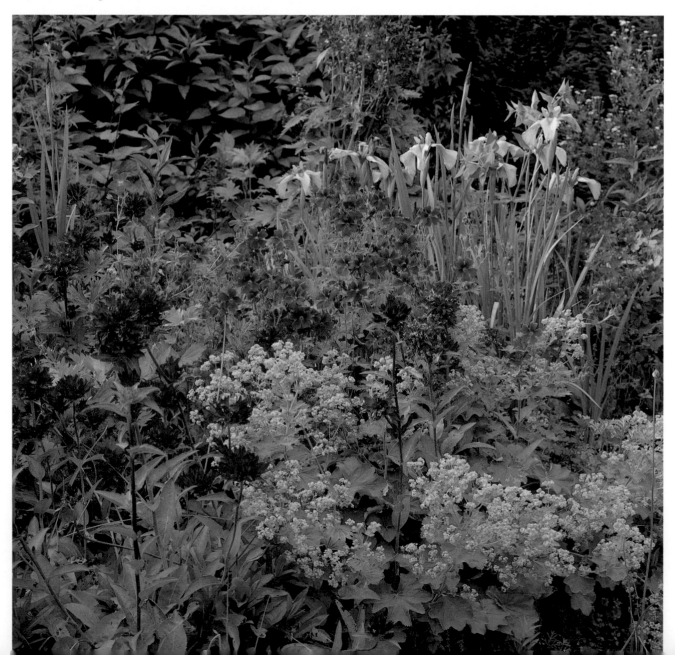

In a detail of the well-balanced planting scheme in one of the inner compartments of the 'framed' garden near Paris (see pages 152-3), pale Iris *'Rose Queen', hardy* Geranium × magnificum *(which the camera has made look softer and pinker than it appears to the eye), lime-green* Alchemilla mollis *and a tall self-seeding* Campanula glomerata *make a sweep of gentle colour. Choosing plants as suitable companions involves thinking about similar growing needs and good foliage contrasts as well as flowering appearance. Both cranesbill geraniums and alchemillas will produce fresh leaves if cut back as soon as flowering is over.*

first frosts. *Geranium renardii* has grey-green leaves and white flowers veined appealingly with streaks of maroon. Revelling in full sun, it contrasts with the more architectural leaves of irises. *G. × magnificum* has deeply cut hairy green leaves, which tint red in autumn, and violet-blue flowers. It grows well under the arching branches of the pale yellow *Rosa* 'Frühlingsgold' and around the base of some of the fan-shaped Hybrid Musks such as pale pink *R.* 'Penelope' or subtle apricot-tinged *R.* 'Buff Beauty'. The taller more upright *Geranium psilostemon* also has leaves that colour, but we grow it for its glorious black-centred magenta flowers, which glow next to silvery-leaved artemisias or tower above neighbouring frothy-flowered alchemillas.

Both their light green leaves and their feathery lime-yellow flower-sprays make alchemillas indispensable as low-profile companion plants over a long season. They perform at the same time as pink- or red-flowered heucheras and heucherellas, creating garden pictures when combined with tall glaucous-leaved *Thalictrum flavum glaucum* with fluffy yellow plumes, and groups of blue-flowered delphiniums. Sedums also furnish sunny front-of-border situations with handsome grey-green foliage and have flower-heads composed of a myriad small stars, which are much beloved by butterflies. They look attractive when bronzed by frosts in winter. Above decorative fleshy leaves, the stiff stems of *Sedum* 'Herbstfreude' hold large pink flower-heads which later turn coppery-red.

Essential border perennials

All through a season, borders offer a series of close-up pictures of plant association. They may be based on gentle gradations of colour harmony or more stimulating contrasts, but in order to succeed they are always composed with interesting textures and masses in mind.

A few of the traditional perennials flower early in the season to accompany spring shrubs and bulbs in sun or shade, or flourish beside mounds of delicate young foliage in main borders. Many small, mainly North American woodland plants suitable for naturalizing in peaty soil flower early in the season. Both semi-evergreen *Phlox divaricata* and creeping evergreen *P. stolonifera* flower in spring to grace the front of woodland beds with saucer-shaped blooms on erect stems in association with drifts of trilliums, erythroniums,

uvularias, jeffersonias and, more prosaic, less demanding omphalodes and pulmonarias. Grey-leaved Virginia cowslips like the same conditions for their lavender-blue bells, but forms of *Phlox subulata* and *P. douglasii* are sun-lovers, a substitute for the ubiquitous aubrieta and alyssum to cascade over border edges. Bulbs destined to flower later in the season may thrust through their fading foliage.

Bold clumps of perennial honesty (*Lunaria rediviva*), with hairy leaves and lavender-white flowers will thrive in light shade alongside cream-flowered *Helleborus argutifolius* and evergreen *Euphorbia amygdaloides robbiae* with its green leaf rosettes and pale yellow bracts. We plant clumps of *Lathyrus vernus*, with purple, pink or white pea-flowers, at the back of our main borders; low-growing and flowering in spring, they associate well with fresh young leaves of later-flowering perennials placed farther forward. Mat-forming *Veronica gentianoides* takes a foreground position. Ice-blue flower-spikes rise above glossy basal leaves.

The mat-forming speedwell Veronica gentianoides, *with pale blue flower-spikes above green leaf rosettes, is a very useful plant for the front of the border. It flowers early in summer, so that other plants can be allowed to flop down over its foliage during the rest of the season.*

I grow it grouped to edge a bed in front of yellow-flowered *Paeonia mlokosewitschii* and as a foil to the evergreen bushy spurge *Euphorbia characias wulfenii*. Slightly later flowering, the much brighter Oxford-blue flowers of *Veronica austriaca teucrium* are brilliant when combined with purple-toned leaves and crimson-coloured roses (*Rosa* 'Rosemary Rose' has suitable leaves and flowers) or with shrubs such as the semi-evergreen *Piptanthus nepalensis* with contrasting yellow pea-flowered racemes. *Erysimum* 'Bowles' Mauve' has a drawn-out season, flowering for almost three months after a mild winter. Its pale magenta flowers shine among grey-green leaves; small creeping evergreen spurges such as *Euphorbia myrsinites* and *E. nicaeensis* spill out at its feet.

Portraits of some classic border perennials demonstrate their role as early summer performers. Most Jacob's ladder (forms of *Polemonium*) bear attractive pinnate leaves and flower at the same time as the first roses. The common upright *Polemonium caeruleum* flowers for many weeks, filling in the comparatively flowerless period between German flag irises and traditional summer perennials. At Tintinhull we grow lilac-flowered *P. foliosissimum* as a wide, sprawling clump next to silvery-leaved *Dorycnium hirsutum* (now *Lotus hirsutus*).

Pinnate-leaved galegas are mainstays of borders. Violet-blue pea-flowered *Galega orientalis* is superb but spreads vigorously; it associates well with the yellow of *Thalictrum flavum glaucum* and the scabious-like flower-heads of *Cephalaria gigantea*. The true goat's rue (*Galega officinalis*) flowers at least a month later, producing an ice-cream effect of blue and pink and tying in nicely with tall campanulas and early garden phlox.

Sun-loving alstroemerias are essential border plants, given unobtrusive staking with twigs when the attractive leaves emerge in spring. *Alstroemeria* Ligtu Hybrids have soft-tinted petals, in a range between rosy-pink, bright coral and cool apricot and yellow, which associate with almost any neighbouring flowers. The seed-heads are attractive, but their fading foliage may be an eyesore. Shallow-rooted plants that flower later help disguise unsightly leaves. The hardier orange-flowered *A. aurantiaca* (now *A. aurea*) – a mainstay of Victorian cutting beds and more tolerant of shade – reaches its peak later to coincide with summer perennials.

By midsummer the hardy perennial standbys are in full leaf and many of them are in flower. Achillea, for

example, will be displaying its flat heads composed of tiny daisy-flowers. When combined with its attractive feathery leaves, it makes graceful clumps to associate with other Compositae such as anthemis, or with artemisias and campanulas, or with contrasting foliage of plants such as kniphofias, day-lilies and later-flowering crocosmias. Those achilleas with pale yellow flowers fit into any border scheme; the tall, more vigorous achilleas (such as *Achillea* 'Coronation Gold') carry flat corymbs of glowing yellow that shout for attention; they are best in strong-coloured schemes with neighbouring orange-spiked kniphofias or scarlet lychnis.

If happily sited in full sun and richly fed, astrantias are superb summer neighbours to showy clumps of daisy-flowered anthemis or silver-leaved anaphalis; they are equally effective in a shady corner rising behind the nodding yellow sprays of the low-growing *Chiastophyllum oppositifolium*.

The aromatic artemisias, often with silvery or grey filigree leaves, act as foils to adjacent flower or foliage colour. Some with insignificant flowers form mounds of attractive foliage for flower-bed edges. They need well-drained soil and full sun and are often short-lived; take cuttings each season. Others such as *Artemisia lactiflora*

In early summer Galega orientalis is dramatic at the end of one of the Tintinhull borders. Somewhat of a 'runner', this goat's rue needs equally vigorous companions or it may overwhelm them in a few seasons. At Tintinhull, to keep planting proportions in balance, it is split up every few years; its contribution to the planting scheme makes this trouble well worthwhile. With completely contrasting habit and foliage effects, silvery-leaved Artemisia 'Powis Castle' and glossy-leaved Acanthus mollis latifolius (not visible in the picture) are ideal neighbouring companions.

have dark green leaves and tall stems bearing tapering cream panicles. Needing a rich moisture-retentive soil, this full-bodied border perennial should be grown in Jekyllian drifts or in bold clumps next to herbaceous plants that need similar conditions, such as yellow-flowered achilleas, cream-plumed aruncus, and later-flowering chelones and purple-leaved lobelias.

Perennial campanulas are essentially companion-able sun-lovers with little absolute distinction, yet sturdy clumps with soft blue, palest pink or white bell-flowers blend into border schemes beside plants with stronger foliage or flower impact. Many of the smaller tussocky types are spring or early-summer flowerers, but the taller forms perform from summer onwards. Thread-leaf tickseed (*Coreopsis verticillata*) has bright yellow daisy-flowers; the paler *C.v.* 'Moonbeam' luxuriates in hot summers and flowers into the autumn. Plant in the front of borders, as neighbours to spring-flowering rock roses or summer annuals such as verbenas or ageratums.

Garden phlox are reliable summer and late-summer flowerers. Both *Phlox maculata* forms, with cylindrical clusters of purple, pink or white-flushed pink flowers, and popular *P. paniculata* cultivars (too many to name) make good clumps between other conventional border plants. Although astilbes will thrive in sun (in Europe – not in the hotter states of America), they are perfect shade-lovers for a woodland garden provided the soil is rich and moisture-retentive during the summer months. Plumed flowers in white, pink and red complement the delicate bronze-tinted foliage. They make good companions for drifts of broad-leaved hostas with lily-like scented flowers or for ligularias with green or bronze leaves and vibrant orange daisies. Japanese anemones are also ideal for shady beds or for the back of a border, their pale white or pink-tinted single or double flowers silhouetted against dark hedging late in the season. Their attractive maple-like leaves are an invaluable foil for plants with more insubstantial feathery foliage all through the summer.

At the end of summer the orchid-like flowers of toad lilies attract interest in shady borders; earlier in the season their pleated shining leaves steal the show as they emerge between hellebores and Solomon's seal. The North American Joe Pye weed is imposing. Its garden form *Eupatorium maculatum atropurpureum* is an indispensable late-summer border plant with purple-flushed stems and leaves and wide flat rosy-pink flower-

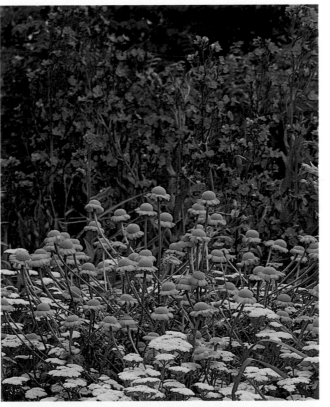

LEFT *In an open bed a clump of a form of blue-flowered* Anchusa azurea *makes a misty backdrop behind the blending yellows of anthemis and achillea. Companion plants must enjoy the same sort of conditions of soil and aspect; all these plants revel in hot sun and need good drainage.*

BELOW *In a garden designed by the Oehme, van Sweden partnership, lavenders and perovskias, both with soft greyish leaves, combine with more strident yellow achilleas to make mounds between tall clumps of swaying grasses. Here the vibrant achilleas, carrying their flat heads on tall stems, brighten the effects with their extreme contrast.*

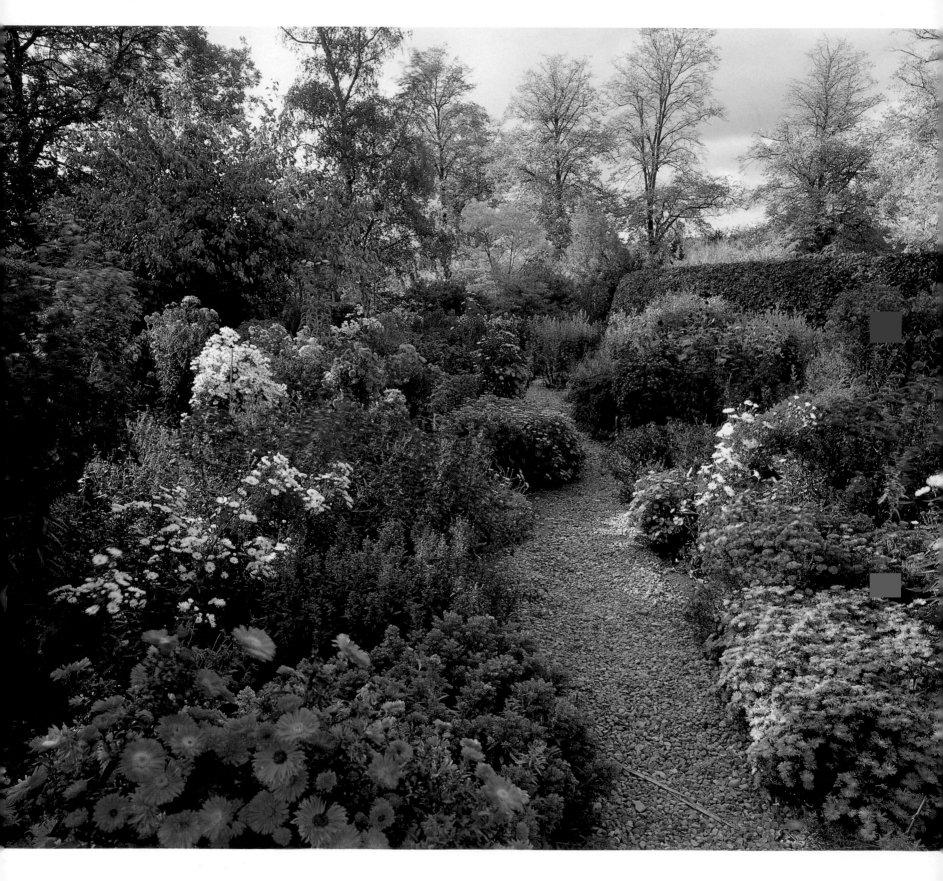

heads; spreading groups are ideal companions to tall spires of blue or white *Veronicastrum virginicum* or turtlehead chelones.

There are many late-flowering asters. These are very desirable and carry the border into winter. *Aster × frikartii* seedlings such as *A. × f.* 'Mönch' or *A. × f.* 'Wünder von Stäfa' have delicately rayed blue flowers above grey-green leaves all through late summer and autumn. Other Compositae are included in fine groups of yellow and bronze daisy-flowered helenium, helianthus and heliopsis, all perennials with undistinguished foliage but providing essential colour in the autumn.

Bulbs in companionable drifts

Those tall bulbs whose visible leaves and stems are almost as important as the flowers may look effective growing under tree canopies, around the bases of shrubs and in beds between groups of border plants. Many bulbs come from areas of extreme climates and need growing conditions similar to those in their native habitats. Not all bulbs, therefore, thrive and multiply in drifts in herbaceous and mixed borders.

Nevertheless, many early flowerers – daffodils, tulips, fritillaries, camassias, Byzantine gladiolus, various forms of bulbous and rhizomatous iris, leucojums and alliums (in approximate flowering sequence) – do survive well and contribute drifts of flowers to coincide with spring-flowering shrubs. However, some such as hybrid tulips are best treated as annuals and replanted each year. Tall hybrid daffodils and some of the small narcissus treasures such as *Narcissus cyclamineus* adapt to flower beds. In borders these bulbs need to be sited where perennial foliage may grow up to disguise fading bulb leaves even before flowering time is over. At Tintinhull we grow alliums in the iris bed, Byzantine gladioli to flower through the low-spreading branches of shrubs, *Leucojum aestivum*, which flowers in late spring, as white spears in a densely planted bed of *Rosa gallica officinalis* and stately spring-flowering imperial fritillaries behind summer-flowering perennials.

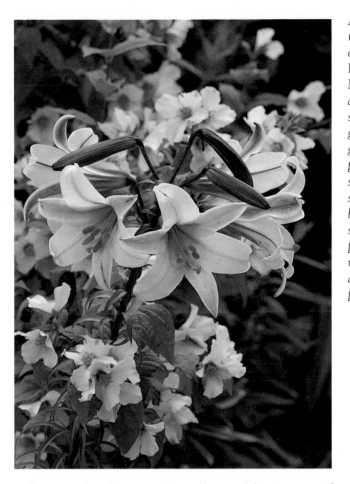

A tall spire of the regal lily (Lilium regale) soars in front of a bush of flowering Philadelphus 'Belle Etoile'. Most lilies prefer to grow around the base of sheltering shrubs or through some ground-covering plants that give their emergent tips protection from damaging late spring frosts. Deciduous shrubs, with low spreading branches casting only light shade in spring, are particularly suitable neighbours, but low-growing anemones or scillas often provide adequate protection.

At Old Court near Malvern double Michaelmas daisy borders, both beds backed by high hedges, are filled with cultivars of Aster novi-belgii *in a range of white and crimson to dark blue, and mauve A. 'Pink Lace'. Too few gardeners use these late flowerers to carry summer into autumn; even fewer can spare space for such a show, reminiscent of Miss Jekyll's wonderful turn-of-the-century daisy borders at Munstead Wood.*

Summer borders may be enhanced by groups of appropriate lilies, *Dierama* species and hardy arum lilies (*Zantedeschia aethiopica*), crocosmias and curtonus (now *Crocosmia paniculata*); as autumn approaches, summer hyacinths (*Galtonia candicans*), crinums and tender *Gladiolus callianthus* precede nerines and amaryllis, which will only thrive in a hot site.

Regal lilies planted in open borders rather than light woodland are susceptible to late frosts, which damage their early shoots and ruin flowering. Provide light but adequate protection by planting them so they grow through branching lithospermums, between biennial honesty plants, behind rhizomatous irises or deep in beds of spreading wood and Italian anemones.

In semi-shade under the canopies of mainly deciduous trees and around the skirts of shrubs, plant bulbs such as erythroniums and trilliums, small corydalis, arisaemas, exotic-looking arums with mottled or 'painted' leaves, and some fritillaries in groups, as they all associate well with other small woodlanders. Other bulbs may spread to naturalize in massed carpets.

42 THE PALETTE OF FLOWERING PLANTS

Filoli in California offers supremely clever examples of massed planting (see pages 154-5). Here a breathtaking sea of white arabis provides a soft ground for hyacinths in spring. In the outer frame a blue form of Hyacinthus orientalis *makes a flowery pattern between the clipped box hedging, while a white form makes a more solid impact in the inner rectangle. Formal, geometric layouts look best when planted with precision and groomed so no leaf or flower is out of place.*

MASSING PLANTS

Often when intimate plant details are forgotten it is general impressions that remain in the mind to be conjured up for future inspiration. Some of the most memorable garden scenes are composed of massed blocks of flowers or leaves – the simplest kind of planting, dominated by a limited number of varieties rather than a restless combination of dot plants.

A great number of plants are individually beautiful and perform well – perhaps with a long period of summer flowering or with fine foliage that sets off neighbouring flower groups – but they are seldom grown as single specimens. Instead such plants are massed for effect, so they appear as one gently undulating almost horizontal sheet of colour and texture. Mainly low-growing, they are vital ingredients in the pattern-making and bedding-out schemes of formal gardens, such as traditional knot gardens and parterres. In less formal garden areas, massing plants – appropriately chosen to suit soil conditions and aspect – make companion drifts to taller permanently planted perennials and carpet the ground below shrubs, seemingly spreading at will with compositions following the natural contours of the land or the canopies of shade created by overhead trees. On a larger scale appropriate plants may also clothe steep banks where mowing or weeding is difficult – the plants eventually meshing together to form so-called 'ground cover'. In the final analysis a smooth or textured lawn contributing to the layout of the garden and linking areas consists of interwoven grasses, which give a restful and purposeful feeling.

For success with massed planting, whether permanent or temporary, the soil of the whole bed must be

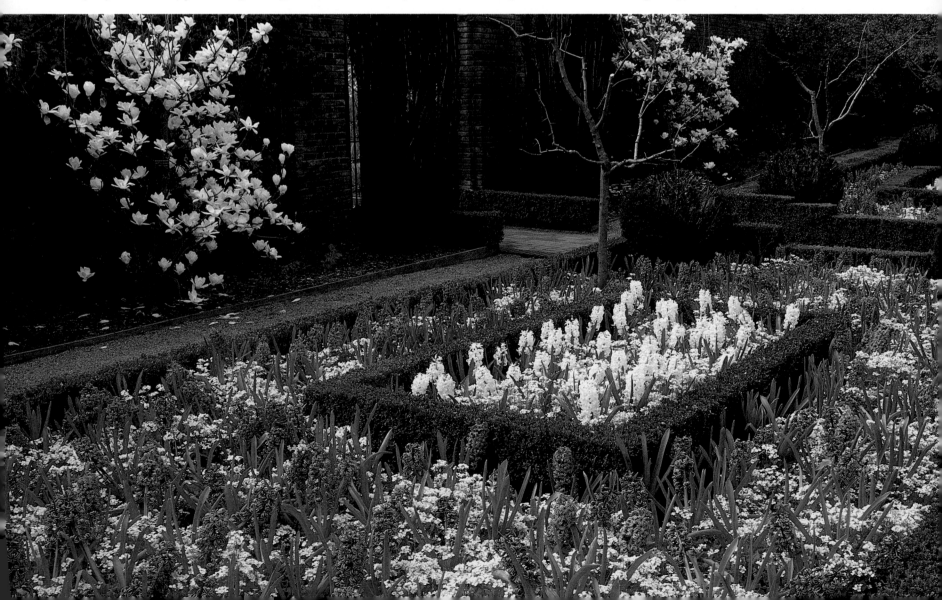

well prepared, cleaned and suitably enriched. Permanent plants need conditions approximating to their native habitat: soil that is too rich will encourage lax growth and promote foliage at the expense of flowers. Mediterranean-type plants and those with silver and grey leaves seldom need heavy feeding. On the other hand, the ground for all quick crops should be rich and fertile; annuals growing from seed to flowering in a few months (or even weeks) need every encouragement, especially if they are to flower over long periods. Soil must be regularly forked over and fertilized each time new plants are put in.

Plants for pure colour
The mainstay of jewel-like patterned planting is the improved hybrid, bred for an especially good flower colour, a long-blooming habit or some other such desirable characteristic. The plantsmanly qualities of natural grace and good overall proportion (whose loss is often deplored when flowering potential alone is developed to the highest degree) are not important in situations where plants are to be tightly massed. The gardener chooses 'efficient' plants that quickly blend together to make an impression of dense colour and texture. Seasonal bedding effects call for considerable twice-yearly effort; the plants should need little attention once established in their flowering positions: adequately prepared and enriched soil and regular dead-heading ensure a long flowering performance.

Spring-flowering annuals include velvety-textured pansies and wallflowers with their rich warm colours and airy forget-me-nots. Bulbs such as hybrid tulips are also treated as annuals: they seldom perform well after their first season, and may be lifted after flowering, dried off and used again in successive years in less important sites. Once flowering is over, spring flowerers treated as annuals are removed to make space for the true summer 'bedders', which are set out after the last frost is anticipated. These plants may be used like embroidery silks to create an excitingly wide range of breathtaking colour schemes.

Many summer-flowering annuals are sown *in situ* in spring. Violas germinate and flower in a quick six-week period. Other annuals, insignificant singly but together making pretty patches or sheets of colour, include clarkias, echiums (such as *Echium* 'Blue Bedder'), lavatera, poached-egg flower (*Limnanthes douglasii*) – both decorative and also grown to attract a hover-fly

that feeds on aphids – toadflax, *Malva moschata*, mignonette, Virginia stock (*Malcolmia maritima*) and night-scented stock (*Matthiola bicornis*), blue-flowered nigellas and phacelias. Some of these plants self-seed. The small knotweed *Persicaria capitata* will seed and flower in the front of borders and in rock gardens, while the Kenilworth ivy (*Cymbalaria muralis*) seeds prettily to make a flat cover between bulbs as well as colonizing wall crevices with its scalloped leaves and yellow-eyed blue flowers.

'Improved' hybrids cannot be expected to perpetuate themselves each year in the same bed or border by self-seeding; their seed will not come true. Most hybrid annuals are therefore grown from fresh seed each year and planted out when all danger of frost is over. A greenhouse may be needed to cultivate these tender short-lived plants. Alternatively nurseries and garden centres sell seedlings at the appropriate time, although their range is often limited and only mixed-colour 'bags' may be on offer. If an appealing choice can be found, however, buying annuals is an ideal solution for those with very small gardens. And by happy accident, this style of planting is particularly well suited to the formality of many town plots.

For making stunning carpets of colour or drifts to enhance border schemes in a sunny site, consider any of the following: ageratums with powder-blue flowers, alonsoas, daisy-flowered brachycome, calendulas, gomphrenas, gypsophila with clouds of white

Wonderfully artificial in appearance, sun-loving zinnias are superb when massed in a formal setting. At Filoli the planting is beautifully manicured, each plant always looking in perfect health and bloom and each massed bed having crisply defined outlines. The antithesis of natural-style gardening, Filoli's geometric layout has precise guidelines laid down for planting type and colour. Its success is a matter of choosing just the right cultivar for each area, and it takes a highly developed sense of colour nuances to get the subtle balance required. The garden maintenance alone requires a very high degree of skill.

LEFT *Not all massed planting is of impermanent annuals. Perennials or shrubs, chosen to grow at just the right level, can be equally suitable for achieving an overall cover and will suppress weeds. Here in Mrs Goossenaert's garden in Holland bergenias flower in spring beneath a pink weeping cherry (Prunus pendula 'Pendula Rosea') and are reflected in the pool to give a double image.*

BELOW *In Phoebe Noble's orchard on Vancouver Island the massed planting of the hardy Geranium macrorrhizum in panels beneath fruit trees is wonderfully effective and contrasts well with the mown grass. Once established, this sort of gardening – simple, yet making a positive statement – is not only beautiful, but (apart from mowing) almost labour-free. This is inspirational and deserves to be copied.*

flowers, scarlet linum, lobelias, mesembryanthemums, marvels of Peru, nemesias, pelargoniums (special cultivars are easily grown from F_1 seed), petunias, small *Phlox drummondii*, salvias, French and African marigolds, tobacco plants, hibiscus and verbenas. Begonias and impatiens (which grow from seed or cuttings) will even perform well in shade.

Tender plants are also effective substitutes for true annuals. Perpetuated from cuttings (like some of the desirable annual hybrids), they are not so susceptible to late frosts if hardened off appropriately and may be planted out earlier than annuals grown from seed, quickly growing together to cover bare earth. Try soft-stemmed diascias, osteospermums, penstemons and verbenas, with the more woody silver-leaved artemisias, argyranthemums, calceolarias, felicias, helichrysums and salvias. Root them in autumn and over-winter in a frost-free greenhouse.

Permanent carpeting

Permanent planting schemes of low-growing shrubs, perennials or bulbs are labour-saving when compared with seasonal annuals. Some hand-weeding is necessary in the first years but, once established in well-prepared ground, the foliage will mesh together to form a light-excluding carpet that suppresses both annual and perennial weeds. (I prefer not to call this ground cover, which has become associated with rather dreary gardening where beauty and appropriateness are sacrificed to function and low maintenance. Good plants may effectively reduce work without diminishing the quality of performance.)

On a large scale, shrubs such as symphoricarpos, hypericums, pachysandra, viburnums, periwinkles and ivies – grown primarily for foliage effects but often producing worthwhile flowers in season – have wide horizontally spreading branches or suckers to cover the ground. On a more manageable scale, in flower beds and shrubberies, select herbaceous clump-formers such as day-lilies, cranesbill geraniums, tiarellas and tellimas that spread, or ajugas, buglossoides, dicentras, creeping Jennies and lamiums, which have colonizing root systems.

Some sun-lovers have the bonus of good flowers in season as well as beautiful foliage throughout the summer. Substitute these for labour-intensive traditional annuals in quite formal schemes or use as infillers for difficult corners of the flower garden. If the proportions are right these plants are as effective in a small homogeneous group as when massed on the grand scale in dramatic parterres or in woodland scenes. It is not that plants of this type lack individuality: they are often beautiful as single specimens, but are even more effective when massed to grow on a single plane, with flowers and/or leaves all at the same height and

A pair of bronze-leaved smoke bushes stand guard outside the gates to the courtyard at Tintinhull. Both are probably seedlings of one of those with darker purple foliage, such as Cotinus coggygria *'Foliis Purpureis' or C.c. 'Royal Purple'. Under their skirts the yellow-flowered St John's wort (Hypericum calycinum) – here contained by stonework to stop it spreading – makes an effective foil to its taller neighbours as well as preventing weed growth. In a situation such as this, where immediate effects are important, I prefer simple plant associations rather than a mixture of many kinds of flower and leaf.*

At La Garoupe on the French Riviera a wide bed partly shaded by a spine of olive trees is planted with a well-established mass of Chasmanthe aethiopica, a tender bulbous plant with orange-red flowers that is closely related to crocosmia. Massed planting schemes do not have to be formal in intent, although this one follows the line of an avenue. Often using a single plant in quantity rather than a fussy mixture produces the most striking effects. The style of this rather exotic bed can be reproduced in more austere climates using hardy plants such as day-lilies instead of the tender drought-loving chasmanthes.

RIGHT *Streamside planting in a garden near the Devon coast is a deliberately informal mix of candelabra primulas and the unusual Portuguese form of St Bruno's lily (Paradisea lusitanica), with grassy leaves and white trumpet-flowers on tall stems. The primulas self-seed in wonderful colour variations and literally cover the soil, forcing out any weeds that germinate. A silver-leaved willow (Salix lanata) also thrives in the moist soil but remains low-growing. To be so effective, this sort of planting must be well maintained; this is not 'wild' gardening, but 'natural' gardening, very much under man's control.*

blending into a distant textured carpet – or cushion. Examples of more compact flowering carpeters include ground-hugging acaenas, dwarf campanulas, creeping snow-in-summer curtaining drystone walls and filling in cracks between stonecrops, saxifrages and scented thymes; also *Euphorbia cyparissias*, *Lamium maculatum* (with white or pale pink flowers and pretty variegated leaves), *Anthemis nobile* (used to make chamomile lawns), prostrate veronicas and seeding violas. Glossy-leaved acanthus, alchemillas, the taller euphorbias, cranesbill geraniums (some forms grow well in shade), and grey-leaved California fuchsias (*Zauschneria californica*) are good on a larger scale.

Some of the plants grown as permanent carpeting are chosen primarily for the colour, shape and texture of their leaves, which are as important through the garden season as any flowers. These plants may be massed in formal patterns or more freely grouped in open borders. Silver- and grey-leaved plants such as shrubby *Senecio* (now *Brachyglottis*) 'Sunshine', artemisias, helichrysum and carpeting stachys provide a leafy foil to bright flower colour. Lavenders, rosemaries, santolinas and good foliage forms of *Salvia officinalis* are all sun-lovers with good-looking and aromatic leaves (and attractive flowers in season). Good foliage perennials for less sunny sites include pig-a-back tolmieas and lamiums with white- and cream-marked leaves (*Lamium maculatum* 'Beacon Silver' and *L.m.* 'White Nancy').

Quieter areas of green offer a restful contrast. Ordinary box bushes may be effectively massed together and clipped and trained into flat-topped blocks or undulating waves a metre or even less in height. This makes an interesting alternative to using box as hedging or topiary shapes.

Choose carpeting foliage to suit aspect and soil: only healthy plants successfully cover bare earth in problem areas. Prostrate junipers with green-textured foliage thrive on dry banks, with liriopes and different forms of suckering and invasive mint, including grey-leaved *Mentha* × *rotundifolia* 'Bowles' (syn. *M.* × *villosa alope-curoides*). In shade, shrubs grown mainly for their leaves include *Lonicera pileata*, large- and small-leaved ivies, forms of euonymus with green or variegated leaves and acid-loving pachysandras (look for the American *Pachysandra procumbens* as well as the ubiquitous *P. terminalis* from Japan). Other shade-tolerant shrubs that also have attractive flowers and/or fruit

are cotoneasters, heathers, hypericums, glossy-leaved sarcococcas (with deliciously scented flowers in winter) and symphoricarpos. All of these are effective spreading through woodland.

Low-growing ajugas with green or coloured leaves and blue spikes, evergreen epimediums, shining-leaved *Asarum europaeum*, *Brunnera macrophylla*, sweet woodruff, hellebores, day-lilies, hostas, omphalodes with starry blue flowers, pulmonarias with marbled leaves, forms of comfrey (*Symphytum*), tiarellas, tellima and yellow-flowered *Waldsteinia ternata* are all suitable for massing in deep shade. They will grow under shrub branches to cover the soil tightly and make an impenetrable weed-suppressing carpet. Some, such as blue-flowered lithospermums, are determined acid-soil lovers (although the related *Buglossoides purpuro-caerulea* is lime-tolerant); other woodland plants that thrive in shade and moist peaty soil are houttuynias, vancouverias, the even more acid-insistent partridge berry (*Mitchella repens*), arctostaphylos, maianthemum and gaultheria.

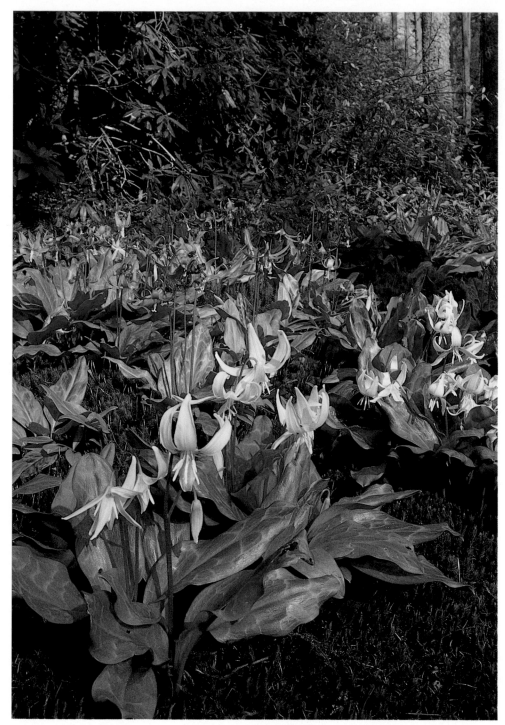

Dog's tooth violets, their attractive spring foliage setting off pink, white or yellow flowers, look their best when colonizing a wood, as at Knightshayes. Pink Erythronium revolutum

with brown-tinted foliage frames E. 'White Beauty' (probably a form of E. oregonum), with large cream reflexed flowers and shining marbled leaves. These choice plants prefer an acid soil but

are not fussy, and will establish in any shady corner of the garden under the branches of deciduous shrubs such as magnolias, which love the same conditions.

Naturalized drifts

Garden scenes where plants seem to have spread at will evoke something of an idea of paradise. Frank Kingdon Ward thought he had found his own paradise when he first glimpsed the Himalayan blue poppy (*Meconopsis betonicifolia*) in south Tibet in 1926: 'Suddenly I looked up and there, like a blue panel dropped from heaven – a stream of blue poppies dazzling as sapphires in the pale light.' Few of us can grow these Himalayan wonders successfully, but other 'blues' such as buglossoides, Apennine anemones or even the more prosaic forget-me-not make vivid garden carpets. I find inspiration in the sweeps of bluebells in a deciduous wood in spring-time.

Real wild flowers spreading in their native habitat are breathtaking and – appropriately adapted – may inspire garden scenes. Unaided by garden-making techniques, spring rains bring golden eschscholzias and blue-flowered lupins to life to cover Californian hills in broad sweeps of colour. Snakeshead fritillaries are more modest in Oxfordshire meadows. In North American meadows native columbines (*Aquilegia canadensis*) create drifts of nodding red and yellow flowers in late spring. In the British Isles primroses and snowdrops colonize banks to make natural tapestry, also in spring.

Bulbous plants that grow and spread in grass are the ultimate in low maintenance, although the grass-care itself involves a considerable number of man-hours each season. Work out a mowing programme to ensure that grasses do not become too competitive and that bulb leaves are not cut too early. In winter yellow aconites carpet a lawn under deciduous trees. Crocus, chionodoxas, muscari, narcissi, scillas and snakeshead fritillaries will all grow happily in mown grass or in a rough orchard. Colchicums, cyclamen and autumn-flowering crocus appear at the end of summer.

Other small bulbs spread to make flowering carpets in beds. Some, such as cyclamen, corydalis, erythroniums and trilliums also produce decorative foliage. Spring-flowering anemones have a brilliant but fleeting period of flower. Alliums, species tulips and leucojums will all naturalize in beds and give the garden an appearance of age and happy maturity.

I love the idea of massing blue- or cream-flowered camassias to create scenes reminiscent of those glimpsed in their native north-west America. In hot climates blue agapanthus become weeds, seeding and spreading to make panels of colour even under trees.

PLANTS TO USE AS BACKDROPS

Background curtains of climbing plants and wall-trained shrubs provide an extra dimension of beauty behind any planting scheme. Climbers, such as roses and clematis, rising high above a border on walls or trellis, and tall shrubs, in free or pruned shapes, may extend planting and colour themes with their foliage and flowers. Other shrubs or small trees, making a continuous line like a hedge or grouped informally as single architectural keynotes, may provide background interest behind a more free-standing border. Many hedges are grown to provide a mass of mainly one foliage colour to link a whole scheme together, but there are plenty of suitable hedging plants that also contribute flowers.

All these backdrop plants combine with other planting to give individual group effects to complement the planting in front. Vertical plants carry the eye upwards and are especially valuable in small gardens: by introducing a third dimension they make the most use of available space.

The cast of flowering climbers
Some climbing plants are vigorous self-supporters and once established do not need tying in to a frame. Parthenocissus species have adhesive pads that fix the tendrils to any surface. Like ivy, climbing hydrangeas have clinging aerial roots: *Hydrangea anomala petiolaris* is the most common species, and the subtle unshowy beauty of its greenish-white corymbs and fresh green leaves makes a fine background to hellebores, shade-tolerant *Euphorbia amygdaloides robbiae*, pleated hosta leaves and ferns. Schizophragma (*Schizophragma hydrangeoides* and *S. integrifolium*) and the related *Pileostegia viburnoides* also have attractive lace-cap flowers and like shade. The tender evergreen *Trachelospermum jasminoides* with its very fragrant creamy flowers is sun-loving and self-clinging on a warm wall.

The best flowering climbers generally need some supports. Vines have curling tendrils, clematis curling petioles which, with a little guidance, thread themselves through any proffered framework, including the branches of other plants. Climbing roses possess recurved thorns, which hook themselves over wires or branches. Scandent plants such as wisteria and honeysuckle use their stems for twining around supports to produce their flowers in the light.

Wisterias are perhaps the noblest climbers of all, suitable for growing on high sunny walls and pergolas and, in warmer climates, up into tall trees. Their long scented pea-flowered racemes in different tints of violet and mauve or white clothe a flat surface with a scented curtain in late spring. They may also be trained as small standard trees, look elegant when planted as an alley and make focal points in a flower bed in which the drooping flower-heads reach almost to the ground.

Honeysuckles' twining stems decorate trelliswork, pergolas and fences with colourful – and often scented – flowers: different forms flower from spring through summer. Seldom very strong-growing, they are useful in small corners as neighbours to tall perimeter shrubs, and some are shade-tolerant. Delicate summer jasmines also scent the air with fragrance. Blue potato-flowered *Solanum crispum* 'Glasnevin' and the more tender *S. jasminoides* forms may be wall-trained and will scramble over fences or unsightly sheds.

Framing a doorway set in golden Ham stone at The Gables, Mrs Gwen Beaumont's garden in Somerset, the shapely leaves and lacy flower-heads of a climbing hydrangea (Hydrangea anomala petiolaris) make a charming picture with nearby plants. By giving height, climbers add an extra dimension to horizontal planting schemes. Almost every garden needs some sort of frame; this can be achieved by relying on the natural shapes of trees or by letting flowers and leaves weave a background curtain over artificial structures.

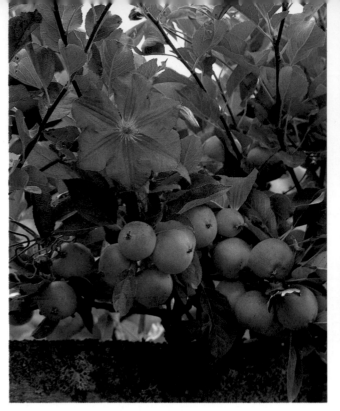

Annual sweet peas (*Lathyrus odoratus*) look wonderful when, like clematis, they are grown on vertical tripods as features in flower beds, in the utilitarian herb garden or even among rows of kitchen vegetables. Plant them four to a tripod in single colours, or allow mixed blues, pinks, mauves and whites to blend in the eye. If regularly picked for the house or dead-headed, sweet peas flower fragrantly for many months.

Clematis and roses

For short periods of flowering some permanent climbers become key features because of the sheer impact of their curtains or garlands of blossom. The most luxuriant flowering climbers will form abstract shapes to carry the planting design upwards – twining through openwork trellis, draping themselves over pergolas or fencing, cascading over roofs, covering the face of stone or brick (perhaps given some framework to help them) or even throwing themselves with romantic abandon high into trees. Less vigorous 'climbers' may fall over balustrading or low walls and sprawl to cover sloping banks. Some climbing plants, however, are best suited when formally trained on supports or walls, where they bring a measured presence to the garden.

Clematis and roses predominate in this category. Different clematis give pleasure for most months of the year – some with a particularly attractive veil of foliage, all with charming flowers (which often become silky

In the best cottage-type gardens orchard trees, vegetables and sweetly scented flowers all grow together within the garden frame. At Chilcombe sweet peas, clambering into twigs in traditional fashion, give

height above neat rows of carrots and beetroot. Behind them climbing roses invade old fruit trees to add a touch of wildness.

Fruit trees play host to other climbers as well as roses (LEFT). Clematis

'Perle d'Azur', one of the best late-flowering clematis, entwines the branches of an apple and flowers as fruit develops in late summer.

seed-heads). Many will curtain walls, twine over trelliswork and up tripods, or clamber through neighbouring plants to make glorious displays with small delicate or wide saucer-shaped blooms providing massed colour. Ferny-leaved evergreen *Clematis cirrhosa* curtains a sheltered wall with creamy flowers in earliest spring. *C. armandii*, another evergreen, carries handsome leaves of leathery texture. Like all clematis, it likes its roots in shade but reaches up to flower in more open positions: a perfect solution is to plant it on the sunless side of a wall and allow it to spill over the summit to drape its fragrant blossom on the sunny elevation as a backdrop to sun-loving euphorbias and erysimums, spring-flowering coronillas and mauve- or white-flowered abutilons and the emerging foliage of sturdy perennials.

The *montana* clematis are vigorous and healthy, requiring minimal attention and capable of clothing a large expanse of wall or adorning substantial trees with creamy-, soft or rose-pink flowers. *Alpina* clematis are scramblers, hanging over low walls or balustrades and clambering into the lower stems of climbing roses. Forms of *C. viticella* curtain walls or grow up into small trees; their profusion of small dark purplish-blue flowers looks lovely behind groups of pink phlox or white cimicifugas. At Tintinhull I have allowed them to cascade over metal umbrellas between similarly toned purple-foliaged and contrasting golden-leaved shrubs. *C. flammula*, beloved by Gertrude Jekyll and used to garland all her pergola schemes, bears scented white flowers. Besides the charming clematis species, as summer proceeds a wide range of larger-flowered hybrids come into bloom above the level of most perennials. They are especially useful for growing on frames to give height to a border, to play their part in colour schemes or to create patterns of their own against leafy or man-made surfaces.

Clematis are perfect companion climbers for roses: they will twine up through rose foliage to contribute their flowers at quite another season or be spectacular flowering in unison. Both genera have such a wide range of colours and flower forms that their effects in combination seem unlimited, from almost chintzy floriferousness to delicate embroidered textures.

The choice of backdrop roses is not simply a matter of selecting a colour that works with adjacent planting but also one of mood and style. The more 'perfect' individual rose-buds or 'overblown' open flowers on a

Clematis *'Etoile Violette'*, with subtle dark violet flowers, performs at the same time as the fragrant climber Lonicera × italica (*formerly known as* L. × americana), between them totally covering the wall behind and above the leaves of day-lilies. The muted contrast of these complementary colours makes a rich backdrop. Many climbers, accustomed in their native habitats to clambering upwards through natural vegetation, like to grow with their roots in shade and then to flower in the open sun. Here the good effects reflect the fact that the site is naturally satisfactory for all the plants concerned.

larger scale deserve to be admired in close-up. On a pergola or archway, clematis and other twining companions can be allowed to clamber up from below to clothe the roses' bare stems. For a 'curtain' of roses to back a bed or border, clusters of little flower-heads set amid fresh green glossy or rich-looking foliage make a foil to flower colours in the foreground. Paler colours help create a diffused effect, but specific yellows, crimsons or deep reds contribute to a more carefully orchestrated overall colour scheme.

Ramblers are best growing over an open framework; climbing roses are for walls. Ramblers are pruned after flowering to promote flower-bud formation on new shoots that will appear in the succeeding spring; when skilfully executed, this pruning and training gives plants a strong aesthetic impact. A well-pruned climbing rose has its branches stretched in horizontal lines away from a main central stem; the young shoots growing from these laterals produce the most flowers.

For many people Ninfa, the romantic garden in the ruined thirteenth-century village south of Rome, must represent a personal vision of paradise – a Garden of Eden in which man remains a spectator. Roses and other climbers (their identity often a mystery, since extant lists of old nursery orders are imprecise) have been planted to clamber over old walls and into the trees to make floriferous backdrops on a grand, wild scale. The effects of colour, scent and beauty are magical.

OPPOSITE In the walled garden at Mottisfont Abbey a great profusion of old roses fills beds and festoons walls. Backdrop roses are pink 'Blush Rambler' on the rear wall and, to the right, the vigorous Moss rose 'William Lobb', with dark crimson flowers. In the bed (at front left) is a solitary pale bloom of 'Mousseline'; beside it is 'Salet', with few flowers; behind is the taller flower-covered 'Belle Amour', of Alba descent. In the centre deep red Rugosa 'Mrs Anthony Waterer' is visible behind 'Mme Pierre Oger' and 'Bourbon Queen'. On the right is the Gallica rose 'Spong'. Underplanted alpine pinks and self-seeded white foxgloves add to the effect.

Many species and species-type roses, however, such as the early-flowering Banksian rose and *Rosa* 'Mermaid' (of Banksian origins), only need their young shoots tied in after flowering. A favourite climbing rose is 'Gloire de Dijon', which has large buff-apricot to pale orange flowers; these, repeated through the summer, open flat to reveal muddled or quartered centres. A warm wall site permits the monthly rose *R.* × *odorata* 'Pallida' (syn. 'Old Blush China') a succession of charming plant associations. At Tintinhull we intertwine *alpina* clematis, with the semi-double pink flowers of the rose, in a narrow border; sun-loving pink nerines and amaryllis thrive below; Algerian iris with its gentle violet flower-sheaths carried through warmer spells in winter is another perfect companion.

The main flowering flush of some of the stronger-growing climbing roses may be a major part of a distinctive colour plan: deep yellow roses, such as 'Golden Showers', with Hybrid Tea-type flower clusters, complement blue and yellow border schemes. Crimson roses (one of the best is 'Crimson Conquest') blend with a foreground planting of purplish-toned leaves and blue flowers. Deep reds and scarlets of those such as 'Guinée' and 'Danse du Feu' may have a special place in richer, warmer colour schemes. The glowing bright blues of ceanothus are softened by pink climbers: in spring double pink 'Madame Grégoire Staechelin' will accompany *Ceanothus* 'Cascade', while 'Old Blush China' may be teamed with a ceanothus flowering in any summer month.

Some of the more rambling types of roses, both species and cultivars, flower early. Forms of tender scented *Rosa banksiae* and the Cherokee rose (*R. laevigata*), with wide creamy-white fragrant petals, make cascading curtains against a hot wall (with some support) or – in favoured regions such as the American South – grow wild and free into tall trees. Others flower just after the bedding roses and more conventional climbers have completed their first round. With clustered heads of small white yellow-centred flowers, *R.* 'Bobbie James', *R. mulliganii* and *R. filipes* 'Kiftsgate' all look effective grown on tall trellises or allowed to climb into trees, their flowering branches plunging downwards. The vigorous *R.* 'Paulii' has a natural trailing habit and will curtain dull walls and banks with impenetrable prickly stems and a single flush of clove-scented white flowers. (A pink form is less thug-like.)

Other ramblers have a modest demeanour, more

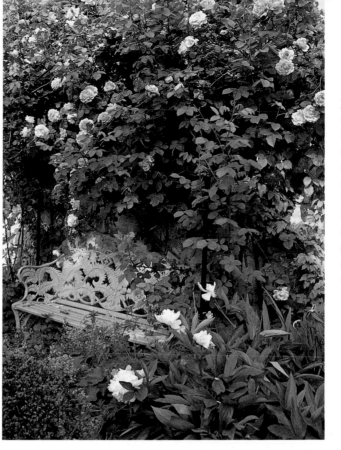

LEFT *The vigorous pink rose 'Constance Spry' and a dark-flowered* viticella *clematis clamber to make a frame behind a cast-iron seat that is almost engulfed by peonies and alchemilla in a garden in southern Holland. Providing height behind borders and beds, plant pictures of this sort give a garden an architectural lift, besides extending the colour range on to a vertical plane.*

Yellows and golds

Yellow flowers and golden foliage never seem heavy in a landscape. Whether seen as folded rose petals, feathery alchemillas, angelica umbels, diaphanous evening primroses or flowering shrubs with winter clusters of spider-like stamens, yellow flowers gently draw the eye and seem to give a feeling of airy lightness. Pale and golden leaves may be used to extend space and apparently push the garden perimeters outwards.

In spring, flowering shrubs seem to possess predominantly yellow flowers; under their skirts smaller aconites and crocuses precede primroses and narcissi. The early yellows are often paired with flattering carpets of blue, violet and mauve flowers, which sets a pattern for flowering schemes during the rest of the season. There are fewer yellow-flowering plants in the middle of summer, although roses, cinquefoils, day-lilies and alchemillas provide a wide choice and range of yellows. In traditional yellow and blue summer schemes copied from nature's spring colours, grey foliage of artemisia and lavender provides further subdued contrast. By late summer the yellows have become deeper and more orange in tone, swinging round towards the browns and bronzes of the prolific daisy-flower families, golden rod, tall verbascums and golden-rayed lilies.

Many yellow flowerers produce good foliage so they are often successfully grown on their own or as specimen groups, or are allowed to seed in paths and paving. Whole borders planned with a range of yellow flowers are also attractive and with care will perform all through the summer.

FAR LEFT *Yellows are always light in their effects and seem to glimmer in a garden setting rather than making blocks of solid colour. Here waxy flower clusters of* Lilium 'Connecticut King' *look relatively heavy beside diaphanous evening primrose flowers. The dark purple foliage of orach (*Atriplex hortensis 'Rubra'*) adds a further dimension and a deep note of contrast.*

LEFT *In a border planting with a yellow and white theme, graceful cephalarias rise above pale yellow-flowered thalictrums and creamy-yellow foxgloves (*Digitalis grandiflora*). White roses act as a foil and are repeated to unite the plant groupings. Silvery-leaved* Artemisia ludoviciana *runs like a thread through the foreground planting.*

RIGHT *In this plant group a bright achillea becomes the strong focal point while yellow-toned neighbours like the retiring Alchemilla* mollis *fade beside it. Grey leaves of artemisia and helichrysum blend as background colour to prevent harsh effects.*

RIGHT *Scarlet-reds and harsh yellows – harmonies from the 'hot' side of the spectrum – were often combined in Miss Jekyll's grand border schemes. Telekia speciosa (syn. Buphthalmum speciosum) and Maltese cross (Lychnis chalcedonica) here make a dazzling partnership deliberately designed to jolt the mind and draw the eye from blander colour associations. Most gardens will benefit from some such vibrant colour scheme carefully chosen to enliven the atmosphere.*

BELOW RIGHT *In an ornamental pot* Pelargonium *'Lord Bute' and dark-leaved fuchsias, with flowers in toned-down reds, combine above the sultry purple-flushed leaves of a tropical coleus. This sort of planting combination is distinctive without being distractingly flamboyant.*

LEFT *The most eye-catching flowers and foliage in this red border are annuals which produce vivid short-term effects, although bee balm (*Monarda *'Cambridge Scarlet') and crocosmias are part of the permanent structure. Scarlet dahlias, verbenas, begonias and* Nicotiana *'Crimson Bedder' glow between the seasonal leaves of ricinus, scarlet-stalked ruby chard and beetroot.* Berberis × ottawensis *'Superba' and* Sedum telephium maximum *'Atropurpureum' have deep purple-toned leaves which pick up the blue pigment of the darker red flowers.*

The range of reds

Pure bright reds with dazzling oranges are probably the most controversial of all flower colours. It is impossible for the eye to ignore red features; they stand out and grab the spotlight, and even their own green leaves intensify the redness. By their demand for attention they provoke strong reactions. Most 'good-taste' gardeners dismiss as violent, even vulgar, many of the colours from the 'hot' side of the spectrum. The purest and brightest scarlets and vermilions – reds without any blue pigment to give more mellow crimson shades, and without the traces of yellow that produce more cooling oranges and browns – are certainly vibrant.

This quality of dazzle may also make bright reds desirable. Conventional colour schemes of pale blending pastels and silvery foliage can become dull: bored with sameness, the eyes and mind refocus with the introduction of contrasting bright colour. In a garden these reds – kept from immediate view and deliberately sited around a corner or behind a hedge – jolt the mind and provide surprise focal points. Our red and yellow border at Tintinhull has for some a jarring quality, but I love its contrast with the toned-down greens, greys, and pale flowers of other areas.

Reds are advancing colours, distorting and fore-shortening distances, but even this may be turned into an advantage. Small, intimate garden areas become cosier, safer and mysterious if deep reds are set against glowing backgrounds of green hedging.

As with the clear and the reddish-blues, there are to all intents and purposes two sorts of red. Scarlet reds and crimson reds may clash violently or, more maturely, harmonize, with the blue pigment in the crimson toning down and softening the harsher electric scarlets. In the border, reds are best chosen in colour harmonies: oranges and yellows on one side, crimsons and violet-toned flowers stretching away on the other.

Flowers in softer reds – darker shades, or paler pastel pinks – are easier to use and provide less to argue about. These soft colours may pair with blues and, indeed, often share blue pigment in their make-up. Purple-toned leaves provide background colour that harmoniously accentuates the 'blueness'. Pinks, especially when salmon- or apricot-toned, seldom work well with yellows. Mauve, on the other hand, is close enough to blue to make an admirable contrast with most pale and bright yellows.

Colour effects in planting

Gardeners should study colour behaviour in the countryside as well as in the garden, and above all learn how painters and other colour craftsmen have built up colour associations in their work. Looking closely at the blending blue-green weaves of Brussels tapestries, for example, helps us to appreciate how foliage tones set the background for every garden scene (just as in nature, where incidents of bright colour are usually small in proportion to the larger masses of background greens, greys and browns in low tones). Perhaps Impressionist artists have most to teach the gardener. It is their vision, repeated over and over again as a series of glimpses, that adds up to our garden views. Many great garden artists trained as painters: Monet planted his garden at Giverny in order to paint it later, and we can study it translated on to canvas. Gertrude Jekyll, unable to continue her career as a painter owing to deteriorating eyesight, applied her colour lessons

(many of them derived from Turner) to perfecting garden borders. From Turner she learned the colour values of mist and spray, ice and snow; later she translated his theories of light and used silvery foliage to make neighbouring flowers seem to glow more brightly. She copied the vibrant evening tones of his paintings by using orange and deep violet flowers together.

The principles of colour manipulation remain much the same although the painter works with exact colour mixes, while the gardener labours in a constantly changing world. Both use colours not only in pleasing associations but also to play tricks to convey architectural and linear effects. Dark solid plants such as yew, rhododendron, heavy purple-leaved prunus or beech trees imply weight, while dense twiggy bushes with pale foliage are light and airy. Flower and leaf colours emphasize aerial perspective; painters and gardeners choose cool blues, dull greys and browns and all pale tints to distort space and give the appearance of depth and distance. 'Warm' reds, oranges, shimmering yellows and solid whites foreshorten all dimensions. Thus the length of an avenue or border may be exaggerated, shapes of flower beds apparently altered, and the eye drawn to certain features.

A gardener cannot change colours by mixing pigments as a painter does, but the colours selected will be similarly affected by where they are placed, which colours they are next to, the relative sizes of all the colour groups and the distance from which they are seen. In the three-dimensional garden with planting on different planes, fresh views and colour sequences are unfolding in new and constantly renewed relationships. Whether in a long border glimpsed across a lawn or as plants tightly packed into a container, flower colours behave logically: seen from close to, colours remain in distinct blocks; from farther away they blend and interweave like a Persian carpet.

The colours actually perceived are influenced by all the other elements visible at the same moment, so producing an almost inexhaustible number of possible permutations and combinations. The human eye tends to exaggerate apparent differences, so that colours that seem quite similar (such as two tones of blue) will look very different when placed together; dissimilar colours will, if anything, look even more different when placed side by side. Completely opposite or complementary rainbow colours, the pure undiluted hues such as yellow/violet, orange/blue and red/green – all of which

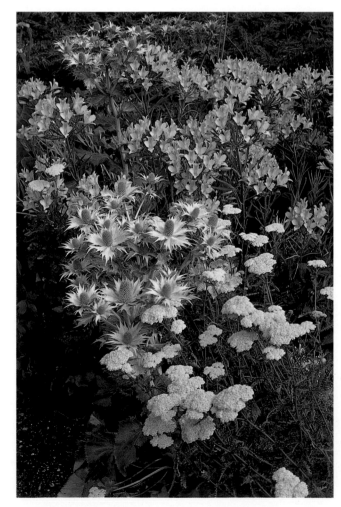

Golden-orange alstroemeria and lemon-yellow achillea are companions to thistle-like Miss Willmott's ghost (Eryngium giganteum) in a border scheme. The almost blue tinge to the silvery leaves and flowers of the eryngium sets off the neighbouring yellows, making them seem brighter and more glowing. Gertrude Jekyll loved to use silvers and greys with pastel colours to make their tints seem stronger, but they are equally effective with the almost strident orange tone of this Peruvian lily.

On the wall at Tintinhull Clematis 'Huldine' makes a curtain of light next to the yellow-green flowers of the shrubby Chilean Cestrum parqui. With petals that are almost translucent and a central boss of greenish stamens, the flowers of 'Huldine' have a quality of whiteness that is easy to use in a garden, flattering neighbours rather than grabbing the spotlight for itself. Tinted whites and pale glimmering yellows are an ideal combination.

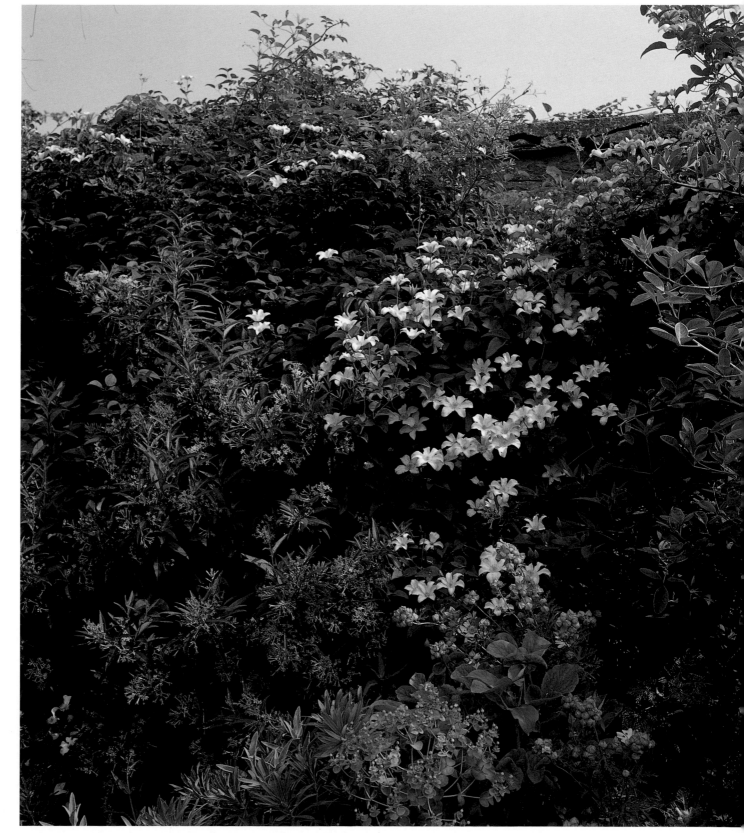

THE NATURAL GARDEN

Approaches to planting
Achieving the natural look
The meadow garden
Waterside gardening
Natural rock gardens

A New England garden
A garden in Holland
A garden in Vermont
On the French Riviera

The essence of natural gardening lies in working with nature rather than against it. Plants are used in ways that they obviously enjoy: they grow with freedom, intertwine with romantic abandon and spread in drifts to match the lie of the land or to complement overhead tree canopies. The natural approach is possible on any scale. True Robinsonian 'wild' gardening, as expounded by William Robinson in the nineteenth century, is most suitable for woodland or for landscapes where trees and hills shape the horizon. The principle of using plants to create such a look of spontaneity, however, may be applied in a pocket-handkerchief flower bed in which hellebores and wood anemones thrive in the shade of a single tree.

This chapter is about growing flowering plants on a modest garden scale, in ways inspired both by the simplicity of nature and by some more intimate wild flower details. In the natural garden, planting schemes appear relaxed and uncomplicated; plants seem to grow as if positioned by accident. Where accent plants are used they subtly enhance the forms and textures of an understated composition rather than punctuate the layout with eye-catching contrasts. Good companionable groups or drifts and natural-looking spreading shapes make abstract patterns, echoing contours and shadows existing in the site.

The myth that wild or natural gardening is virtually labour free should be exploded at the outset. Such gardens may mean less work, but what work there is – from the planning stage onwards – is skilled and sensitive. Natural planting should look as if it requires low maintenance, but this casual appearance is sustained only by selective hand-weeding and considerable annual juggling of plants to retain the relative proportions between the groups. To paint a garden picture informally composed of shapes, flowers and leaves, the natural gardener must have not only a sense of beauty but also a deep knowledge of plant types, their relative growing rates and general needs – skills less vital to the pattern-making formal gardener whose horticultural skills combine with those of the architect.

Mirabel Osler's garden pond in Shropshire has just the right 'natural' touch. The plants look as if they have arrived spontaneously, thriving in the moist soil to spread in drifts that push out into the water's edge. The pond itself has an appropriately informal air, with no hard lines. To keep such a scheme in balance is a demanding task: vigorous plants need firm management.

APPROACHES TO PLANTING

To the real ecologist, gardening with anything other than native species is artificial. In the British Isles adherence to this principle would mean that flower gardens were fairly dull. As a result of the Ice Age, and the islands' subsequent separation from the continent of Europe, the native flora of Britain is not rich in species. Using native plants only would result in charming meadows of delicate wild flowers – suitable for the outer fringes of the garden, perhaps – but the flower garden as a whole would undoubtedly be impoverished.

In many other regions of the world, such as North America, Asia and Australia, which have a wide range of climates and physical conditions, there is a huge diversity of plant material and gardeners have more exciting possibilities for native plant gardens. Most gardeners, however, even if keen on naturalistic results, will want to use foreign plants and good hybrids and cultivars to enhance effects. The gardener's individual skills are employed to give exotic plants growing conditions resembling those found in their native habitats and to grow highly bred garden plants as naturally as possible.

Some naturalistic planting is more psychological than real. An alternative to confining the palette strictly to native flora is to use 'old-fashioned' species in unsophisticated cottage-garden styles of planting. This tradition harks back to a pre-industrial time when gardening was uncomplicated by horticultural sciences and the flood of new plant introductions after about 1600. It may not satisfy the purists, but its rejection of highly bred nurserymen's specimens in favour of unimproved species plants may achieve appropriately simple, natural effects. A few standard fruit trees (if possible old varieties) and some old-fashioned cottage-garden flowers – roses, peonies, columbines, irises, fritillaries – interplanted with rosemary, lavender and lettuces indicate the theme.

Framing wooden steps at the edge of a garden on the Long Island shore, wild flowers flourish in profusion. Here European ox-eye daisies, naturalized as wild flowers in North America, mingle with day-lilies escaped from garden cultivation and a variety of grasses to give the approach a very natural air. Even a native plant purist who declines to use exotics will accept the presence of plants that have been grown around the house for centuries.

Pioneers of natural planting

The earliest and in many ways most influential advocate of the natural garden was William Robinson, who wrote *The Wild Garden* in 1870 at a time when gardening fashions, dictated by the great houses and their influential head gardeners, had established a highly artificial style. Tender bedding-out plants, changed two or three times a year, were being used to implement elaborate colour patterns and massed effects; gardening skills and techniques were intended to demonstrate man's control over nature while showing off the wealth of the garden owners. Hardy plants, both native and introduced, had been relegated to the cutting borders in kitchen gardens; some of the best only survived in smaller rectory and cottage gardens.

Robinson's naturalistic approach seemed revolutionary to his contemporaries, who misunderstood or distorted many of his ideas. He advocated that groups of hardy native and exotic plants (mainly perennials and bulbs) should be encouraged to grow and spread in natural drifts on sloping banks, under the branches of deciduous trees at the edge of woodland, or in moist soil by watersides. After planting, it was hoped, they would multiply naturally and eventually look as if they owed nothing to man's artistic or horticultural interference.

Other pioneering spirits and collaborators such as Gertrude Jekyll took his themes and broadened them for use in the flower garden as well as in the outer areas where garden perimeters fade into countryside. In order to achieve the natural look, the flower garden was treated as if each constituent part provided conditions suitable for certain sorts of plants, and emphasis was put on using plants that were appropriate to each site. There were few obvious climax or architectural plants; instead, blending groups set a theme of happy association and companionship. All this, of course, concealed careful manipulation: the soil and aspect of the site would have been thoroughly considered and, where necessary, adapted and improved in order to give the plants the best chance of success.

Not all naturalistic concepts have come from Britain. Modern gardeners draw on ideals fostered by designers and nurserymen such as Karl Foerster who worked in Germany between the two world wars. Foerster encouraged the use of flowering perennials and grasses in landscapes, and an escape from formality in plant arrangements. Jens Jensen, working in the Mid-

In this New England garden a winding pathway of soft pine-needles leads under the trees and contributes a sense of direction and space. Even plants as sophisticated as hostas, originally from Asia and 'improved' by nurserymen over the last twenty years into a thousand cultivars, assume a natural look when planted in a simple, unpretentious way. William Robinson knew them as funkias and described them as 'noble' plants suitable for massing or edging in shrubberies. Groups of one kind of hosta do not look too exotic and make excellent ground cover.

western states of America, particularly around Chicago, advocated using American native plants in naturalistic designs at a time when most American gardeners – still mainly inspired by traditional European layouts – were choosing imported plants from Europe and sometimes even American natives that had been improved by European nurserymen before returning to be used in gardens in their place of origin.

The new American-style gardens for the 1980s, laid out by Oehme, van Sweden and Associates and planted with prairie grasses and perennials, carry on this tradition today: they are essentially naturalistic in concept. Planting is not confined to American natives, but includes broad sweeps of tufted flowering grasses interlocking with massed rudbeckias, sedums and ceratostigmas, imitating nature at its best. All these pioneers, whether sticking to a 'natives-only' policy or allowing the addition of suitable hardy exotics, choose plants that are suitable to the region and those that are in keeping with the theme of the bed or border.

Nature's inspiration

Like the painter arranging pigments on a canvas, the gardener planning a natural garden must think in terms of creating a balanced composition, using the plants to give height and depth, width and lightness (conveyed by habits of growth and foliage colour), colour and texture, exactly as if he or she were working inside the frame of a picture. Strong accent plants should be arranged in groves or informal groups rather than paired to frame vistas or planted in regular patterns.

A momentary breathtaking glimpse of a foreign countryside embellished with native flowers, exotics to the onlooker, growing wild across the landscape may provide inspiration for garden schemes. The varied climate and scenery, and rich native flora, of North America offer such examples: in the southern states glorious backdrops of wisteria and Spanish moss, along with the Cherokee rose (*Rosa laevigata*) – an escaped introduction – festoon the evergreen live oaks (*Quercus virginiana*); pink-flowered cranesbills (*Geranium maculatum*) flourish by the expressway in the woods of Connecticut; and on Vancouver Island swathes of camassias grow along the shore.

LEFT *Wild garlic* (Allium ursinum) *with dark green leaves and white starry flowers makes an attractive, if pungent, weed-suppressing cover in moist woodlands. Here at Levens Hall it carpets the ground under the branches of the wide beech alley beneath which few plants can thrive.*

ABOVE *Pink-flowered* Allium karataviense *emerges above a mat of sweet woodruff in a charming incident in Catherine Hull's garden on the North Shore near Manchester, Massachusetts. Low-growing spreading plants, if not matting too thickly, make foils for bulbs to push their way through.*

Nature's effects are intended to be improved on by the gardener. Some magical scenes I recall are set in gardens skilfully planned to give truly natural effects, making use of suitable native and introduced flora. I remember with pleasure a field of native meadow anemone (*Anemone canadensis*) in Lincoln Foster's garden in Connecticut – a mass of starry white flowers that made a broad sweep beside a steeply gushing stream. Only a few yards away, on a rocky outcrop, sun-loving European euphorbias (the cypress spurge *Euphorbia cyparissias*) had colonized shallow open soil to seem equally at home. At Mount Cuba, Delaware, small American east coast native flowers spread in broad drifts between mountain laurel and dogwood, while along the stream in the valley Asian primulas had been allowed to establish themselves in natural profusion.

Some of the best small American gardens are those stolen from woodland, where planting follows nature's patterns as closely as possible. By thinning out a few trees to make patterns of light and shade, native acid-loving plants such as maianthemums, arctostaphylos, mitchella, eye-catching arisaemas, bloodroots, heucheras, bluets (*Hedyotis caerulea*), red- and yellow-flowered *Aquilegia canadensis*, sweet rocket (introduced, but now naturalized in New England woods), as well as exotic shade-loving hostas and ferns, spread in natural drifts between dogwood, mountain laurel and native rhododendrons. Biennials (or even annuals) are encouraged to self-seed *in situ* and establish themselves without obvious human interference.

These American examples are matched for me by some in the British Isles. At Glendurgan, Cornwall – a superb natural-style garden – advantage is taken of steep slopes and a mild climate to grow many rare introduced plants: native English cowslips, for example, flower in the rough grass in front of flowering Japanese cherries. Many other great European gardens furnish magnificent scenes of naturalistic planting, closely echoing the magic of recalled scenes of nature. Even if it is not possible to match precisely the particular growing conditions, soils and climates, it may be feasible to introduce similar scenes or incidents into a garden, eliminating obvious signs of control and the appearance of artificiality.

At Sheffield Park, Sussex, giant lilies (*Cardiocrinum giganteum*) are grouped in dappled shade in the woods. White foxgloves glow in the dusk at Knightshayes Court, Devon, and at Winterthur, Delaware, drifts of

pink and white azaleas spread out beneath the tulip trees, and in their turn are underplanted with broad sweeps of native phlox or May-apple and European bluebells. There is nothing simple about any of these gardening triumphs. The giant lilies will only flourish to their full potential if richly fed (Gertrude Jekyll, who used to have manure-filled pits dug for each stand of bulbs, was amused by casual visitors who thought her successes were easy). The white foxgloves at Knightshayes represent years of weeding out mauve-flowered interlopers. The melting colours of the waves of azaleas at Winterthur with their accompanying sweep of colonizing woodlanders have been achieved only after years of patience.

Some gardens may already contain natural features that suggest a theme for naturalistic development, as well as indicating the actual plant types that may be grown – a stream bed, perhaps, beside which to encourage moisture-loving bog plants. The flower

Lenten roses flower en masse at Knightshayes Court. With flower colour varying between cream and blushed purple, Helleborus orientalis hybrids, often attractively marked, flourish in shady borders. They like rich feeding but need little attention other than tidying of their foliage during the flowering period in early spring. Good colour forms can be selected and grown on from divisions but, left to their own devices, these hellebores will volunteer plenty of good quality seedlings to colonize a suitable site.

garden may spread into natural woodland, carpeted with drifts of low-growing shade plants and with taller woodland perennials. In some gardens, open banks and meadow valleys provide natural sites for sun-loving colonizers. In others, layers of stratified rock may become the foundation of a natural rock garden for alpine plants that like to put down deep roots in search of moisture (see Natural rock gardens, page 94). Features such as these set the scene, and the planting range may be extended with suitable plants from all parts of the world, so that natives already *in situ* or added discreetly thrive beside drifts of similarly happy exotics.

Themes from elsewhere

For the natural gardener in search of a theme, paintings, carpets, tiles and porcelain may all provide inspiration. The association between art and gardening is a recurrent theme: the romantic landscapes of painters of the school of Claude Lorrain may well have helped to inspire the development of the English landscape movement in the eighteenth century. In its turn, the new landscape ideal, which swept away geometric layouts and plant regimentation to replace them with soft curves and contours, directly influenced the more natural ways of growing plants developed by William Robinson.

The baroque Dutch paintings of the seventeenth and eighteenth centuries – in which snowdrops and anemones, roses and peonies, irises, fritillaries and tulips, lilies and dianthus are displayed together in exuberant if seasonally impossible profusion – may provide a point of departure. When planning a theme for a flower bed, the gardener may emulate the free-style effects of the paintings to follow the seasons. Lavish, informal arrangements overflowing and arching out of elegant vases are worth copying in containers and borders.

The close connection between the Impressionists and their gardens has already been mentioned. Monet created his famous garden at Giverny so that he could paint it and Renoir treasured and preserved the timeless atmosphere of his garden and olive grove at Les Collettes as inspiration for his paintings. Impressionist canvases may act as a direct inspiration to gardeners. Some of the paintings done at the end of the nineteenth century also capture a freedom and exuberance of flower-bed style that deserves study. In the United States, Childe Hassam's portrayals of Celia Thaxter's island garden off the coast of Maine during the 1890s show impressionistic sweeps of flowers growing naturally.

More formal representations of flowers may even stimulate ideas for the natural garden. In the patterns of Persian carpets, stylized flower shapes and colours blend and mingle inside firm geometric structures. The same effect may be achieved within the manicured edges and horizontal lines of backing walls and hedges, the crisp architecture providing a foil to the free-style inner planting. Borders at Hidcote, Sissinghurst and Tintinhull are of this type, described by Vita Sackville-West as 'maximum informality of planting in a formal setting'. Similarly, the flowery meadow glimpsed through the window of an Italian master's painting of the Madonna or the Annunciation may seem horticulturally unrealistic but nevertheless has a charm that merits emulation.

ACHIEVING THE NATURAL LOOK

Whatever your chosen theme, the essence of natural gardening lies in selecting plants that flourish in the soil and climate of the locality and in using them as nature would. This same principle holds good whether your garden is favoured with features lending themselves to naturalistic development, or is a city backyard or suburban rectangle. However urban the site, growing flowers in a natural way involves careful consideration of the soil of the locality so that from the outset the right plants are chosen.

No 'natural' garden, even one in which only natives are grown, will survive without constant reappraisal. Hardy plants growing in conditions they enjoy may quickly get out of control and spoil the balance of the composition. Inevitably some plants grow faster than others; the toughest survive, the weakest go to the wall. To achieve the desired casual look you need to know in depth the habits and requirements of individual plants and their relative rates of growth in successive years.

In theory, introduced plants will do best in any garden site if the conditions approximate to those of their natural habitat. In practice, many good garden plants are no longer 'natural' species, but have been improved to satisfy particular garden conditions. Some requirements are obvious: sun-lovers need an open situation, and shade-lovers prefer woodland conditions – or at

One way of achieving a natural look is to choose garden plants with an ebullient, informal habit so that they cloak man-made structures with flowers and foliage. At Ninfa in Latium, south of Rome, climbers grow in profusion over the old walls of a ruined village. Here pink climbing roses sprawl with luxuriant abandon in the seventeenth-century walled garden. A wonderful assortment of old and new roses thrive in this climate, where the hot sun ripens the wood for next season's performance.

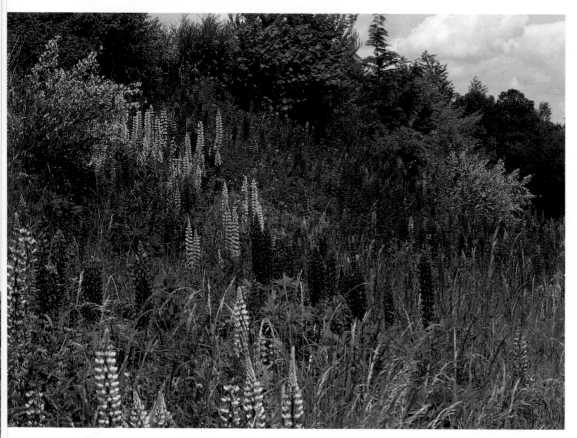

Along a Dorset roadside hybrid lupins with violet-blue, mauve and pink flowers – descendants of the original Lupinus polyphyllus *from western North America – have seeded and naturalized in the grass. The blending tones of these seedlings weave together subtly to give a charming relaxed colour effect that would enhance any garden scheme. Allowing plants to self-seed in a haphazard way often produces effects that are as exciting as carefully planned garden programmes.*

Periwinkles, often relegated to poor shady sites, flower brilliantly when given more open situations and richer soils. Blue *Brunnera macrophylla*, with forget-me-not flowers in spring, thrives in deep shade; its thick leathery heart-shaped leaves look attractive all summer.

Hardy herbaceous geraniums are prolific flowerers, with colours ranging between mauve, pink and violet, and their mounds of elegant cut leaves fill in gaps between taller perennials or shrubs and fall forward over flower-bed edges for softening effects. Lady's mantle, with gentle light green leaves and feathery lime green flowers, is another spreading perennial that epitomizes the natural look. Grown in drifts at the base of taller plants, it fits into any flower scheme.

If beds are backed by walls, climbing plants – allowed to grow into natural shapes rather than fanned and tied to wires – give a soft curtained backdrop. Draped over walls and climbing up trellis, they also disguise and sometimes completely hide rigid lines of architectural detail or unsightly landscape features. Twining through the branches of neighbouring trees, climbers such as the flame creeper give an air of romantic and wild profusion.

Annuals and biennials

The jungle effects created by the free-style planting of woody plants, hardy perennials and bulbs are further enriched by biennials and annuals that are encouraged to seed themselves in haphazard groups and drifts to colonize any patch of bare soil. The crafty gardener may well direct events by scattering seed (never using a hoe or hand-cultivator) in available spaces.

In spring, biennial honesties (forms of *Lunaria annua* – known as the silver dollar plant in North America) will thrive and spread in the dappled shade of a fruit tree or ornamental cherry. Its mauve flowers make a striking colour contrast to the pale yellow bracts of the almost evergreen perennial spurge, *Euphorbia amygdaloides robbiae*, or the smaller *E. cyparissias*, both of which spread in similar sites. A white-flowered honesty (*Lunaria annua alba*) may flower at the back of beds where shade-loving perennials take over later in the season and if isolated comes true from seed.

Biennial forget-me-nots (forms of *Myosotis sylvatica*) may be allowed to seed freely after flowering each spring and will happily multiply in any shady corner. Plants can be pulled up after flowering is over. Brighter blue flowers and sturdier plants are obtained in named seed packets; they should be sown in early summer and transferred to their flowering sites by autumn.

Biennial foxgloves, for sun and shade, are excellent in an informal garden. The ordinary *Digitalis purpurea* has a dingy pink flower, but white-flowering seedlings, as at Knightshayes Court, may be selected to add grace and interest to a border. The southern European *D. ferruginea*, with coppery-yellow flowers, looks exotic but is not too glamorous for the natural garden. Although a perennial, it is best treated as a biennial.

In open situations statuesque angelicas, evening primroses, tall silvery thistles (forms of onopordum), silybums with green leaves veined with white, and thistle-flowered Miss Willmott's ghost are all worthwhile biennials that mix well with groups of permanent shrubs and perennials; all are species and come true from seed.

The floppy horned poppy (*Glaucium flavum*) with greyish foliage and bright yellow papery flowers will sprawl at the front of a sunny border. Some of the biennial mulleins seed as single specimens between groups of perennials. They provide height, while prolifically seeding violas and verbenas carpet the ground, filling up space at the front of borders.

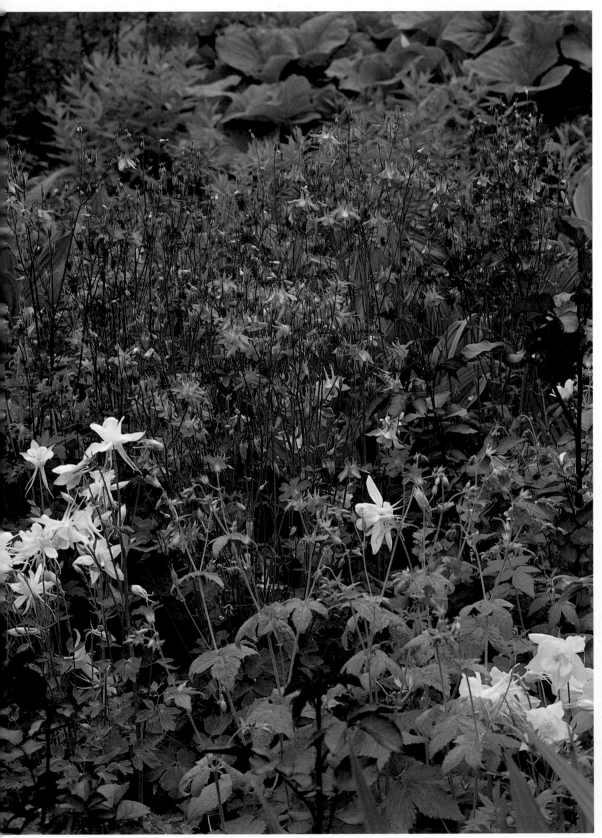

LEFT *Columbines (mostly the ordinary Aquilegia vulgaris with flowers in tones of pink and blue) seed freely in a border in the Walled Garden at Wallington in Northumberland to enhance an early summer scene. Later, as other plants come into flower, the columbines can be dispensed with; as long as a few are allowed to set seed, a selection of new plants will always appear in the following season.*

BELOW *At ground level in Jim Reynolds' Irish garden a patch of pink cranesbills (Geranium × riversleaianum 'Russell Prichard') and little violas – the old-fashioned heart's ease, a prolific seeder – mingle without damaging one another's growth.*

Some annuals, or flowers that may be treated as annuals, are self-perpetuating seeders and look appropriate in natural flower beds. Cultivation of the tall grey-leaved opium poppy (*Papaver somniferum*) is discouraged in the United States and is illegal in public gardens, but I love this plant with its crowded heads of folded white, pink or red petals and encourage it to establish itself as a permanent annual feature; allow the best forms to seed and pull out the least interesting. The catchfly (*Silene armeria*) has oval grey-green leaves and bright rose-pink flower-heads in mid- to late summer and will seed in sunny spots at the front of borders. Venus's navelwort (*Omphalodes linifolia*), with its lance-shaped silvery leaves and whitish flowers in summer, and the tiny ground-hugging knotweed *Persicaria capitata*, with pale pink flower mop-heads, enjoy spilling out on to hot paving or growing between stones.

A display bed of annuals including corn cockles, clary, poppies, marigolds, cornflowers and love-in-a-mist demonstrates the intense effects possible if the flowers have no competition. To achieve this apparently natural profusion, the ground must be cleared each season to prevent coarse grasses and perennial weeds creeping in to weaken flowering potential.

Some tobacco plants such as *Nicotiana sylvestris* seed *in situ* after flowering. Others, such as the very tall and almost woody *N. glauca*, seldom appear spontaneously in the temperate climate of the British Isles; in hotter regions such as California, though, this species seeds freely and has become a roadside weed.

Many annuals are climbers, twining through small trees and shrubs that have flowered earlier in the season and flinging themselves over adjacent plants to give an even more pronounced natural feel. Self-seeding canary creeper (*Tropaeolum peregrinum*) and Chilean glory flowers (*Eccremocarpus scaber*) may well swamp other less vigorous neighbours. Growing up to 3m/10ft in a season, the latter is a perennial in warm climates, and a self-seeding annual in colder regions.

THE MEADOW GARDEN

Meadow gardening is of two kinds: the permanent meadow, of mixed bulbs, annuals, biennials and perennials that are able to survive competition among grasses; and the annual flowering meadow, which is made anew each year in freshly cultivated soil. The permanent meadow, which is never cultivated again once it has been established, may reflect nature at its very simplest, as in the wild flower garden; bluebells and primroses colonize grassy slopes in deciduous woodland, a sea of lesser celandine with fritillaries and leucojums grow in English water meadows in Oxfordshire, and ox-eye daisies flourish on steep banks.

The annual flower meadow, on the other hand, may reach an intensity of dappled colour realized only by alpines in natural meadows when, as the snow recedes from grasslands in spring and early summer, they are in their full flush of bloom. On the California hills native flowers, sheets of annual golden eschscholzias and blue-flowered lupins, bloom after the first spring rains.

But the meadow garden need not be restricted to native regional flora: Flanders poppies, *Agrostemma githago*, *Rudbeckia hirta*, annual phlox and violas create a riot of kaleidoscopic colour. American and British gardeners, with such different native flora, interpret the term meadow gardening in different ways. British native meadows may be a bit dull; a mixture of native and exotic plants will much improve the interest. In North America a gardener can more easily afford to be a native flower freak since he has a greater repertoire of splendid flora on which to draw.

In Suffolk Country Park an annual meadow garden is on a grand scale. Colourful field poppies, cornflowers, corn cockles and daisies mingle against a green background to conjure the image of a rich medieval tapestry or a 'flowery mead'. Although some plants such as the poppies will self-seed, this wealth of colour will not return each year unless the ground is rotovated and resown with a mixture of desirable flower seeds.

Essentially, meadow gardening implies gardening that is done in grass. Much of the success of this sort of gardening depends on creating and maintaining the conditions in which meadow plants will thrive and spread. Meadow gardening does not have to be on a large scale or be part of a larger layout. Meadows may be intimate pockets of planting right against the house or in the front garden. A meadow, sharply delineated by mown grass pathways or other edgings, may seem to take the place of a perennial or mixed border as part of the inner flower garden.

Whether started from scratch or made on a patch of uncut lawn or rough part of the garden, meadows need a foundation crop of various grasses. Mixed with them, hardy flowers, including bulbs, perennials, biennials and annuals are encouraged to naturalize and spread. Their greatest competitors are the vigorous grasses, which gradually tend to push out some of the flowers. Meadows with native or a mixture of native and exotic hardy flowers are easiest to establish in poor soil; Sussex downlands are rich in native flora. In rich soils, grasses, thistles and other hedgerow weeds, including Queen Anne's lace, will usually get the upper hand and most of the flowers will disappear over a period of years. For this reason, ideal as they may seem for the purpose, kitchen gardens, fertilized over decades, are not suitable sites for meadow gardens; nor are old borders and beds, abandoned for economy, or areas of mown lawn where grasses, tightly cut each week in the past, have needed heavy feeding to promote growth.

Meadows may be made by gradually adding bulbs and herbaceous plants to an existing orchard or any rough grass area, the poorer the better; an appropriate mowing timetable using machines with adjustable blades will allow plants to develop leaves and flowering stems and also allow time for seeding. Alternatively, meadows may be established in fresh ground that has been cleaned and rotovated; a grass and flower seed mix, chosen for the soil type and climate, includes perennials, biennials and annuals. Bulbs and established pot-grown plants may be added; planted out individually, they will help to speed up effects but are only feasible for an area of modest size.

Unfortunately, some desirable plants, as well as unwanted weeds, are natural thugs and if left alone will overrun less pushy neighbours, so – however relaxed the garden style – it will be necessary to restrain some plants and encourage others. Grasses, ornamental cow parsley, thistles, nettles, bindweed and brambles, which are colonizers in outer meadows and woods, are popular with many conservationists as part of local ecology (butterflies need nettles to survive). However, in common with undesirable aliens such as ground-elder (which was introduced to Britain to be eaten as salad by the Romans), they love the same conditions as many garden plants, particularly the sites in which bare soil has been improved by cultivation. Such plants need to be controlled.

Both native plants and escaped foreigners can take over when provided with conditions that suit them. In English meadows, strong-growing grasses and even primroses may push out colonies of snakeshead fritillaries, native narcissi, cranesbill geraniums and cowslips as effectively as the farmers' chemical sprays. By watersides, sedges and meadowsweets may be overrun by imported giant heracleums (*Heracleum mantegazzianum*). In North America the European purple loosestrife (*Lythrum salicaria*) is strangling native skunk cabbages (*Lysichiton americanus*) and blocking waterways; in the southern states the kudzu vine (*Pueraria lobata*) is killing native trees and shrubs with its tangled grasp.

The kinds of flowers selected will depend on whether the meadow is in an open sunlit area or in partial shade, as well as on the type of soil. Some meadows are designed to put on a display all through the summer; others for a shorter spring show.

Bulbs such as aconites, snowdrops, crocus, scillas, snakeshead fritillaries, tulips and anemones may be naturalized in grass that is cut quite short during the previous autumn and returned to lawn as soon as possible after the spring flush of flowers; the area may be mown within about six weeks of flowering. Meadows for early and midsummer performance may be brightened with native grassland species – white ox-eye daisies, blue bachelor's buttons, poppies and cranesbill geraniums. In England native orchids, flowering in midsummer, will seed by late summer, allowing the meadow to be cut before having its second fling with colchicums, autumn-flowering crocus and sternbergias in early autumn.

In North America, where there are native flowering plants suitable for every possible meadow environment in different climatic regions, schemes are especially inspirational and wide-ranging. In the north-east a late-season perennial meadow is truly labour saving:

native butterfly weed, eupatoriums, heleniums and heliopsis, purple coneflowers, Michaelmas daisies, golden rods, yarrow and coreopsis glow with waist-high tangled colour among non-invasive grasses; a few naturalized aliens such as day-lilies, teasels and lythrums increase the range. In shadier sites native aquilegias, *Geranium maculatum*, false indigo, claytonias, monardas, dwarf *Iris cristata* and woodland-type Michaelmas daisies grow at different heights.

In the wetter Pacific north-west, where conditions more closely resemble those in the British Isles, established meadows are always threatened by invading perennial grasses and thistles, and acid-loving plants multiply in woodlands and by roadsides. In the Midwestern prairies, where winters are very cold and summers very hot, meadow gardening has assumed a more serious conservation aspect: restored prairie areas (the region's natural habitat now almost wholly destroyed by agriculture) represent a natural plant community in which alien plants may too easily upset nature's balance. Even in controlled garden meadows, plants should be restricted to the innumerable native prairie flowers and grasses as exotics spread too easily.

WATERSIDE GARDENING

Moist places in the flower garden, the edges of streams and ponds, and their calm water surfaces, are all ideal spots for natural flower gardening. For damp spots in the inner flower garden there are spreading clumps of plants that thrive in moisture-retentive soil, such as astilbes, cimicifugas, *Euphorbia griffithii*, filipendulas, hostas, some lobelias, suckering *Lysimachia clethroides*, and ligularias with beautiful heart-shaped leaves and orange flowers. Large-leaved rheums and rodgersias are suitable if the scale is right. As well as their attractive flowers in season, all have interesting foliage through the summer months. The round- or broad-leaved plants can be set alongside those with contrasting spikes such as *Lobelia cardinalis* or the sword-like leaves of irises: yellow flag iris (*I. pseudacorus*) grows in any soil; Japanese *I. ensata* (syn. *I. kaempferi*) and *I. laevigata* need acid soil.

Ponds with natural contours can be edged with groups of plants, the natural effect enhanced by leaving part of the bank clear and encouraging drifts to spread companionably, rather than using single specimens.

The gently sloping banks of ponds and streams, too, provide perfect sites for drifts of hardy flowering plants. Choose spring- and summer-flowering primulas, bog irises, purple loosestrife, rodgersias, *Lysimachia punctata*, peltiphyllums, ostrich plume (*Matteuccia struthiopteris*) and royal ferns (*Osmunda regalis*), marsh marigolds (*Caltha palustris*) and yellow, white or ivory globe flowers (forms of *Trollius*), as well as hostas, astilbes and meadowsweet.

Acorus calamus, with fragrant foliage, bog arums, and various sedges and rushes actually grow in shallow water around the edge. The so-called hardy arum (*Zantedeschia aethiopica*) cannot withstand frozen water around its roots, but will survive low temperatures if the crowns are safely below water level. If winters are not too cold, *Gunnera manicata* from Brazil, with giant bristly, deeply lobed leaves, is a magnificent waterside plant; flowers are conical spikes of dull green followed by orange-brown seed-pods; at the end of the summer season, bend their dying leaves over the crowns to provide frost protection.

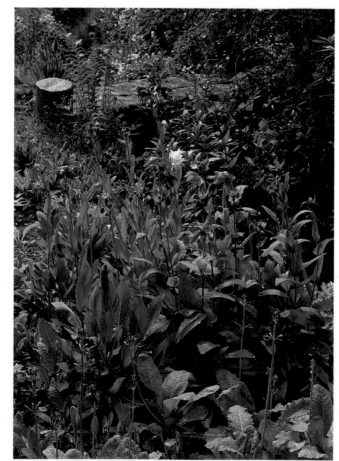

At Kildrummy in Scotland the conditions of acid soil and high atmospheric humidity suit both Himalayan poppies and Asiatic primulas which flourish as they would in their native habitats. Once established, these Robinsonian drifts of plants should be self-perpetuating, but a fine balance is required between providing the moist but not waterlogged soil necessary for meconopsis species and keeping conditions damp enough for the primulas, which do best in more moisture-retentive soils.

Aquatics – plants such as waterlilies that are physiologically adapted to live in soils without oxygen – thrive at various levels in shallow or deeper water. They cannot be grown successfully in swiftly moving streams or where there are changes of current, but lying on the still surface of ponds they further enhance the informal effects of the natural garden and bring nature into formal layouts. In summer their leaves and flowers break up patterns of clear reflecting water, and their spreading horizontal shapes make calm contrast with the fussier silhouettes of neighbouring plants. They only flower satisfactorily in sunlight, but their shining leaves give an exotic tropical air to patches of water in deep shade.

In the Fountain Garden at Tintinhull where the planting is predominantly white the American *Nymphaea odorata* with pointed white petals and greeny-purple sepals flourishes in the shallow water. In the Pool Garden where the water is deeper, *N.* 'Marliacea Rosea', *N.* 'James Brydon' and *N.* 'Escarboucle' bear red and crimson flowers that tone with the hot colours in an adjacent border.

To maximize the naturalistic effects of water features, choose plants that require the same soil type as found in the rest of the garden – unless the pond is in a separate area and can be visually isolated. Plants with quite different requirements and unsuited to an environment often produce a jarring note. Although it is possible to create entirely artificial conditions and to meet plants' different soil and drainage requirements, in practice it is quite difficult to isolate growing areas from the natural environment in any permanent way; water soon leaches through and 'reconverts' the area to its natural conditions.

A water or bog garden will deteriorate more rapidly than almost any other part of the garden. All garden schemes need constant adjustment to make sure that the more vigorous plants do not monopolize space – or that there are no unwanted intruders – but the lush conditions at the water's edge make vigilance particularly important. Even aquatics may spread and take over all the water surface of a pond, leaving no space for sky or trees to be reflected; ideally at least a third of the water surface should be kept clear of spreading leaves. Most of these summer-growing plants are rapid colonizers and have to be divided every few years.

It is not always easy to maintain a clear water surface, especially in a water feature situated in full sun.

LEFT By the water's edge at Heslington Manor in York a candelabra primula (Primula 'Inverewe') grows among grassy-leaved Acorus calamus 'Variegatus'. Behind, waterlilies float on the still surface of the lake. At water margins, as in all natural gardening, there is a constant need to adjust finely tuned planting proportions as some plants increase and spread more quickly than others.

ABOVE In the bog garden at Saling Hall in Essex, pale hosta flowers and tall yellow flower-spikes of Ligularia przewalskii rise from among the elegant tracery of fern foliage and contrasting large-leaved darmeras. All of these plants flourish in good moisture-retentive soil. An ornamental pot provides just the right focus to the lush jungle effects of the planting.

BELOW *Sun-loving plants that enjoy free drainage thrive and spread by seeding at Roquebrune on the French Riviera. The daisy-flowered* Erigeron karvinskianus *colonizes the walls and terraces with its delicate pink and white blooms.*

BELOW RIGHT *In a cool damp corner of the garden at Kildrummy Castle in Scotland,* Primula *'Guinevere' and* P. sieboldii *flourish amid moss-covered rocks and moisture-loving ferns. In drier climates such humid conditions require some sort of misting system, which immediately destroys the natural look.*

Vast amounts of algae develop quickly and turn clean reflecting water into a green soup. The quick-growing summer-flowerers. – waterlilies, water hyacinths and lotus (*Nelumbo*) – are all oxygenators that play a part in keeping water surfaces clear. Most ponds in full sun will also need further oxygenating plants such as Canadian pondweed (*Elodea canadensis*), that live below water and compete fiercely with the unsightly algae for carbon dioxide.

NATURAL ROCK GARDENS

Windswept alpine slopes in Switzerland and crags and peaks in the Rocky Mountains are the natural homes of countless garden plants. Their special features of soil and climate, however, are not easy to reproduce in an ordinary garden. Many alpine specialists abandon the naturalistic attempt and instead grow their plants in greenhouses where conditions may be totally controlled, or construct raised beds with specially prepared soils in sun and in shade.

The great alpine gardener Reginald Farrer had outcrops of local limestone in his garden at Ingleborough, Yorkshire, where he could satisfy the conditions needed for his precious mountain plants. Many of the grand Edwardian gardens had rockery areas built with limestone slabs brought especially from the Lake District. This is hardly practical or appropriate today.

Although rock gardens are ideal adjuncts to the flower garden, adding new possibilities to the range of plants that may be grown, it is not easy to create a natural-looking rock garden area, or to site it next to other features in the garden. When grown in gardens true alpines, usually snow-covered in winter in their native mountain habitats, need excellent drainage so that their crowns remain dry in winter, as well as deep pockets of soil so that their questing roots can seek moisture during growing periods. They do not require rich feeding. A rock garden, well designed to achieve natural effects, is most often successful if the plant range is limited. Grit-covered sloping screes on an open site with specially prepared drainage, rather than complicated arrangements of rocks, often provide suitable and visually acceptable growing areas. Mediterranean-type plants, with aromatic and silvery leaves and fragrant flowers, after suitable adjustments for soil preferences, will also thrive in these beds, enjoying conditions of heat and drainage similar to their native lands.

Sun and good drainage also suit bulbs from South Africa, shrubs and perennials from California and Chile and some plants from low latitudes in Australia that will survive cold winter temperatures. At Blake House in California, with a view across the bay to the Golden Gates, a sun-facing rocky outcrop has become the home of Mediterranean cistus, Australian melaleucas, New Zealand meterosderos, South African bulbs and native California sun-lovers that naturalize freely and give a wonderful unplanned air to the garden. In drier zones in California, sloping gardens are planted with succulents, which store moisture: agaves, cacti, sedums and sempervivums all thrive, and their glaucous leaves fit naturally into the landscape.

In most natural gardens, however, rock garden areas are best planted simply, with quite ordinary cascading sun-lovers such as mossy phlox, candytuft, cottage-garden pinks, diascias, rosemaries and many silver-leaved plants that will grow between prostrate junipers, ceanothus and brooms. On the shady side of a slope ferns and moss, bloodroots, tiarellas, *Campanula latifolia*, epimediums, roast-beef iris (*Iris foetidissima*), Solomon's seal and grasses such as the tufted luzula will thrive among shrubs such as arbutus that are tolerant of dry soil and shade.

Slopes that provide essential drainage without introducing the harsh lines of retaining walls or raised beds obviously best capture the requisite spirit of relaxed informality, but, even on flat ground, scree-beds may be specially prepared to ensure that water drains away. Plants in ill-prepared beds are far more likely to be killed by water freezing around their crowns than by low temperatures. Many plants from higher altitudes will also survive such conditions if protected from excessive moisture in winter by cloches.

In plantswoman Margaret Charlton's garden north of Vancouver, British Columbia, rough stone walls and terraces maximize the potential of a steep south-facing site and create 'rock garden' conditions that suit a wide range of native and exotic plants. In the foreground are flower-heads of Erysimum 'Bowles' Mauve', *Iris sibirica and* Persicaria affinis 'Dimity'. *Behind, yellow doronicum mingles with the spiky foliage of Crocosmia 'Lucifer', and leafy rosettes of* Barbarea vulgaris variegata *set off sedums, alyssum, catmint, phygelius and penstemons.*

A NEW ENGLAND GARDEN

Catherine Hull's rock and woodland garden to the north of Boston is outstanding in its combination of superb plantsmanship with delicacy and taste. The ground falls steeply below the house to provide a naturally varied terrain and in the 1970s the landscape designer Fletcher Steele constructed a pool and pergola, giving the garden a focus around which Mrs Hull has arranged her planting. Natives and exotics grow happily in association in just the way William Robinson recommended in *The Wild Garden*. The rockery – often a tricky subject in garden design – is made with natural stone to look as if it has always existed, and drifts of little woodland plants glimpsed under native trees have the same effect of permanence. All the plants, including many quite fussy alpines, are given conditions in which they thrive.

ABOVE *The foliage of a clump of Solomon's seal, also known as David's harp, provides a distinctive texture in the dappled woodland shade and clothes the stark base of a tree trunk. The plant's graceful lines are particularly attractive in this variegated form, Polygonatum odoratum 'Variegatum', the white leaf-margins clearly visible in the shaded sites in which it flourishes.*

LEFT *In early summer white-flowered dodecatheon, native to North America, thrives in pockets of soil on a rocky outcrop, giving a restrained picture in light shade. To create the best effects Mrs Hull uses simple drifts of one plant type only, rather than 'dotting' plants about more restlessly. Such simple garden schemes disguise great skill and plantsmanship.*

LEFT Mrs Hull uses a low-growing columbine (Aquilegia flabellata pumila) to make a little drift of sophisticated flower colour in the rock garden area. From Japan, this columbine falls into William Robinson's 'exotic' category, but looks perfectly in keeping with the spirit of the site. Planting pockets amid well-placed rocks provide natural-looking frames to set off such small-scale plant treasures.

ABOVE Native American plants such as the little woodland Phlox divaricata spread in drifts in areas where some sunlight penetrates, and biennial Lunaria annua self-seeds to naturalize companionably. Constantly changing light filtering through the tree canopy enhances the natural planting effects. The limited colour range of this flowery mass with its delicate tints and shades sustains the simple mood.

A GARDEN IN HOLLAND

Mrs Goossenaert's garden in the south of Holland is hidden and sheltered from the road by evergreens, so that the areas that open out around the house as you approach along a narrow drive come as a surprise that turns to enchantment as a wealth of plant pictures gradually reveal themselves.

Many good plants establish a strong foundation for gentle naturalistic schemes that seem to flow between one part of the site and another. Each garden view is framed by taller trees and shrubs to make a picture, while at a lower level the planting style is more relaxed and seemingly unplanned. The use of height to break up the space into different areas disguises the extent of the garden, and the resulting air of mystery adds to the feeling of unstudied organization. This sort of gardening –

a mixture of sophisticated planning and a spirit of *laissez-faire* – is the most difficult of all to carry out successfully. It calls for a sure sense of design, well in evidence here, and Mrs Goossenaert also understands the needs of individual plants, juxtaposing those that need sun and good drainage, and accommodating those that enjoy shade. Occasionally more formal elements and intimate or restful areas help to give the garden coherence and provide an important degree of contrast.

Often limited in size by natural topography, Dutch gardens tend to excel in plant association pictures rather than grand effects: when space is restricted, it is essential to be selective, using only the best available plants to create stunning seasonal colour compositions. Mrs Goossenaert deploys this tradition of plantsmanship to equally good effect in her not-so-small garden.

ABOVE *A white-flowered clematis (Clematis 'Moonlight') clambers up through a rose into the light to contribute its flowers in season. Intertwined climbers above head height help to make the garden seem relaxed and jungle-like; in reality even these simple effects require considerable manipulation and expert guidance. Plants growing together must enjoy the same conditions, in this case rich feeding and sunlight.*

LEFT *A graceful silver-leaved bush of Buddleja alternifolia 'Argentea' is planted in a sea of silver-leaved Stachys byzantina to give a wonderful effect, further enhanced in summer when the branches of the buddleja are wreathed with fragrant lilac flowers. It is these touches of brilliance in plant association which distinguish this garden from the run-of-the-mill.*

An inviting seat in a spring meadow in the Goossenaert garden. In the grass cuckoo flower or lady's smock (Cardamine pratensis) flowers with the early daffodils, in this case Narcissus 'Dove Wings', and tulips to make a charming scene. This sort of 'wild' gardening is not as easy as it seems; the cuckoo flower should be allowed to set seed and the leaves of the daffodils to wither before the grass is cut. Most of the highly bred tulips will continue to flower when naturalized in grass for many years, their flowers gradually getting smaller and more 'natural'-looking than when grown in specially prepared compost in ornamental pots or beds.

LEFT *In spring the flowers of* Clematis montana rubens *appear when the great* Wisteria sinensis *is also in full bloom. In native habitats climbing and twining plants grow upwards towards the light, clinging to each other to gain support. Both vigorous and hardy (although wisteria flower buds may be damaged by a late frost), wisteria and clematis can be judiciously trimmed after flowering to keep their relative proportions in a garden scheme.*

BELOW LEFT *Dark ivies, leaves of* Hosta sieboldiana *and flowering hydrangea make a restrained autumn picture in which leaf association is as important as the more fleeting flower effects. This garden is full of* such carefully managed scenes, each isolated to give delight and surprise as you make a garden tour.

BELOW *Another part of the garden in late summer where flowers dominate the scene. Stately plume poppies (*Macleaya × kewensis*) and a Rugosa rose with the small-flowered* Clematis viticella *'Purpurea Plena Elegans' growing through it perform above the glaucous leaves of* Hosta sieboldiana. *Using plants with fine foliage in a mixed border gives satisfactory effects all through the season. From spring to autumn the leaves of both plume poppies and hostas act as a foil to all neighbouring flowers.*

LEFT *In a summer border backed by a weeping silver pear (Pyrus salicifolia 'Pendula'), white spikes of* Lysimachia ephemerum *rise behind an exuberant mass of mallow, phlox, campanula and anthemis. Although these effects look easy and relaxed, in practice a border planting like this needs constant grooming to maintain such a balanced picture.*

BELOW *In an intimate corner a more formal note is struck with trimmed box shapes grown in pots to sit on paving. Silver-leaved cotton lavender sets off the more solid greens. The hardy deciduous Ceanothus × delileanus 'Gloire de Versailles' flowers in late summer.*

A GARDEN IN VERMONT

In essence a 'natural' garden reveals its secrets by degrees; the element of surprise is strong. Unlike a formal garden with a prescribed pattern, or even a border composition viewed across a lawn, the more natural scheme is planned to beckon and entice.

This garden is in the southern Vermont countryside. Although they have split the garden into different 'rooms' each with a distinct scheme, Wayne Winterrowd and Joe Eck have kept planting schemes simple. Trees and shrub shapes dictate the spirit of the garden; they frame the sky overhead and make canopies below which flowers spread in drifts in the summer season. All this is not achieved without a lot of trouble; it is a tribute to the owners' skills that winter protection with evergreen brush makes it possible to grow a wide range of plants beyond their own zone 4 without marring the feeling of spontaneity.

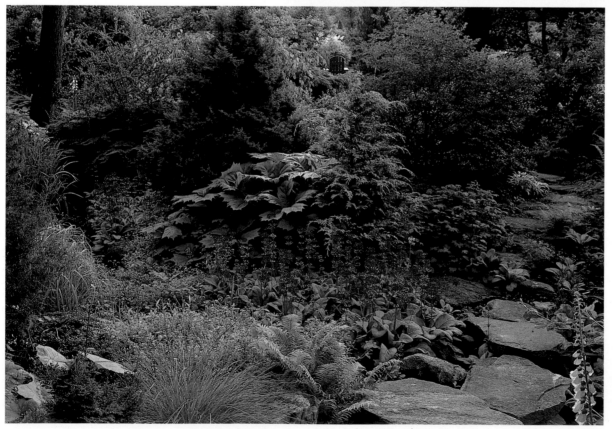

ABOVE *Stepping stones by the stream bed lead to the focal point,* Robinia pseudoacacia 'Frisia' – *described by Wayne Winterrowd as 'the colour of fresh butter all summer'. In the foreground sparkling blue* Meconopsis betonicifolia *contrasts with variegated glyceria leaves and* Primula japonica 'Postford White'.

LEFT *Moving from shadow into sunlight in the stream garden, pyramidal* Chamaecyparis 'Boulevard' *and bronze-tinted* Rodgersia aesculifolia *provide a background to a drift of pink-flowered candelabra primulas* (Primula japonica) *and blue water forget-me-nots. In this garden statements are made with foliage and the weaving patterns of flowers add their seasonal effects.*

BELOW *Beds surrounding a lawn laid out on three levels with retaining walls built of fieldstone from the site are planted to flower through spring, summer and autumn. The scheme maintains a sense of lightly jumbled informality, with well-nurtured perennials growing in free luxuriance. Peonies, Siberian and bearded iris, hardy border geraniums, day-lilies, phlox, platycodon and asters secure a succession of bloom. On the stone walls scented pinks enjoy the sun and free drainage.*

RIGHT *Self-seeded foxgloves are lit up by sunlight in a clearing. True Robinsonian planting depends on encouraging plants to establish themselves so as to appear natural rather than guided by artifice. For this, plant expertise is as important as an eye for composition. Throughout this garden pines and junipers establish an evergreen framework which gives a strong feeling of unity to disparate planting themes, each of which is appropriate to its situation.*

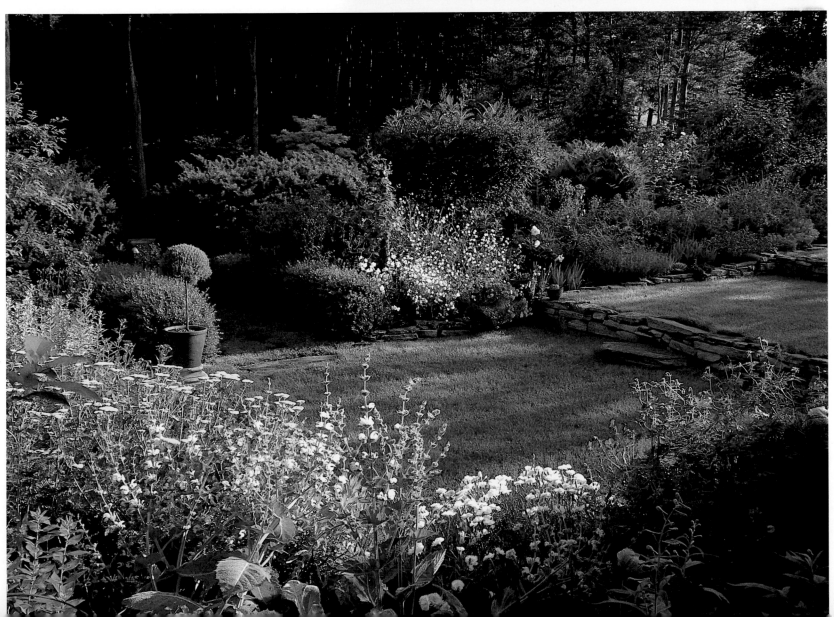

ON THE FRENCH RIVIERA

Some of the most beautiful gardens in the South of France were made between the two World Wars and their terraces and elegant steps reflect the leisured life of those days. Plants here grow only during the winter, as the almost rainless summers are too hot and dry. Silver-leaved plants, with small hairs protecting them from the sun's blast, and those with aromatic foliage containing protective oils flourish best – both native *garrigue* or *maquis* plants and exotics from similar habitats elsewhere in the world.

At Roquebrune Mrs Norah Warre went farther than most of the 'winter gardeners', taking advantage of a favourable microclimate to grow an amazing range of plants from regions with comparable climates, including South African daisies, rare Australians (such as the red-flowered *Templetonia retusa*) and plants from California. Frosts are virtually unknown at Roquebrune; its aspect is protected from icy northern winds, and mature trees now provide further shelter. Lawrence Johnston, who gardened in a colder inland valley at La Serre de la Madone, used to send Mrs Warre newly discovered plants that he could not manage and she grew them successfully in her coastal garden.

Today many of Mrs Warre's rarer plants have gone, but tall Aleppo pines give shade and thriving exotics, naturalized after more than half a century, frame the sea views.

An introduction from Tasmania, Olearia phlogopappa 'Comber's Pink' with mauve daisy-flowers held between silver-green leaves, flourishes beside a pale pink form of Paris marguerite (Argyranthemum 'Mary Wootton'), and spikes of English lavender. Eucalyptus trees, American agave and aloes give a more exotic flavour above sheets of the South African daisy bush (Osteospermum ecklonis), with almost white flowers, blushed blue underneath.

ABOVE *A line of Aleppo pine* (Pinus halepensis) *along the edge of the terrace gives protection to an orange tree above a drift of German iris. Here exotic plants, revelling in the climate, have become naturalized to give a jungle effect probably far removed from the original owner's intention. Tender roses from Burma and elsewhere in the Far East, such as* Rosa gigantea *with wide open single white flowers, grow extravagantly to curtain the old terrace walls. The flowering profusion produced by allowing the strongest plants to succeed is possible only in this very favoured microclimate.*

RIGHT *On one of the terraces pines and eucalyptus give some shade from the scorching sun to allow vegetation to cover the old terraces, blurring their more formal lines.* Osteospermum ecklonis *carpets the ground in a glorious flowering jungle. The garden in maturity, in spite of comparative neglect, still reflects Mrs Warre's plantsman's knowledge; the abundant tender exotics seed and spread today as they would in their native sun-soaked lands.*

THE
FLOWER
BORDER

Border styles
Schemes and themes

Crathes in Scotland
Stonecrop, New York State
Ashtree Cottage, Wiltshire

The flower border is where plants are brought together not for their individually striking qualities but for the part these plants play as neighbours and companions in an integrated scheme. A border consists of a series of plant groups that link together in a three-dimensional planned picture of jigsaw-like complexity rather than the flat pattern of a knot or parterre. Adjacent flower and leaf colours may be exciting in themselves, but it is for the contribution they make to the whole composition that they are chosen and arranged. Even the most architectural plants, although used to contribute overall design effects, are chosen to enhance the whole scheme and not for any key qualities that draw the eye.

It is the planting style or plant themes rather than the location that define the term border. Originally borders marked the line of lawns, edged paths or ran along the base of walls or hedges. Nowadays the term is used much more loosely; all flower beds in which the planting varies in height and depth and is in different planes are called borders – even an island bed may be a form of border.

BORDER STYLES

Flower borders can be planted with all types of plants. Traditionally they were composed of hardy clump-forming herbaceous perennials with seasonal leaves and flowers at their peak between midsummer and early autumn. Nowadays this sort of scheme is usually supplemented with spring bulbs, early-flowering perennials and drifts of summer annuals for a much more prolonged display. Alternatively a border might be predominantly of shrubs, carefully chosen to flower in succession through the months; the addition of some bulbs and low-growing herbaceous perennials, planted to flower beneath the sweep of deciduous branches, may produce extra seasonal displays.

Borders may also be mixed – that is, planted with a combination of trees and shrubs to give year-round structure and to provide pockets of shade, which are

At Benington Lordship double borders show an eye to design, with repetition of groups of perennials such as clustered spikes of yellow Lysimachia punctata, magenta Geranium psilostemon (in the foreground) and airy greenish lady's mantle making emphatic blocks of colour. Foliage of sword-like iris, arching day-lily and pale-rimmed Symphytum × uplandicum 'Variegatum' set off the more brilliant flowers.

filled in by the seasonal growth of other plants such as upright 'border' perennials in conventional groups as well as shade-tolerant sprawlers and bulbs, biennials and annuals. Many borders in small to medium-sized gardens are of this type.

In practice, the kinds of plants used in each scheme overlap – it is really a matter of personal choice and time available, and there do not have to be too many rules. I prefer to have a few shrubs in a mainly herbaceous border as they give some 'body' and help appearances in winter; they are the permanent feature around which the other plants are replanted and rearranged. All our borders at Tintinhull are of this type. Others find conventional border plant groups, which can all be divided and rearranged as one major spring or autumn task, less demanding.

Whatever plants are used within a border, planting styles can range from the very formal, with repetitive architectural plants and a series of repeated colour patterns flowing through the scheme, to the completely informal or natural style discussed in the previous chapter. Some borders are given a formal outline by crisp box edging; others are backed by horizontal clipped hedges that provide a unifying continuous line of colour to frame the planting in front.

The 'English' herbaceous border

The traditional summer herbaceous border, with its quintessentially 'English' look, developed when beds of hardy perennials, grown as cutting flowers for the great house, were rescued from their Victorian oblivion in the walled kitchen garden and introduced as a focus of attention in the flower garden. The heyday of these great borders was the Edwardian age, when labour was plentiful to groom the plantings. Other garden areas provided interest outside the brief summer weeks when the herbaceous plants were performing.

Herbaceous plants can grow only when ground temperatures are above 5°C/40°F – producing leaves, stems, flowers and seeds in one short season. Hence the temperate climate in England, with no winter or summer extremes, enables a wide range of plants from many variable climates to be grown and borders tend to reach a peak of performance. The flowering periods of many non-native plants are extended by the cool nights and relatively cool days of summer, and seasonal rains maintain growth rates during the hottest part of the year.

ABOVE *In Peter Wooster's Connecticut garden shrubs, grasses, perennials and tender 'fillers-in' texture late summer borders edging trimmed grass paths. Such a personal planting style that disregards the rules dictating plant types can achieve exciting results,* different plants being used each year to set off the more permanent inhabitants.

OPPOSITE *In Francis Cabot's garden north of Montreal the growing season is short but strong perennials, often snow-covered in winter, thrive and* especially enjoy the cool summer nights. Delphiniums, tall Thalictrum flavum glaucum, creamy astilbes and bright yellow ligularias are densely planted so that leaves and flowers interweave.

In the garden at Tintinhull we have to get the borders to look good throughout a six-month opening period from April to October. Foliage plants – like sedums and Japanese anemones, which perform from spring to autumn and have beautiful flowers in late summer – become high-priority choices giving the whole scheme an air of luxuriant permanence, and setting off neighbouring clumps of more seasonal flowerers. This border in the Cedar Court is shown at midsummer. It is backed by climbing roses (Rosa 'New Dawn'), scented honeysuckle and intertwining clematis, which flower a little later. In flower are Hybrid Musk roses and clumps of catmint (Nepeta 'Six Hills Giant') – both of which will bloom again in the autumn – and × Heucherella tiarelloides with pink plume-like flowers. A large clump of the white-flowered form of the invasive fireweed or rose-bay willow herb (Epilobium angustifolium album), one of my favourite border perennials, dominates the scheme. The seed of love-in-a-mist (Nigella damascena 'Miss Jekyll') is scattered annually between the rhizomes of bearded irises (now hardly visible) in the narrow frontal border where the globe-shaped Allium christophii also flourishes.

Gardeners all round the world can seek to capture the ethos of the English border style by creating plant associations using perennials that are appropriate to their particular climate and soil. The challenge is greatest in countries with hot summers, especially those where nights are hot. Many herbaceous plants will not tolerate intense heat, especially if it is accompanied by high humidity. For this reason it is more difficult to establish and maintain an English-style border in the south-east of the United States than it is in California. Fortunately, however, many nurseries now give guidelines indicating the tolerance of individual plants to humidity and heat as well as zoning them for frost hardiness. At the other climatic extreme, in cold regions, the main problem is the very short season during which herbaceous plants must make their growth. The fact that the ground may be frozen all winter has compensations, for blankets of snow cover (or thick mulches) protect most border plants from the ill-effects of cold.

Providing winter protection for borderline plants is only one of the tasks of maintaining the herbaceous border. Clump-forming perennials need to be split up and divided every few years or they will cease to flower well. Stems and leaves are cut down each year some time between autumn and the following spring. The soil is mulched and new soft growth is staked and tied in early summer. Gardeners who like their garden to look neat during the winter months will complete the cutting down as soon as leaves fade and stems start to rot; others choose to wait until spring approaches. Those keen on organic methods simply cut down all the stems and leaves, letting them lie where they fall; the new spring shoots push through and in time the dead material rots down to make a mulch.

For the gardener who wants the best possible results in the border at all times, the annual spring or autumn tidy-up is not enough. He or she will spend many hours each week throughout the summer supervising the overall appearance and adjusting the plant relationships within the border. There is always something to do. Fading leaves can be trimmed, dead flower-heads removed, and stalks cut back to encourage other plants to grow over and into the neighbouring flower groups that are already past their peak. Seed is gathered and cuttings taken when appropriate.

In practice the short season of true 'herbaceous' borders is often extended by the welcome addition of bulbs planted in drifts between the perennials. Tulips (small species or the taller hybrids that are treated as annuals), Dutch and English iris, alliums and camassias are at their best in spring and early summer; thereafter their untidy foliage is effectively disguised by the leaves of summer-flowering perennials. Sun-tolerant lilies (and shade-lovers, if planted in the shadow of taller perennial clumps) flower in midsummer, followed by crinums, *Galtonia candicans* and *Gladiolus callianthus* (long known as *Acidanthera bicolor*) in later months. Amaryllis and nerines will only flower well if given a warm site in full sun, ideally at the base of a sheltered wall.

Many annuals are also suitable for growing in companionable clumps and drifts to cover bare soil between groups of perennials. Whereas perennials flower only once in a season (even if over a long period), annuals will bear flowers all summer. In many ways, being temporary and seasonal, they are easier to handle than permanent plants: grown from seed and planted out after the last frosts, they may be fitted in between existing plants just before flowering time.

In the borders at Jenkyn Place in Hampshire colour planning and the proportions of the plant groupings are superbly and thoughtfully executed. Stone edging frames a beautifully maintained wide border planted with large clumps of traditional hardy perennials. Feathers of creamy Aruncus dioicus and cloud-like sprays of Crambe cordifolia back mounds of Geranium × magnificum that flow out over the stone. White and purple forms of Dictamnus albus as well as the dark-flowered Lychnis coronaria at the front of the border continue the colour theme.

Borders designed by the late Peter Coats at Buscot Park in Oxfordshire are mixed in content, with small trees, shrubs and perennials contributing to the very successful effect of purple, grey and golden foliage combined with blue-toned and yellow flowers. The blunt-nosed lime-green flowers of Euphorbia characias wulfenii *match the yellows of shrubby* Phlomis fruticosa *in front of dark-leaved* Berberis × ottawensis *'Superba'. 'Blue'-toned* Geranium × magnificum *and catmint spill over the low box hedge.*

Indeed, annuals can also be effective on their own. Plants chosen especially for their capacity to bloom over a long period without needing their dead-heads removed can be grown from seed and after the initial labour of planting out make a floriferous border that needs relatively little attention. Ageratums, cleomes, godetia, convolvulus, lavatera, nicotiana and salvias can be arranged in groups, the taller towards the back, so that as you walk along the border their colours gradually unfold and blend into each other to create the feel of the traditional herbaceous border in its summer glory.

The shrub border

Composing a flower border using only shrubs calls for a grander time scale as well as a different approach to space. Once planned and established, a shrub border is relatively undemanding to maintain, but there are two important considerations to bear in mind at the outset.

Firstly, these woody plants will take time to reach their full potential. Secondly, since the shrubs will be permanent features, all neighbouring plants chosen must enjoy the same conditions of soil and drainage.

Flower displays are transitory, but shrubs chosen to flower successively will ensure a summer-long performance in the border. Strong architectural plant forms and displays of coloured leaves in season provide year-round interest.

Before planting consider the characteristics of the main plants that set the theme – the natural shape of the shrubs, the foliage colour and texture, seasonal flowering and fruiting performance, and density of growth. (Some woody plants, especially evergreens, are dense and heavy, giving weight to a scheme; others have twiggy growth and pale leaves that bestow an air of lightness.) A balanced border design will include: round-shaped bushes such as evergreen osmanthus and smoke trees; some bushes with branches that fan out from the base, such as Hybrid Musk roses, philadelphus and suckering symphoricarpos; and some that will give definite vertical accents, such as abutilons and variegated buckthorns. Nevertheless, as the border is primarily to be of flowers, it is important to choose good flowering shrubs rather than concentrate too much on foliage textures and shapes. A border scheme should not end up as a Victorian shrubbery.

Consider carefully where to position the shrubs. Plant single specimens so that, on reaching maturity, their branches will just touch those of their neighbours without marring their own graceful outlines. The branches of shrubs planted in groups may interlock, but should not encroach on neighbouring specimens or groups. Creating instant effects by overplanting will give trouble in later years. Planting up a shrub bed is not like planting a forest where alternate trees or lines of trees can be removed at a later date to allow the main specimens (all of similar types) to mature.

Each shrub in a border is an individual with its own growth rate and requirements. When newly established it needs room to breathe and space to put down its roots. Above all, it needs light and adequate moisture. Do not, therefore, surround young shrubs with seasonal annuals or even perennials that have no part in the border's final scheme – tempting though it may be to fill the empty spaces. Unless handled very carefully, such quick-growing infilling plants may all too easily injure the vulnerable young shrubs.

If you have the right sort of acid soil with a low pH and woodland to provide a sheltering canopy, planting low-maintenance azaleas and rhododendrons can be very effective. In this corner of Princess Sturdza's garden in northern France the shrubs – denying light to the soil beneath – are underplanted with shade-tolerant bluebells in a simple scheme. Shallow-rooting shrubs such as these resent attempts to fork over the bed, but appreciate rich top-dressings of organic mulch which help prevent weed germination. These woodland plants look their majestic best grown in appropriate conditions, as they are here, but look ridiculous in smaller borders or open sunlight.

Once established, shrub borders are never dug again unless some of the shrubs have to be removed. A thick organic mulch, applied annually, with the addition of some general fertilizer as growth restarts in spring, will keep the soil fertile and the plants healthy.

All the woody plants in the border need some annual work with pruning shears to ensure a successful performance the next year: dead flowers and flowering shoots must be removed to promote new growth. Shrubs that flower in the spring and early summer generally produce next year's flowering shoots after this year's performance is over and should therefore be pruned immediately. Those that flower towards the end of summer do so on wood produced in the current year and may be pruned back in spring, when frost-damaged shoots are also removed.

RIGHT On a more intimate scale, a shrub border in a town garden depends on shapes and foliage colours more than on flowering seasons. Golden-leaved holly (Ilex × altaclerensis 'Golden King') and Hydrangea macrophylla 'Quadricolor' make effective neighbours in the scheme, but the picture captures a moment when the hydrangea's lace-cap flowers are held on long stems above the variegated leaves and give an extra richness.

The mixed border

A glorious mixture of small trees, shrubs, perennials, biennials, annuals and bulbs arranged as flowering neighbours, the mixed border contains the planting elements of the herbaceous border and the more utilitarian shrub border. However, it is the groups of herbaceous plants that dictate the spirit of the composition, providing firm impressionistic colour patterns, particularly during the summer months. Today the majority of planting schemes are of this type, bringing the natural or cottage-garden style back to the border. No single plant is of major importance for itself: each one is part of the whole scheme.

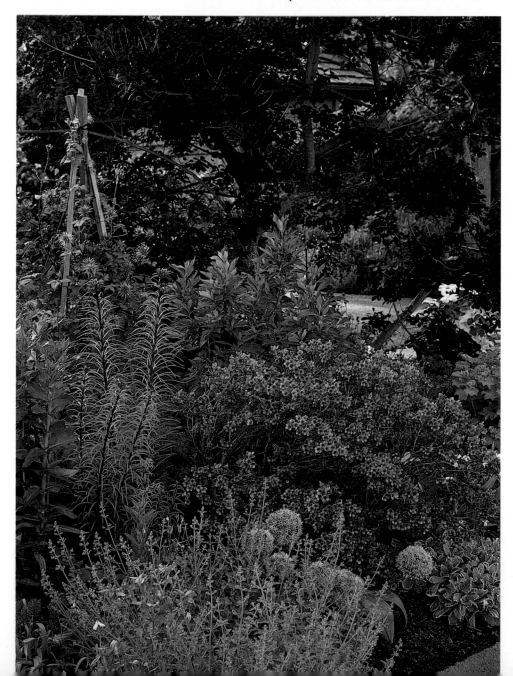

Unlike the shrub or herbaceous border, a lasting blueprint is almost impossible in the mixed border: the relative shapes and proportions change each year and the balance of the composition depends upon the individual's eye rather than on following a rule book. Success also requires a good knowledge of plant needs and behaviour. Over a period of years, if 'soft' material is not divided and replanted, the mixed border can easily turn into something closer to a shrub border, and the impact will gradually be lessened.

Many of the best turn-of-the-century border layouts were of mixed planting. In one of Gertrude Jekyll's borders, for example, woody plants might include a graceful, broad-canopied tree to give overhead protection for spring bulbs and hellebores, while shrubs such as spring-flowering spiraeas and viburnums, autumn hydrangeas and caryopteris, interplanted with drifts of bulbs, extended the season of flowering perennials. Jekyll selected annuals and tender dahlias to enhance permanent planting, sometimes even sinking prepared pots of lilies or similar exotics between more mundane and reliable groups of plants.

The mixed border, with so many different plant elements to consider, is the most complicated border scheme to both plan and maintain. It calls for the skill of the architect in balancing heights and shapes in different planes of planting, as well as the two-dimensional eye of the painter working in one plane. Few gardeners today achieve such amazing results as Gertrude Jekyll and her contemporaries, who had the benefit of skilled assistants in this most labour-intensive form of gardening. Most modern gardeners are better advised to attempt something simpler than the highly orchestrated schemes so dear to the gardeners of the past.

Although perennials set the theme for the mixed border, the small trees and shrubs are put in first. Unlike the shrub border, they should not be planted so that their branches interlock at maturity. They are feature plants, chosen to give an integrated year-round structure to the less sturdy clumps of seasonally growing perennials. If time for gardening is limited, restrict the choice of plants to those that need relatively little attention. Select small trees that cast dappled rather than heavy shade: among those that look good in a border are the very slow growing paperbark maple (*Acer griseum*) and box elder (*A. negundo*, especially its variegated form), dogwoods including *Cornus mas* and

RIGHT *The borders designed by the late Peter Healing at Kemerton are among the most inspiring in England. Although such perfection requires knowledge, skill and lots of hard work as well as a gift for colour arrangement, I think it is worth trying to emulate this achievement. Here a form of Buddleja davidii and a climbing clematis on a tripod frame lower planting of a floriferous Michaelmas daisy, seasonal dahlias, Salvia farinacea and verbenas, including the airy V. patagonica.*

OPPOSITE *The border in Susan Riley's garden in Victoria, Vancouver Island, is of mixed planting: shrubs, perennials and bulbs all play major roles in the completion of the scheme. A dark purple-leaved smoke bush (Cotinus coggygria 'Foliis Purpureis') overshadows a pink Rhododendron lepidotum, while lower-growing herbaceous plants and the attractive spherical flowers and handsome leaves of Allium karataviense fill in the foreground. Lilium regale will flower later in the season. This sort of planting is the most visually satisfying: shrub shapes and branches give substance to a scheme while allowing more gently billowing soft-stemmed plants to fill in the detail.*

C. kousa (and of course the American dogwood *C. florida* if it will do well for you – it needs hot summers), laburnums, styrax, halesias, Judas trees, redbud (forms of *Cercis*) and clerodendrums. Among slow-growing shrubs that need little annual cutting back are smoke bush, choisya, the lower-growing Rugosa roses ('Fru Dagmar Hastrup' would be my choice), deutzia and the shrubby potentillas. Mediterranean cistus actually resent being pruned, but are relatively short-lived. In regions with cold climates many shrubs need their unsightly frosted shoots trimmed in spring.

Herbaceous plants should be sturdy enough not to require staking; avoid those that need routine dividing. I avoid labour-intensive delphiniums which need constant attention (rich feeding, staking and protection against slugs) and go for plants such as astrantias, campanulas, eryngiums, eupatoriums, day-lilies, phlox (which do need dividing but never staking), hardy herbaceous geraniums, perennial honesty and catmint.

Choose bulbs and low-growing carpeters that increase naturally without frequent replanting: all the usual scillas, chionodoxas, bluebells and good forms of wood and Apennine anemone for spring; agapanthus, alliums, camassias and lilies for summer display.

To keep the balance of the planting in trim, all borders need some revision in spring or autumn: in the mixed border, where the permanent shrubs create more shade each year, the 'soft' plants will need to be shuffled about more often than in the perennial border, in which there is no competition from woody plants.

In a very broad border with a tall wall or hedge as backdrop, a narrow gravel or paved path towards the back of the planting allows access for maintenance within the main bulk of the border and for any pruning, clipping or training required by backdrop plants. The bed at the foot of a wall can be specially prepared to accommodate the needs of climbing plants and trained shrubs curtaining the man-made surface so that they do not interfere with those of the main scheme. A path also helps to contain the greedy roots of a background hedge as they try to spread into the main planting area and compete for water and nutrients.

SCHEMES AND THEMES

A border is often glimpsed as a whole from a distance, but is also viewed in detail from close to, and slowly unfolds new incidents of textured colour as it is passed. The series of static plant pictures revealed has not only different nuances from different angles but also shifting permutations as spring, summer, autumn and winter bring changes in appearance and new associations.

A coherent border plan ensures that the whole entity hangs together and works. Most schemes benefit from a unifying theme. This may be provided by the repetitive use of trees, shrubs or perennials chosen for a particular quality of shape or colour. Whether the rhythm is formal or informal, this repeated note turns the whole scheme into an integrated composition.

When making a plan, try to conjure up in three dimensions the colour sequences that unfurl from week to week as different flowers reach their peak then fade. Following the example of Gertrude Jekyll, flower colours may be orchestrated to unfold in different themes based on harmonies or contrasts. As noted earlier, she combined the 'hot' tones of orange, scarlet and crimson in a harmonizing gradation of colours and introduced the cooler colours – blues, greys and pale yellows – in deliberate contrast. At Crathes Castle the main borders, with weaving blues and mauves in earlier summer, become 'warmer' with gold and bronze flower colours as autumn approaches.

Even more important than colour associations is the overall look of the border, the impression of deliberate order. Repeating shapes, colour features and plant groups at least once in any line of vision creates a calming effect; this is particularly valuable in a small garden such as that of Ashtree Cottage, where views of the border are framed by planting that echoes similar themes. Sometimes plants and flower colours are repeated in a studiously regular rhythm to produce formal, mirror-like effects. At other times – like painting a picture – a more free-style composition gives balance and repetition but not exact symmetry, as in Francis Cabot's garden near New York. At Tintinhull we compromise between these two positions. Certain symmetrically placed feature plants hold the border designs together; their choice and disposition depends on a sense of balance. Repeated colour groups aim at stability rather than a mirror-image effect, striving after a naturalistic yet controlled pictorial result.

Successful borders depend not only on making an aesthetically pleasing composition but also on satisfying the plants' growing requirements. Apart from the fact that it will not flourish in the long term, a border scheme will have the wrong 'atmosphere' if adjacent plants do not naturally enjoy similar soil and similar day-to-day feeding and watering.

Mainstays of a classic border, such as phlox, peonies and dahlias need rich feeding. Grey- and silver-leaved plants all require well-drained positions in poor soil in full sun – their silvery appearance is derived from the short hairs that protect the leaves from strong sun rays, enabling the plants to survive long periods of summer drought in their natural habitat. Mediterranean plants such as artemisias, silvery thistles and artichokes will thrive as neighbours.

There are inspiring borders everywhere, magical projects that introduce new plant and colour combinations to lift the heart of the observer. They also

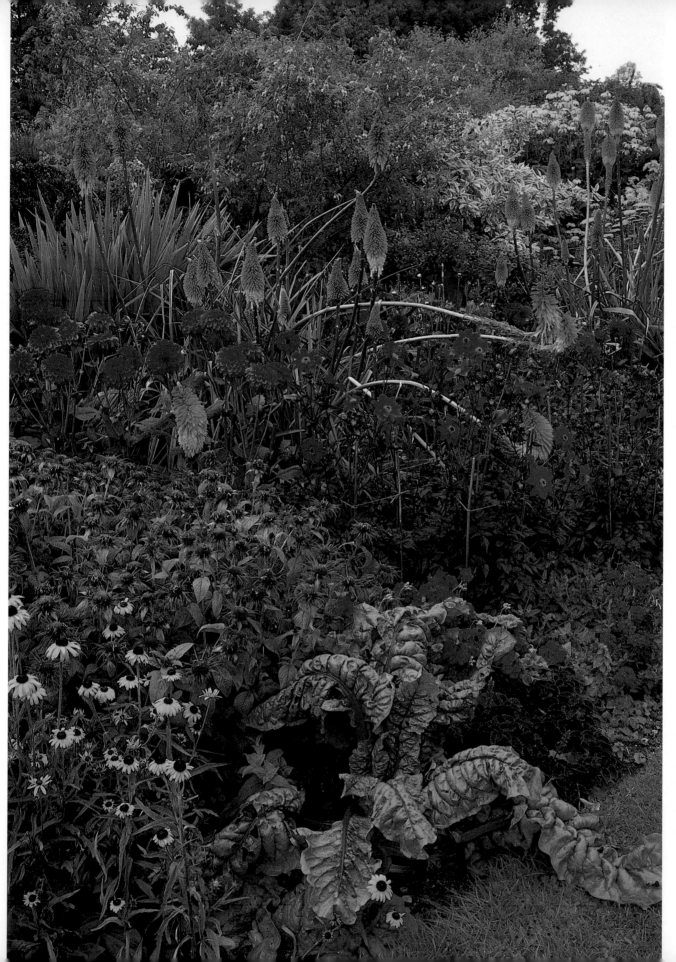

Another border at Kemerton is of 'hot' colours, with flowers of orange, scarlet and yellow matched against red-toned foliage. But the colouring of leaves and flowers gives only part of the picture: textures and shapes of petals and foliage, and even the way they are held, affect the way we see plants as individuals and the roles they can play in planting schemes. In this border red hot pokers, with flower-spikes of tight orange petals grading down to yellow at the base and held on tall stems above rush-like foliage, are a complete contrast to the daisy-flowered semi-double dahlias with their dark bronze-purple leaves and to monardas (Monarda 'Cambridge Scarlet') and rudbeckias in the front of the bed, with wide ray florets around central coloured discs. The red-stemmed crinkled leaves of ruby chard are a striking feature at the edge. I also love the way the graceful arching Rosa moyesii, with its coloured hips, adds an extra dimension at the back of this bed without making too solid a background.

When choosing border companions, the habit and behaviour of each plant has to be considered in detail as well as what you require of the scheme. I prefer the kind of strongly accented heights and depths seen in this Kemerton border to lower, flatter schemes with all the plants growing at one level.

provide models for adaptation. Looking at good borders, especially those in a climatic region similar to the gardener's own, is far more useful than spending hours with graph paper on the detail of the planting.

Planning plant groupings

The artists of the traditional herbaceous border have much to teach gardeners about combining plants to make a beautiful composition on a large scale; many of the visual considerations of deploying flowering plants as neighbours apply even to the more stately pace of shrub borders. But it is with perennials and their bulbous counterparts as supremely unstable building blocks that the glorious effects of herbaceous and mixed borders are achieved.

Apart from possessing soft stems that die down in winter, herbaceous plants have few characteristics in common. Plants such as verbascums and delphiniums soar to head height and more, in contrast to ground-hugging veronicas, creeping mossy phlox and spreading diascias. The flowers are even more varied: peonies and poppies have flat, papery petals that convey strong colour messages. Others – achilleas, eupatoriums and silvery thistles – have tiny airy flowers that form broad, flat flower-heads. The petals of some herbaceous flowers are arranged in a single layer, giving a translucent, ephemeral effect; others are double, providing greater weight and solidity. Astilbe, artemisia and golden rod have feathery flower-heads, while eryngiums and angelicas have spherical umbels.

Although some, such as giant kale or silvery onopordum thistles, are grand enough to stand alone as architectural features, plants are rarely used singly in an herbaceous border; most are planted in groups, as either blocks or triangles. Large municipal borders are often planted in blocks, which makes staking and tying easier but produces a regimented look, destroying all sense of riotous profusion. Triangular shapes are commonly used to plant the garden on paper, but even this method can have an almost too precise military effect. Gertrude Jekyll's preference was for planting in narrow drifts. This means that a number of colours, rather than those only on each side of the group, 'touch' each other, and may be put to great artistic effect.

The size of the groups will depend on the desired effect. If colours are to remain distinct and separate from whatever distance they are viewed, the groups need to be large. If colours are to blend and interweave (except at very close range), the groups should be small. Any groupings, however, must be scaled according to the area of the overall scheme.

The height as well as the potential spread of each group of plants is an important factor in planning the border. Planting with tall groups only at the back and a graduation in heights towards the front can produce a rather unnatural effect. I like to mix the heights in the different planes by creating an arrangement of peaks and valleys which flow through the border. When the tallest plants are at the back to frame foreground planting, smaller plant groups can also grow in their shadow. William Robinson, writing before the end of the nineteenth century, puts the point well:

Do not graduate the plants in height from the front to the back as is generally done, but sometimes let a bold plant come to the edge and . . . let a little carpet of a dwarf plant pass in here and there to the back, so as to give a varied instead of a monotonous surface. Have no patience with bare ground, and cover the border with dwarf plants; do not put them along the front of the border only. Let hepaticas and

The 'border' is defined by a stream in this garden on the Devon coast. Planting a successful scheme is like painting a picture, though plants behave even less predictably than pigments on canvas. Moreover, the palette is limited to those that suit the site; water gardening presents a great challenge as few woody plants are available to give height and substance. Here the composition is dominated by architectural New Zealand flax (Phormium tenax purpureum), with a drift of scarlet candelabra primulas, a scattering of Japanese irises (Iris ensata and I. laevigata) and more primulas in bright painterly colours beneath.

In the pool garden at Tintinhull one border has pale-coloured flowers; the other, across the canal (and also shown on page 71) has red, yellow and cream flowers. Originally designed by Mrs Phyllis Reiss, both today still reflect her vision. They are linked by silvery leaves repeated at intervals along the front of each bed. All the plant groups grow at different rates, so the whole scheme needs constant revision to keep the right proportions of 'spread'. Shrubs and strong-growing perennials tend to grow beyond their allotted space so that there is less and less room for the seasonal planting essential to give the garden the lift it needs, especially towards the end of summer. In general we try to organize a progression of weekly or monthly flowering bursts to peak in different parts of the borders rather than expecting them to be full of colour all through the summer. In quieter moments good foliage plants such as silver eryngiums, miscanthus, sisyrinchiums and variegated symphoricarpos still give interest.

double and other primroses and forget-me-nots, and dwarf phloxes and many similar plants cover the ground among the tall plants . . . at the back as well as the front. Let the little ground plants form broad patches and colonies by themselves occasionally, and let them pass into and under other plants.

As plant groups spread at different rates, parts of a border will need replanning very frequently. Almost as soon as the best possible results have been attained it will be time to do some dividing and reallocating of space. Creating a border is like doing a complicated jig-saw with pieces that are always changing.

Timing the display

Some borders in grand gardens are planned to reach a seasonal peak at a particular time, but in most modest-sized gardens a single border has to look good at all times of the year. This does not mean that the whole bed has to be continually in flower – that would be impossible to achieve. Nor is it easy to try to spread spots of colour through the whole length of a border during the entire season. The best effects are obtained if each part of the border scheme is planned to peak at a particular period, creating a series of progressive seasonal bursts. At these moments flowering plants become stars, like principal actors in a play; at other times, when not in flower, these plants play supporting roles or may even be temporarily off-stage. Managing plants through the gardening season is very much like directing a play through its performance: good timing and synchronization of impact is all-important as both flowers and leaves in turn reach their peak and fade away to make room for new combinations. At any time quieter sections of foliage structure – attractive plant shapes and leaf combinations – make a rich setting for the fleeting scenes played by floral colours.

The importance of herbaceous foliage

The three-month season of peak activity can be extended, and the border's period of beauty lengthened, by choosing flowering plants that have good foliage shape and colour both early and late in the summer. Emphasis is given to contrasts in leaf shape, texture and colour through all the summer months, as well as to the plants' flowering qualities. Sword-like iris leaves, crocosmia, day-lilies, kniphofias and leafy aga-panthus contrast with the more rounded shapes of

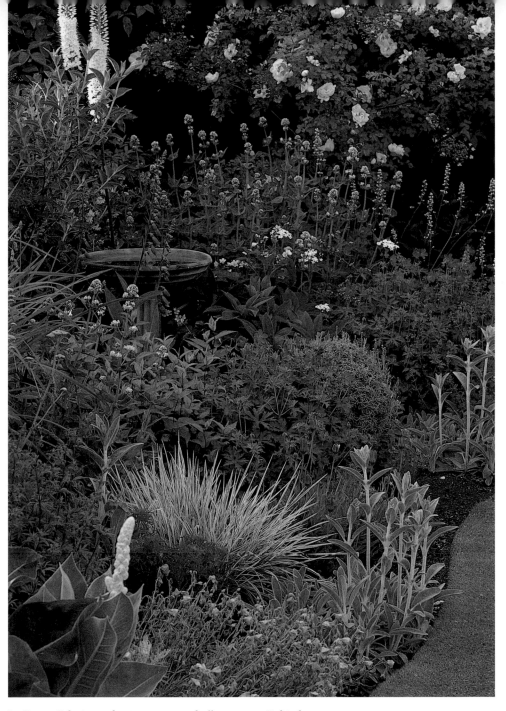

In Susan Riley's garden in Victoria, Vancouver Island, good foliage plants are a high priority for setting off more fleeting seasonal flowers. Silvery Stachys byzantina, verbascum, helianthemum *and* santolina, *the spiky variegated leaves of* Phalaris arundinacea picta *and a tall grey-leaved buddleja are foundation plants that look good all summer. Behind, soaring spires of* Eremurus himalaicus, Rosa 'Nevada' *and a drift of white valerian with some blue cranesbills (*Geranium 'Johnson's Blue'*) blend to make a quiet picture with the pink helianthemums and pink-backed floret rays of* osteospermum *flowers.*

Bunchberry, the charming low-growing dogwood Cornus canadensis *– a denizen of acid woodland in the north-eastern American states – is a wonderful carpeter, with attractive leaves and white four-petalled flowers followed by red berries. Its creeping habit makes it a perfect infiller between tall shrubs that require similar conditions. Most of us would give anything in order to be able to grow it. Here in Le Vasterival, Princess Sturdza's garden, it undercarpets rhododendrons and azaleas in the woodland.*

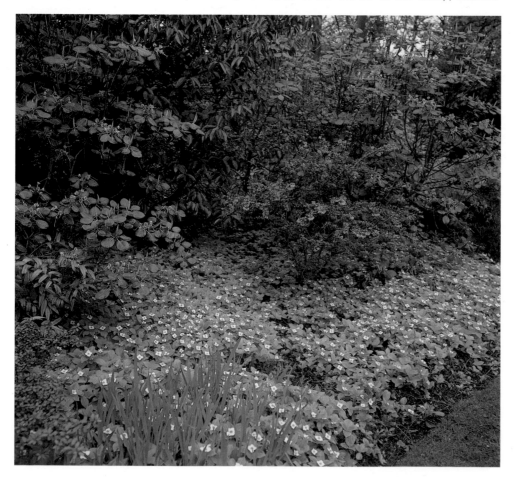

create pronounced contrasts of light and shadow. Judicious pruning will keep plants within prescribed bounds, although fierce cutting back also stimulates renewed growth.

Shrubs for year-round interest

Many shrubs suitable for the small or inner flower garden blossom in spring; far fewer provide blooms in summer or late summer. In spring, choose from abutilons, chaenomeles, *Choisya ternata* (but be wary of the garish golden-leaved *C.t.* 'Sundance'), corylopsis, cytisus, daphnes, forsythias, magnolias, osmanthus, yellow-flowered *Piptanthus nepalensis, Paeonia suffruticosa,* spiraeas and viburnums. For gardens with acid soil, camellias, rhododendrons, pieris and vacciniums may be combined for magnificent, mainly spring, effects, even though they are more suited to woodland scenes.

Summer-flowering border shrubs include both shrub and bush roses, papery-flowered cistus, pink and white deutzias, the dazzling pink-flowered kolkwitzia (*Kolkwitzia amabilis* 'Pink Cloud' is the best), mauve-flowered lavenders, scented philadelphus, potentillas, pyracantha (with berries in autumn), syringa and weigelas. In late summer in most temperate regions (earlier in hot climates) evergreen abelias and arbutus, buddlejas, smoky-blue caryopteris, fuchsias, hydrangeas, hypericums, indigofera, *Itea ilicifolia,* lavateras, perovskias and romneyas all have a high proportion of flower to leaf.

Silver- and grey-leaved shrubs will contrast with more ordinary green foliage in the border, and also provide flowering interest in season. They need full sun and good drainage. Artemisias, helichrysums, lavenders, phlomis, santolinas and shrubby senecios are all worth considering. In regions with a mild climate try leptospermums, hoherias and daisy-flowered olearias. Shrubs with golden, variegated or purple leaves may give stunning results if carefully planned.

There are also shrubs that flower or bear fruit through the winter months. Almost all are scented, and usually their flowers are a tight bundle of fragrant stamens – soft, papery petals would be easily damaged by frost. Mahonias, honeysuckles, shade-loving sarcococcas, many viburnums and witch hazels are good winter performers. Cotoneasters have red or yellow berries that last until Christmas, viburnums carry lustrous, translucent red fruit, while shrub roses bear apple- or flagon-shaped scarlet or orange hips.

Ground-level companions for shrubs

The best companions to shrubs are small bulbs and low-growing herbaceous carpeting plants that will spread beneath the branches and thrive even when lightly shaded during the summer. They will cover the bare earth in the valleys between the shrubs and extend the seasonal colour range of the border. Spring bulbs of the sort that feature in the natural garden are ideal, massed around the base of deciduous shrubs. Those – such as alliums and camassias – that need summer baking during dormancy are not so useful and are best in association with groups of perennials in an open site. Later-flowering drifts of lilies combine well with light-foliaged shrubs, such as corylopsis, caryopteris and perovskia, that allow plenty of sunlight to filter through their branches.

Most lilies can be planted so that they push their spring shoots up through the branches of low-growing and almost prostrate shrubs – in spring their frost-vulnerable tips benefit from the additional protection.

Choose shrubs that do not have too dense a habit or too extensive a root system. *Salvia officinalis*, artemisias, cotoneasters, romneyas, and creeping roses and lithospermums are companions for sun-tolerant lilies; in more shady situations they associate with hydrangeas, sarcococcas, stephanandra and symphoricarpos. At Felbrigg Hall, Norfolk, colchicums in late summer make a band of colour in front of a shrub border in which buddlejas, cistus, hebes, hypericums, fuchsias and potentillas have a long period of performance.

Shade-tolerant herbaceous perennials do well when planted under shrubs in a border, although they may need repositioning as young shrubs grow and take up more space. Sun-lovers, however, only do well while areas are still open to the sky. The most suitable low-growing infill perennials are some of the more pushy plants that will drift from patches of open sunlight into the shady areas under the branches. These include acanthus (although preferring to flower in full sun, except in hot climates, it has glossy shade-tolerant leaves), ajugas, *Alchemilla mollis*, *Asarum europaeum*, astrantias, *Brunnera macrophylla*, *Buglossoides purpurocaerulea*, *Chiastophyllum oppositifolium*, dicentras (although the blue-grey leaved forms will lose their leaf colour), shade-tolerant euphorbias, fragrant sweet woodruff (*Galium odoratum*), hardy cranesbill geraniums, hellebores, hemerocallis, hostas, small blue *Iris cristata* or taller clumps of *I. innominata* (both prefer an acid soil), omphalodes, periwinkles, pulmonarias, all forms of Solomon's seal and false Solomon's seal (*Smilacina racemosa*), creeping potentillas, comfreys (forms of *Symphytum*), tellima and the delicate bronze-leaved *Tiarella cordifolia*.

Biennials, especially self-seeders, are as easy to use in the shrub border as they are in the more relaxed natural garden. Those that flourish and multiply in sun and shade include evening primroses, foxgloves, feverfew, honesty, sweet rocket, *Smyrnium perfoliatum* and some of the columbines. The old-fashioned *Aquilegia vulgaris* with clumps of blue- or plum-coloured flowers is very decorative; its various forms are more tolerant of shade than the modern long-spurred hybrids.

Shrubs, perennials and low-growing creepers combine to make the gold and purple border at Tintinhull one of Mrs Reiss's most imaginative schemes. The tall bronze-leaved shrub is Sambucus nigra 'Guincho Purple'; *with purple-leaved* Berberis thunbergii atropurpurea *and* B.t. 'Atropurpurea Nana', *it contrasts with the golden* Cornus alba 'Spaethii', *which is 'stooled' each spring so that its bark will remain red.* Rosa 'Rosemary Rose' *has dark bronze-tinted leaves and crimson flowers. Along the front creeping* Persicaria vacciniifolia, *once better known as a polygonum, and bright blue* Veronica teucrium *flower in the semi-shade. Many plants will flower as well in half shade as they do in full sun, often benefiting from the cooler conditions.*

CRATHES IN SCOTLAND

Gertrude Jekyll visited Crathes at the end of August 1895, and later wrote: 'The brilliancy of colour masses in these Scottish gardens is something remarkable. Whether it is attributable to soil or climate one cannot say: possibly the greater length of day, and therefore of daily sunshine, may account for it . . . The flowers of our July gardens, Delphiniums, Achilleas, Coreopsis, Eryngiums, Geums, Lupines, Scarlet Lychnis, Bergamot, early Phloxes, and many others, and the host of spring-sown annuals, are just in beauty.' Whatever the cause, and cooler nights are an additional bonus, the flower borders at Crathes are among the best in the British Isles today. Certainly the hardy perennials thrive to grow taller than in the south, and colours seem more glowing, with flowering extending deep into autumn.

Although the borders were already distinguished, they have changed much since Miss Jekyll's day. They were considerably enlarged by the taking in for ornamental purposes of much of the walled ground still used in the 1890s for fruit and vegetables. The majestic yews are thought to date from 1702, but the main layout within the old walls under the castle owes its inspiration to Sir James and Lady Burnett of Leys. The new mixed and herbaceous borders which they designed from the 1930s are in a series of colour harmonies and themes. The formal Colour Garden below the east walls of the castle was given a spectacular scarlet, crimson and yellow scheme of mixed shrubs and perennials, with dark purple-leaved shrubs such as smoke bush providing weight, all surrounding central features of yew and a small pool. In the lower gardens hedges were introduced to create concealed secret areas all with strong colour or seasonal themes. There are white borders, June borders, main borders where the autumn colour of bronze, orange and gold flowers predominates, as well as a Golden and a Red Garden with a strong emphasis on foliage plants.

LEFT ABOVE *The mainly white borders crossing the lower walled garden, with a clipped Portugal laurel as the central focal point, reach their peak in July. They are mixed in composition, with various forms of scented philadelphus and smaller Hebe albicans as shrubby accents, and with*

drifts of bulbs at lower levels. Strong perennial groups include the tall flower-spikes of Veronicastrum virginicum album, featheryheaded Aruncus dioicus 'Kneiffii', the white-flowered Tradescantia × andersoniana 'Innocence' and silvery anaphalis.

LEFT BELOW *Tall Cotswold hybrid verbascums make a foreground point in the main double border leading to the Portugal laurel, and indicate the yellowish-gold tones to come later. Unobtrusive netting stretched over the whole bed in June supports the all-perennial planting.*

ABOVE *The main borders in the central portion of the lower garden create the finest colour effects at Crathes. Early in the season they seem mostly blue and pink. Backed by roses garlanded on chains, the tightly packed perennials here include delphiniums, achilleas, catmint and the*

startling magenta cranesbill Geranium psilostemon, with blue Veronicastrum virginicum to the right and leaves of plume poppy in the centre foreground. Later, as bronze and gold daisy-flowers emerge, these borders glow with harmonies from another section of the spectrum.

LEFT 'Hot' colours fill the Colour Garden in late summer. In the left-hand border purple-leaved *Perilla frutescens* and the sultry red foliage of Swiss chard 'Vulcan' are lit by red nicotianas, scarlet celosias, deep salmon Agastache 'Firebird', Cuphea ignea and C. miniata 'Firefly' and orange Tithonia rotundifolia. *Plants opposite have golden, creamy yellow or variegated leaves:* Weigela 'Florida Variegata', *the tall grass* Miscanthus sinensis 'Strictus' *and the shrubby* Salvia officinalis 'Icterina' *make a background for rioting lady's mantle and spires of* Heuchera richardsonii.

RIGHT *Shrubs, perennials and annuals harmonize in the beds between the enclosed flower garden and the house. On the left tender* Helichrysum petiolare, *pink-flowered* Salvia involucrata *and white argyranthemums are grown each year from cuttings;* Ageratum 'Southern Cross', *purple-leaved perillas and the azure-blue* Salvia patens *are raised from seed.* Monarda 'Croftway Pink', Rosa 'Bonica', Anthemis 'E.C. Buxton' *and silvery stachys survive the winters to make a more permanent frame. On the right helichrysums,* Senecio vira-vira *and variegated plectranthus provide a leafy background to agastaches,* Aster novae-angliae 'Andenken an Alma Pötschke', Argyranthemum 'Mary Wootton', *and native* Eupatorium purpureum.

STONECROP, N.Y. STATE

The inner flower borders in Francis Cabot's garden are framed by walls, hedges and trellis, all decorated with climbers and trailers or formal espaliers. In this setting hardy herbaceous plants interweave with exotic annuals and tender woody rarities grown from seed or cuttings to peak in late summer. A modern evocation of the Jekyllian masterpieces of the Edwardian age, Stonecrop's success depends upon just three dedicated gardeners with a rare interest in the unusual plants.

Colour schemes inspired by Jekyll but in no slavish imitation exploit rainbow harmonies and contrasts, extending the range to encompass nature's subtler tints and shades and mellowed pigments. There is a complex planted colour wheel. But colour is not the be-all and end-all: the groups of plants, often repeated in each visual glance, establish a firm architectural pattern which matches the strong lines and gives a purpose to the whole conception.

ABOVE *In a broad sweep of border, ornamental kale 'White Peacock', silver-leaved cardoons and artemisias and variegated erysimum provide the cool foliage setting for blue salvias (Salvia farinacea), yellow daisies, white antirrhinums, white cleomes (Cleome 'Helen Campbell') and the tall Boltonia asteroides 'Snowbank', this last a plant seldom grown in England. A Russian vine (Fallopia baldschuanica, syn. Polygonum baldschuanicum) clambering on the trellis at the end of the walk sustains the cooler-toned picture created by the plants in this bed. Nobody can call this kind of planting labour-saving; the task of raising the annuals, tending the perennials and, above all, orchestrating them into subtle colour harmonies each season calls for skill and dedication on the part of the small team of gardeners.*

ASHTREE COTTAGE

Ashtree Cottage lies under a spur of the cold downs just north of Stourhead, in Wiltshire, where winters are long and late frosts are expected. The soil is mainly low pH, allowing Mrs Lauderdale to experiment with many acid-loving plants to add to the shrub roses and traditional border perennials which she grows so well. Given the harsh weather conditions she is very successful, proving once again how loving care and good and wise cultivation can overcome difficulties.

At Ashtree Cottage a narrow rose-clad pergola shelters the almost centrally placed main pathway running from the entrance drive to the house. Thickly filled borders, backed by solid hedges, line the rectangular garden; gently curving edges contain rich tight planting of trees, flowering shrubs, graceful shrub roses, delphiniums and phlox, while lavender, catmint and roses alternate in the light and shade of the narrow beds under the pergola frame. Old apples, a 'new' medlar, white-flowering prunus and a weeping silver-leaved pear give height to the lawn areas and fill the garden with blossom in spring. Unusual trees such as the horizontally branched *Cornus controversa* 'Variegata' show a plantsman's interest.

The planting schemes seem casual but are far from haphazard; repeated themes such as grey and silver foliage and strong clumps of blue delphinium hold the design together. At every viewpoint framed 'pictures' make the garden seem much larger than it is. Behind the house, another garden opens out with views to the high downs.

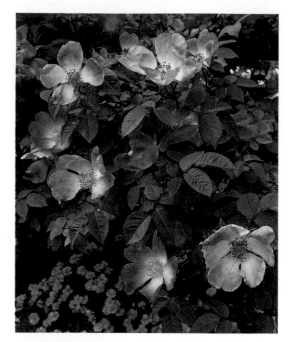

ABOVE *A detail of the companion planting at Ashtree Cottage: the Gallica hybrid* Rosa *'Complicata', underplanted with pinks.*

LEFT *A view from the pergola pathway shows a border group against the southern hedge. Purple-leaved sage and silver-leaved perennials and shrubs provide a setting for white-flowered phlox and white Jacob's ladder. The 'silver' group includes a form of Russian olive,* Elaeagnus angustifolia caspica, *with scented yellow flowers in spring, the tall* Cynara cardunculus, *with wide divided leaves, and low-growing* Stachys byzantina *which creeps along in the foreground.*

LEFT *Another view from the pergola is framed by blue delphiniums and blue-flowered* Viola cornuta *which twines among the stems of the long-flowering pink Portland rose 'Comte de Chambord'.*

BELOW *Nearer the house creamy* Sisyrinchium striatum, *with iris-like leaves, grows and seeds beside some Dutch bulbous iris whose pale blue flowers make a strong accent. Beyond, blue and white forms of* Campanula persicifolia *spread through the border.*

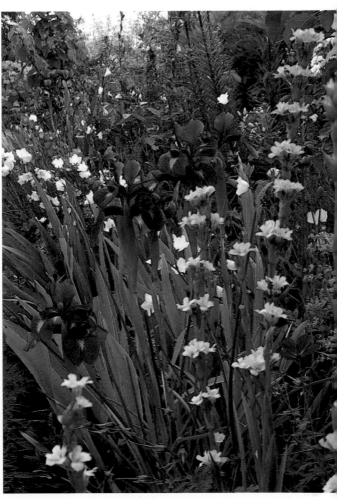

THE FRAMED GARDEN

Framing techniques
The living frame
Flowers framed

Chilcombe in Dorset
A garden near Paris
Filoli in California

Frames direct and focus the gaze and present garden scenes as pictures. Gardens designed to exploit framing devices to the full depend on geometry and repetition; plants are manipulated into preconceived schemes and little seems left to chance. This was the fashion that dominated Western gardening until the middle of the eighteenth century; it had a vigorous renaissance in the nineteenth, and is frequently evoked by gardeners of today. In fact there are few gardens where traditionally inspired schemes cannot be adapted or reinterpreted, if only for one small part of the layout: a more formal atmosphere near the house is possible even in a garden where natural effects prevail.

In modern small gardens, with limited and therefore doubly precious planting space, formal styles help create planting opportunities. Garden divisions provide backing for border schemes, and small flower-packed beds – edged with box or framed with brick, stone or gravel – give unity and purpose to a site that might otherwise be meandering lawn. Even the smallest garden can have vistas lengthened by linear or aerial perspective. On a tiny terrace decorative pots of flowering and foliage plants may be put to effective use.

This architectural approach to the garden, of plants framed or framing to create deliberate effects, and the placing of accent plants or massed plants in patterned beds or containers, seems to be the complete opposite to natural gardening. Yet inside this structure, planting styles can be quite wild and free. Any border may be given a frame whether it is planted with strong-growing perennials of different heights or in a more regimented fashion. An arrangement of informal mixed planting in a fine stone or terracotta urn is formalized by its container. Even meadow gardens, with flowers growing in rough grass, may be sharply delineated at the boundaries by mown paths so that they become flower beds set in smoother lawn; in the 'beds' themselves the grass provides a green frame for pointillist colours.

The classically laid out garden at Hazelby House is divided into a series of linked 'rooms', each with framed views into adjacent areas. The geometric garden, with horizontal divisions and vertical hedges, makes the most economical use of space. Here plants frame architectural features – the raised copper bowl, the trellised archway and, on a lower level, the pathway of patterned bricks. At the same time the architecture defines and limits space, and provides satisfying contrasts with the flowing lines and shapes of plants.

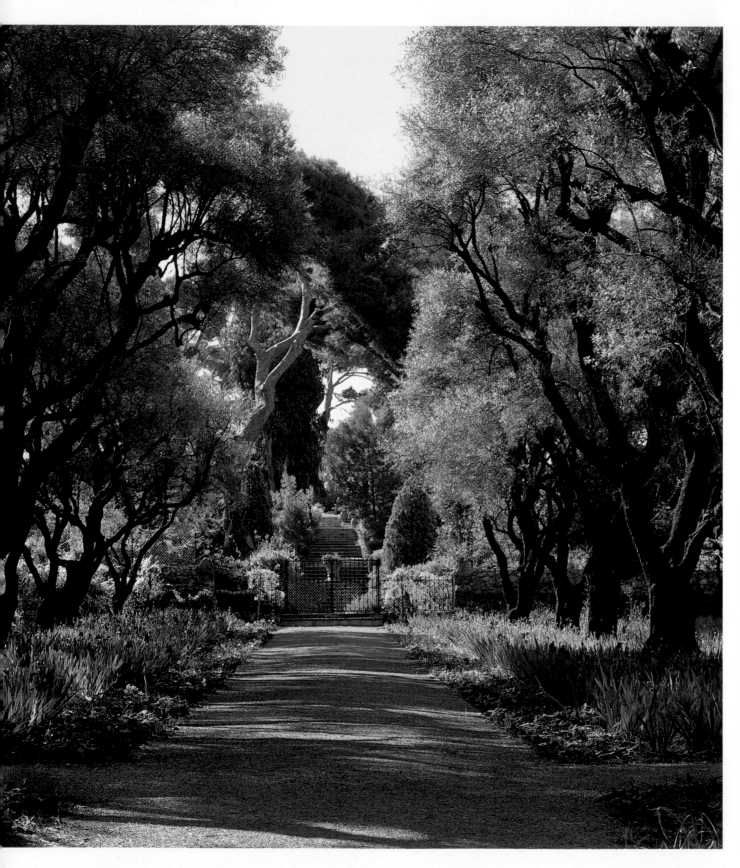

OPPOSITE *Michael Balston makes effective use of symmetry and repetition so that architecture and plants complement one another, hard materials contrasting with the soft billowing shapes of roses and perennials. Overflowing roses line the edges of the main 'frame'. The focal point, the rose-covered archway, reveals a more distant view, at the same time accentuating the graceful outline of the armillary sphere in the foreground. Finally the sphere itself is set off by groups of roses and catmint.*

LEFT *In the Mediterranean sunshine at La Garoupe an avenue of ancient olive trees borders the pathway, giving a sense of distance and framing the steep stairway beyond. The olives shelter tall German irises under the welcome shade of their branches; later in the season the iris flowers are succeeded by clumps of pink cyclamen. Not every garden can be on such a grand scale, but almost all views are best if framed and narrowed to accentuate a distant feature. Avenues can be of trees, shrubs or quite small plants, statues or vases; the size is not important if the eye is correctly directed along a central vista.*

FRAMING TECHNIQUES

The formality inherent in framing involves using symmetry to achieve completeness in each view, with plants regarded as architectural accessories in much the same way as 'hard' garden structures. Deployed in pairs, sets and blocks, key plants with strong outlines – or massed plants marshalled into regular shapes – establish balance, create rhythms and help to manipulate perspective.

A pair of plants such as tall crambes with huge airy umbels of white flowers flanking a seat or ornament emphasizes its role as focal point within the garden area. Plants in a line – continuous as in hedging, or making the separate rhythmic punctuation marks of an avenue – not only delineate the geometry of a layout but will also direct the eye along an axis, emphasizing perspective. Design features found in the great gardens may be adapted for smaller landscapes; the avenue of limes stretching into the horizon to frame a distant temple or hill can be reproduced in miniature with clipped evergreens or by using elegant terracotta urns to line a simple garden path that ends at a welcoming seat or at an accent plant.

When plants reinforce the invitation extended by a path or gateway, they make very compelling framing devices – the frame not playing an enclosing role, but calling attention to something beyond the garden enclosure. A pair of architectural key plants or low box domes surrounded by bulbs and creeping flowers can effectively frame a gate or doorway, or enhance some new flowery delight glimpsed through the opening. Even the most panoramic views are improved when narrowed; by deliberately framing garden vistas and planting schemes, their importance is enhanced. At Newby Hall, Yorkshire, in two rectangular beds flanking a central grass path, branching amelanchiers create a white flowering screen in spring to frame the perennial borders that stretch down the lower slope. In late summer their leaves turn rich crimson and gold.

At Tintinhull converging lines of catmint reinforce the garden axis, framing a distant view into a neighbouring cider orchard. Wings of dark yew, pillars clothed with honeysuckle and graceful arching roses – the grey-leaved Rosa 'Wolley-Dod'*, with shell-pink flowers – all play an architectural role in this composition, contributing different patterns of leaf and flower colour through the seasons.*

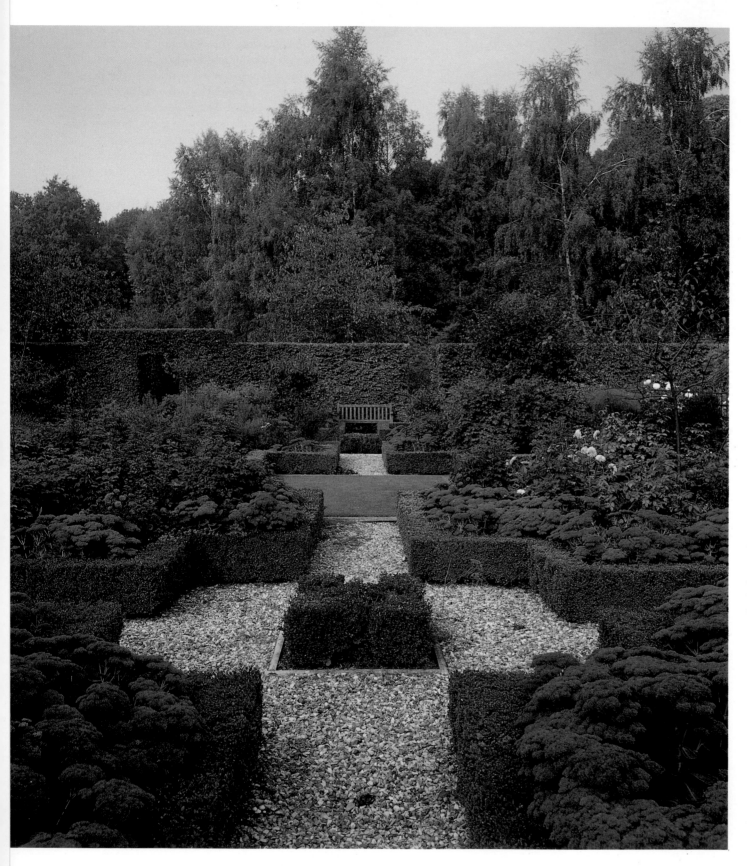

In one of the compartments of this garden near Paris (see pages 152-3), low box hedges framing Sedum 'Herbstfreude', with flat densely clustered pink flower-heads, have been planted symmetrically to give formal definition to the layout. The immaculate gravel and the panel of grass enhance the atmosphere of order, while a tall hedge makes a background to the centrally placed seat. Even the more distant trees play their part in shaping the skyline – something that gardeners can easily overlook at the planning stage. Trees create their own patterns of light and shade and movement; they add an extra dimension to a garden view, having a more human scale and quality than a backdrop of buildings. Here the airy shapes of the birches contrast with the stricter lines of clipped hedging. As well as establishing the garden's style, the trees, hedges and horizontal ground-patterns also create a firm framework in which more free-flowing plant and flower shapes, colours and textures can come and go with the seasons.

THE LIVING FRAME

Flower gardens are framed and accentuated by the permanent planting of trees and shrubs that define space with their shape, outline and mass. On the scale of a whole garden, there is an essential element of contrast: smooth lawns enhance dense trees and shrub canopies that move gently in a breeze, providing movement between shade and sunlight. More solid and static evergreens lend stability and weight.

Trees and hedges set the style of the garden; they also create the design frame inside which flowering associations are assembled to make a satisfactory composition. At Crathes Castle massive L-shaped blocks of yew define space in the centre of the Colour Garden, providing a contrasting focus with mixed borders of red- and orange-coloured flowers in the outer beds. Similar effects are seen at Blickling, Norfolk, where blocks of yew known as the 'Grand Pianos' create a focal point within the great parterre area of more ephemeral flower beds. At Filoli, California, Irish yews with naturally architectural shapes contrast with the flowing lines of flowering plants and provide solid blocks of sombre colour to offset paler tints and fleeting flower performances. In the outer garden, brightly coloured flower beds are framed by a golden-leaved locust tree (*Robinia pseudoacacia* 'Frisia'), cylinder-shaped Irish yews and olive trees, theatrically backed by wild countryside studded with live oaks.

Sombre foliage, used as a living backdrop for colourful foreground planting, is able to achieve dramatic garden contrasts that shout for attention and linger in the memory long after gentler, more reticent schemes have been forgotten. At Packwood House, Warwickshire, the old yews known as 'The Multitude', silhouetted against the sky, make a startling backdrop to colourful flower beds along the brick terrace; elsewhere in the garden low yew hedges grown as buttresses against a high wall frame more intimately the beds of different coloured roses. In the topiary garden at Levens Hall, Cumbria, massed summer-flowering verbenas, contained inside box hedging, set off the giant yew and box shapes behind.

Tall enclosing hedges

In many framed gardens tall hedges break up the broad sweep of lawns into different areas in a manner reminiscent of the style of the seventeenth century. In the garden at Hidcote, Gloucestershire, a series of hedges in different, sometimes mixed, plant materials divide the whole area into a sequence of green rooms deliberately based on Renaissance ideals of symmetry and proportion. These hedges also provide the background frames for luxuriant border planting of hardy plants and roses. The Hidcote style – a combination of formal layout with great informality in planting – has been a major influence on English gardening since it was laid out in the years before the First World War.

Hedging plants that are to make permanent garden compartments or boundaries need to suit the site well enough to grow into more or less regular 'walls' of foliage.

Dark evergreen yew, with its dense tight growth, makes a particularly satisfactory architectural framework for the garden, and enhances the colours and shapes of individual flowers. Its sombre green appears almost black outlined against the sky. Sometimes its intensity and matt effects create almost too much contrast: pure white flowers become dazzlingly bright and garish when outlined against its dark leaves. At Tintinhull we have softened the effects by interweaving grey

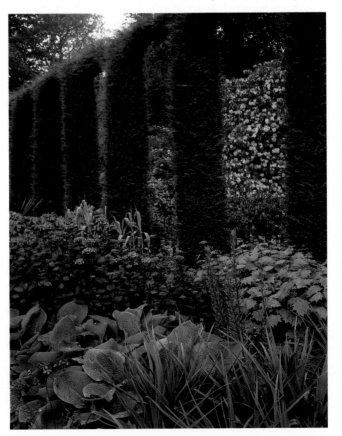

Lady Londonderry used Moorish-style arcades instead of solid hedges to separate the Spanish Garden from the 'wilder' woodland areas at Mount Stewart in Northern Ireland. In the 1930s she planted the Monterey cypress, but the National Trust has replaced this with Leyland cypress, which they consider more appropriate and better suited to tight clipping. Planting in the Spanish Garden is a mixture of formality, with sword-like phormiums contrasting with more naturalistic groupings of Kirengeshoma palmata, Hydrangea *'Preziosa'* and Hosta sieboldiana elegans *which link the scheme with the more relaxed planting style glimpsed through the arches.*

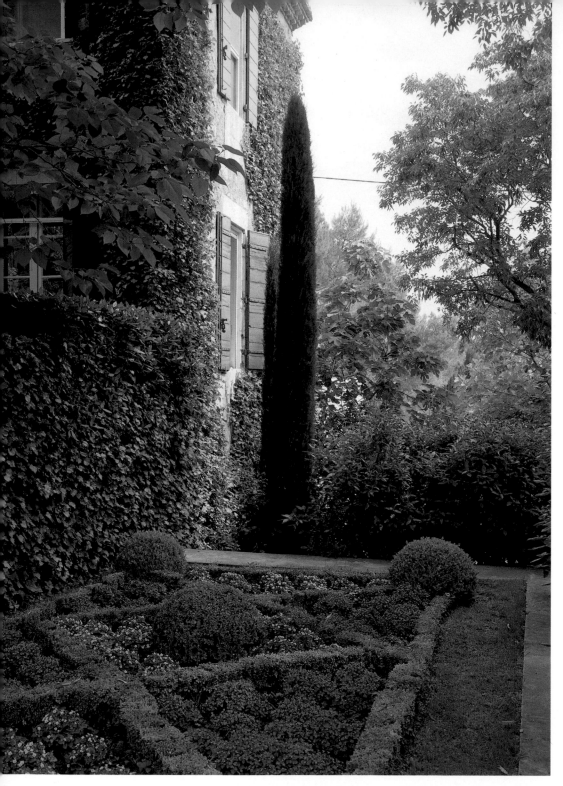

and silvery foliage plants between the flowering plants and the yew and searching for white flowers that are gently tinted with pale pink, cream and blue rather than using those of 'laundry' brilliance.

Old yew hedges become interestingly mounded and give any garden an air of antiquity. When yew grows too high and wide it may be rejuvenated by cutting back to the main trunk; this operation is usually done one side at a time to avoid undue shock to the plant. In regions that experience cold winters, such as the north-eastern United States, forms of Japanese yew (*Taxus cuspidata*) are substituted for the common English *Taxus baccata*. A group of hybrids between the two includes *T.* × *media* 'Hicksii' and 'Hatfieldii', which like to grow into pyramidal form and are most suitable for hedging.

Hollies are beautiful slow-growing hedging plants. When still immature, their tips may be severely damaged by frost in a cold spring. Once established, their glowing leaves contrast well with flowers and pale perennial foliage. The spineless *Ilex aquifolium* 'J.C. van Tol' is worth considering; in the north-east United States the Japanese holly *I. crenata* makes a more sober background. Some elegant American hollies such as *I. opaca*, which needs acid soil, do best in areas where summers are hot. The new very attractive *I.* × *meserveae* hybrids produced in Long Island have a distinctive blue bloom to the leaf. Hardy in extremes of cold and heat, they may well be the hedging holly of the future. *I.* × *m.* 'Blue Angel', 'Blue Prince' and 'Blue Princess' all make strong-growing hedges.

In cold climates the most satisfactory conifers for hedging are the various forms of the slow-growing lime-tolerant eastern hemlock (*Tsuga canadensis*) with dense green leaves that are as decorative and useful as yew. In milder regions such as coastal gardens in the British Isles and the more southerly states of the United States, the Chilean yew (*Podocarpus andinus*) forms an excellent framing hedge for planting schemes as well as a thick evergreen screen.

Among deciduous trees, beech and hornbeam hedges are attractive backgrounds to flowers; in spring and summer the foliage is a fresh green, and clipped hedges keep their buff-coloured dead leaves all through the winter. Tapestry hedges of mixed copper and green beech are sometimes chosen to add interest. Field maple (*Acer campestre*) produces fresh young green leaves that turn a brilliant yellow, sometimes flushed

Ann Cox Chambers' garden in Provence, where sunlight is strong and shadows are important for coolness, has a small knot garden in a corner by the house. The pattern outlined in clipped box and punctuated by box domes is infilled with Exacum affine in alternating blocks of mauve and white. The contrast of a soaring Italian cypress, framed by the more bushy shape of a fig tree, provides just the sort of carefully thought out dramatic incident that good gardeners can use to prevent their planting becoming too bland.

with crimson, in late summer; in Europe it is an ideal perimeter hedge linking garden and countryside.

Roses can make informal hedges to frame inner planting or borders. Suckering Rugosas with fresh apple-green crinkly leaves and scented flowers succeeded by orange or scarlet hips are excellent as background hedging. Ground-cover roses such as *Rosa* 'Max Graf', with its glossy foliage and clear pink yellow-centred flowers, make an informal weed-suppressing frame at a lower level.

Low pattern-making hedging

In the last few years planting low hedging to accentuate formal flower-bed patterns has been found to be more labour-saving than natural planting: modern herbicides control weed growth, and mechanical shears and strimmers have replaced manual tools to make hedge clipping simple and economical. These new beds can be set in stone paving, concrete or reconstituted stone, patterned brickwork, gravel or cobbles, or in a combination of all these different materials. Once laid, they need less maintenance than grass, and plants can tumble over the edges without doing damage.

Tidy horizontal lines of box, lavender, tender rosemary, santolina or thyme, clipped annually, are the most common choice for low hedging, sometimes with fanciful finials or domes to accentuate corners. The scale and type of planting in the beds affects the choice of edging material. Different sorts of box, which may be kept neatly manicured with almost vertical sloping sides and a flat top, are best: few other hedging plants look so good throughout the year. Any box-edged bed appears quite purposeful even when no plants are obviously performing in it; a panel of plain grass is restful framed with cut box.

By far the most common species selected for low hedging is European box: forms of *Buxus sempervirens* or the dwarf Dutch *B.s.* 'Suffruticosa', known since the seventeenth century. If well maintained and clipped every year in early summer, it will keep a narrow outline, making it particularly practical for marking out parterre patterns. In colder climates, substitute forms of Korean box (*B. microphylla*), which have dense bright leaves. European box grows slowly over many years to heights of 3m/10 ft (the 5.5m/18ft hedges at Powis Castle are unique), but most box hedges are restricted to a height of 38–60cm/15–24in, with a spread of about the same extent. Dwarf box grows up to

30cm/12in high, but may be kept much lower; in some parterres it is allowed to grow to only 10–15cm/4–6 in, and coloured gravels are substituted for flowers in the interstices.

European box is known in the United States as American box. There, it tends to grow quickly into mounded shapes; in the hot summers it is difficult to keep its edges crisp and well defined. Broader box hedges, sometimes grown in double rows at different heights (mimicking the sixteenth-century style), may be magnificent, however.

As an alternative, there are a number of hollies that retain a tailored shape. Japanese hollies such as *Ilex crenata* have tiny box-like leaves and may be clipped into dwarf hedges; preferring an acid soil, they may survive cold winters and hot summers. Other American hollies such as inkberry (*I. glabra*), with its dark shining leaves, and yaupon (*I. vomitoria*), with its small box-like leaves, are heat- and drought-resistant. Forms of Dahoon holly (*I. cassine*) thrive where hot summers are accompanied by high atmospheric humidity. In mild areas I have seen *Trachelospermum asiaticum* trained to make a low hedge.

The hardiest hebes also make low compact containing hedges. Grey-leaved *Hebe pinguifolia* 'Pagei' and *H. albicans*, with more glaucous leaves, are salt- and wind-resistant, so they are especially suitable for seaside planting. They need no clipping and bear small dense white flower racemes. Hebe and *Ruta graveolens* 'Jackman's Blue' surround beds of pale pink, yellow and blue flowers in the formal Italian Garden on the lower terrace at Mount Stewart, County Down, in Northern Ireland, where the climate is very mild.

Lavenders, with grey-green linear leaves and flowers ranging from low-toned blues and mauves to pink and white, develop as more informal hedges, each bushy plant growing angular and woody with age. This adds charm in a number of hedging situations, but the lack of definition makes most lavenders unsuitable for formal pattern-making.

Both rosemary and silver- or green-leaved cotton lavender (*Santolina chamaecyparissus, S. neapolitana, S. rosmarinifolia rosmarinifolia* and various cultivars), which has lacy or finely divided foliage, will grow quickly in well-drained soil in a sunny position; they need cutting back each season in spring as they also have a tendency to become woody and are unsightly when bare at the base.

LEFT Ceanothus × delileanus *'Gloire de Versailles'* is set off at Chilcombe by an edging of pink erigerons and companion planting of the biennial musk-scented Salvia sclarea turkestanica. *Low-growing flowers do not detract from the natural shapes of shrubs such as ceanothus.*

BELOW LEFT *At Herterton House in Northumberland, a corner of the physic garden displays a brilliant combination of low-growing plants in a formal way. A central bed of variegated ground elder* (Aegopodium podagraria *'Variegatum') is framed by bands of armeria and London pride. Plants do not have to be woody to play a formal role: these perennials are clearly defining the garden layout.*

Non-woody edging plants

When considering plants to frame a planting scheme there is no need to be confined to clipped woody species. Low-growing evergreen perennials may be tidied into straight lines or allowed to grow in natural ground-hugging shapes. Wall germander (*Teucrium chamaedrys*), silvery stachys, London pride, *Saxifraga moschata* and alpine strawberries are all good containing plants as are leathery-leaved bergenias with mauve, pink or white flowers and the less coarse *Chiastophyllum oppositifolium* with its yellow tasselled flowers. Set in informal lines, such plants can be controlled or allowed to drift forwards into flower beds and over neighbouring stone or brickwork. As well as providing a foil to the inner flowers, they produce their own bloom in season to extend the sequence of colour.

Gertrude Jekyll loved to plant old-fashioned lamb's ears (*Stachys byzantina*) in gentle drifts round the edge of rose beds, softening the harsh appearance at the base of the branching bushes; nowadays the non-flowering form *S.b.* 'Silver Carpet' is popular. To create similar effects, Miss Jekyll also substituted drifts of lavender for a line of continuous hedging. On the raised terrace at Knightshayes Court, Devon, grey and silver plants edge pink-flowered geraniums and dianthus. Small evergreen thymes with green, grey or variegated aromatic leaves are sun-lovers; they often frame herb-garden beds and may be sheared into shape in spring.

Even perennials that do not retain their winter leaves are suitable edgers. Catmint with its misty blue flowers rising in waving wands above soft grey-green leaves is one of the best. New foliage replaces the old if flower-stems are removed as the flowers fade; flowers will be produced again in late summer. Lady's mantle, with its lime-green flowers arching over light green leaves, is another worthwhile edging plant that may spread under shrubs or fall over the pavement. Some of the herbaceous cranesbill geraniums may also be used as ribbon edging; choose those with attractive leaves all summer as well as seasonal flowers. Less vigorous plants such as mossy phlox, low-growing campanulas and veronicas, sedums and the more tender suckering South African diascias all do well framing small-scale flowering schemes.

ABOVE *A classic knot design outlined in box is filled in with cotton lavender (Santolina chamaecyparissus), a Mediterranean plant grown for centuries in more northerly gardens, and with ageratums, which were introduced from tropical America only in the early nineteenth century. Gardening patterns that date back centuries can be executed with more recently discovered plants provided that the house is not typical of a particular period. Designed by Bruce Kelly, this garden is in Long Island.*

ABOVE RIGHT *At Filoli in California the designs of the different garden areas are scrupulously formal. Here linear beds outlined in box and edged with aubrieta are planted in spring with blocks of flowers. The strict colour effects accentuate the precision of the schemes: polyanthus in mixed colours are segregated from blue varieties by lines of box. Later in summer new colour schemes are implemented and the now bare standard rose bushes come into play.*

FLOWERS FRAMED

Many gardeners like to choose flowering plants appropriate to the style of their house, or to take inspiration from some distinct period theme. In the sunken garden by the old Tudor palace at Hatfield House, Hertfordshire, only seventeenth-century plants form the typical knot patterns, while at Westbury Court, Gloucestershire, flowers known by 1700 grow inside the simple parterre edgings.

In the sixteenth century germander and hyssop, both with midsummer flowers, were standard plants for knot patterns (along with savory, thrift, santolina and thyme) although straggly in habit. From the 1620s box and cotton lavender were also used. As well as the more decorative herbs, typical infilling flowers in these schemes would have been irises, bluebells, crocuses, anemones, columbines, foxgloves, primroses,

At Levens Hall in Cumbria the famous topiary garden is dominated by strange and fantastic shapes in clipped yew and box, their contours set off by low-growing massed annuals. The original garden was designed at the end of the seventeenth century, but many of the topiary pieces, including those of golden-leaved yew, were replaced or renewed more recently. The wonderful spread of Verbena rigida is not historically authentic as the South American verbenas were not introduced until the nineteenth century, although the related vervain was known in the Middle Ages. Antirrhinums, on the other hand, could have been part of the original planting.

cowslips, violas, Jacob's ladder, wallflowers, daisies, peonies, pinks, sweet rocket, fritillaries, native narcissi, lilies and roses – all of which had been grown for centuries. More recently introduced exotics such as crown imperials, tulips and hyacinths from the Middle East and plants such as marvels of Peru and sunflowers from the New World were welcome additions.

By the end of the seventeenth century, despite the fashion for flowerless parterres in the French style, many more plants were becoming available for garden experimentation; a wide range of new bulbs and perennials is listed by contemporary writers. During the next 200 years the stream of new plants became a flood, with colourful petunias, verbenas, salvias, eschscholzias, phacelias and lobelias from all corners of the world providing brighter and brighter hues for bedding-out schemes. In their heyday the Victorian 'bedders' had a greater choice of such plants than is available today.

Historical authenticity of course is not essential in this sort of gardening. The mauve verbenas which set off the topiary shapes at Levens Hall, some of which date from the late seventeenth century, were not introduced until the nineteenth century; in other beds marigolds, which could have been used in the original garden, are grown.

Historical schemes can be inspirational rather than defining a series of rules and may be adapted to suit any size of garden. Jacobean mansions display their appropriately restored seventeenth-century gardens, but the smallest suburban front garden may now be laid out with flower beds edged with box, lavender or santolina, containing any plants or only those known to the gardeners of the period. A Victorian terrace house may have an appropriate Victorian garden with flower beds edged with pebbles and pathways framed by rose-wreathed arches.

At Eastgrove Cottage near Worcester, flowers and foliage, mainly good perennials, are separated by the firm line of a hedge, which provides definition as well as a backing to the two schemes. In the foreground beds penstemons give a good show, while at the back the biennial Salvia sclarea turkestanica, phlox, Miss Willmott's ghost (Eryngium giganteum), achillea and hostas, with the shrubby perovskia, make a setting for the welcoming seat.

Modern flowering schemes are typified by carpets of impatiens, with vigorous modern hybrids flowering prolifically all summer in the sun or shade. But some annuals have more interesting qualities than others. I love the bedding echiums (*Echium vulgare*) with 'mixed' blue, mauve and purple flowers that spread like a soft carpet in the Blue Garden at Crathes Castle, as well as the taller gomphrenas I have seen surviving the heat of summers in Midwest America. I grow the straggling *Salvia sclarea* in a ribbon in our kitchen garden at Tintinhull, and the massed cosmos at Pontrancart in Normandy are positioned so the ferny leaves and airy pink flowers are gently stirred by the wind. Carpeting plants need not be annuals. At Barnsley House, Gloucestershire, a central pathway of flagged stones is framed by panels of green lawn and flanked by old Irish yews; shrubby pink- and white-flowered rock roses (*Helianthemum*), which open their flowers only when the sun shines, make an interweaving patterned carpet with silvery-foliaged neighbours.

Inside low hedges the coloured foliage of shrubs or perennials may be used as foundation planting, massed so that taller flowering bulbs may push up through the foliage in season. Santolinas, variegated or purple-tinged *Salvia officinalis*, and green-and-white variegated lamiums may be hosts to alliums and lilies. Even the variegated form of ground elder may be contained to form a background carpet for bulb flowers. In the White Garden at Sissinghurst, Kent, white tulips push through lamium in a flower bed contained by boxwood.

In a lasting and labour-saving scheme demonstrated in the Fuchsia Garden at Hidcote in Gloucestershire, a simple layout of box-edged beds separated by brick paths frames massed spaces of blue-flowered *Scilla siberica*. Permanently established hardy fuchsias, cut to the ground just before the scillas flower in spring, grow up above the bulbs to flower throughout the summer months.

Flowers in containers

The emphasis on manipulation and management, with carefully thought-out arrangements intended to look contrived, is the essence of pictures in the framed garden. Groups of plants in ornamental pots, contained but overflowing, may convey the baroque spirit of a seventeenth-century Dutch flower painting – the plants growing naturally, but with nothing natural or simple about the way they are presented. Just as the Dutch painter had to wait through the summer for each plant to flower in turn in order that their blooms could all be captured realistically on his canvas, so should the gardener plant a container so that it produces a succession of flower and foliage effects for as long as possible. Planting spring bulbs in layers at different depths ensures that they flower at slightly different times. All plants in one container must like the same conditions of soil and aspect, even if they perform in separate seasons. Between each planting the soil is renewed and enriched.

The simplest planting scheme for containers comprises massed annuals, with bulbs, wallflowers, forget-me-nots and pansies for spring followed by summer bedders. Arrangements may be restricted to one plant or one colour. The most traditional container-grown spring bulbs are tulips, which, if a range of types is chosen, may flower for at least six weeks. Favourite summer annuals include pelargoniums, lobelias, petunias and ageratums. All these plants look more appealing if mixed with grey or silvery helichrysums to establish a pattern and enhance the flower colours.

More ambitious schemes for containers introduce woody perennials to act as key or accent plants. Cordylines, phormiums, glaucous-leaved argyranthemums with daisy-flowers (improved versions of Paris daisies), pink-flowered *Anisodontea capensis* and fuchsias are all successful focal points in sunny sites. The soaring chimney bellflower makes a climax plant for the centre of a decorative urn or may be massed for stunning effects in a large container or old cistern. Tender blue-flowered felicias with green or variegated leaves (forms of *Felicia amelloides* or *F. amoena*), silver-leaved *Helichrysum petiolare*, *Senecio vira-vira* and *S. compactus* (now correctly *Brachyglottis compacta* – similar in appearance to *S.* 'Sunshine', but smaller), red- and blue-flowered salvias (which like a lot of water) and small hebes all do well in pots if given adequate moisture and free drainage.

Around the base of these key plants, summer-flowering perennials and annuals ebb and flow as in any planting scheme: diascias (many are tender perennials), red-flowered linums, blue-flowered salvias and verbenas and more run-of-the-mill annuals such as scented tobacco plants, lobelias and petunias, preferably obtained in single colours for a specific scheme. Lilies and hostas, which tolerate shadier sites, thrive in pots containing richer soil.

In winter schemes conifers, hollies (clipped into various topiary shapes) and pyramids or domes of box become central container features. Trailing ivies or lamiums provide colour through the bleaker months, with small bulbs and taller tulips coming up through their low foliage in spring. The edging theme may be extended by training ivy to form a chain or low hedge around the container rim. In a mild winter pansies will flower for three months and forget-me-nots and wallflowers come into bloom for spring display.

Planting an annual scheme in an ornamental container is like arranging a vase of flowers for the house, with living flowers, leaves and the pot itself all contributing to the whole. Here silvery senecio (S. vira-vira) interweaves a scheme of zonal pelargoniums and the dwarfer Pelargonium 'L'Elegante', which will scramble down the sides. Planting is deliberately subdued to fit into the overall garden scheme, with pale-coloured flowers enriched by the silver leaves to give a gentle tapestry effect.

CHILCOMBE IN DORSET

At Chilcombe the walled and hedged garden is laid out in a series of squares and rectangles so that all shrubs and flowers are seen against a background of masonry or foliage. Each separate and secret enclosure could be a garden complete in itself, defined and limited by its perimeter hedge and having its own micro-climate in which a wide selection of tender plants flourish. In considering design and the importance of providing a background structure for the flower garden, we must remember that walls and especially wind-filtering hedges are the traditional means of providing shelter. They thus serve a dual purpose, both framing the flowers and improving the aspect. Even when strong gales blow at Chilcombe, plants in these inner garden rooms hardly stir. Furthermore, the garden lies on a steep south-facing slope and benefits from a mild coastal climate; most frosts simply roll away into the valley below.

John Hubbard is a painter whose wife Caryl is also involved in the art world. They use their knowledge of colour to create garden pictures, framing each scene as if it were a two-dimensional painting. They have made the garden together using the basic structure, already divided into a series of rooms, that they found on their arrival. The main garden lies below the house. Here espalier fruit trees, trellis-work arbours for roses and clematis and hedges of mixed beech and yew all make vertical divisions, given broader shape by old spreading fruit trees. On the horizontal level pathways in grass, cobbles or paving define the edges of flower beds and lead the visitor's feet from one secret garden room into another where a different planting theme dominates. None of this means that the garden is either too formal or too diverse and restless. On the contrary, straight lines at head height or ground level are constantly blurred and softened by overflowing plants; a repetition of plant groups in different sections lends stability and effectively links the disparate themes together.

RIGHT *In one of the most intimate garden 'rooms', framed on one side by espalier fruit and on another by a rustic pergola, the planting, mainly of highly scented flowers or plants with aromatic leaves, is distinctly Mediterranean in feel. The air is still and heat is held in by surrounding vegetation and reflected by the cobbled paths. The flowers themselves are in small repetitive groups rather than in broad drifts. Here regal lilies, grey-leaved* Stachys byzantina *and southernwood are backed by* Knautia macedonica, *with small dark purple flowers, and blue-toned salvias.*

RIGHT *The herb garden and salvias in full flower framed by the rose-clad pergola. In the foreground* Gillenia trifoliata, *used by Indians in North America as a physic, reinforces the 'useful' theme; it flowers beside the marbled-leaved mother of thousands (*Saxifraga stolonifera). *Climbing and rambling roses with leafy foliage turn the pergola into a shady walk, a strong contrast to the intensity of sunlight and heat in the open garden beyond.*

LEFT *The cobbled paths marking out a cross to divide broad flower beds and plants in pots give the same garden area an almost formal aspect. The Mediterranean atmosphere is enhanced by aromatic herbs. Good King Henry (*Chenopodium bonus-henricus), *variegated thyme, pot marigold (*Calendula officinalis), *curry plant (*Helichrysum italicum), *both purple- and variegated-leaved sage (*Salvia officinalis *'Purpurascens' and S.o. 'Icterina'), Jackman's rue (*Ruta graveolens *'Jackman's Blue') with glaucous leaves, origanum and lovage (*Levisticum officinale) *all grow in profusion, scenting the air with old-world fragrance.*

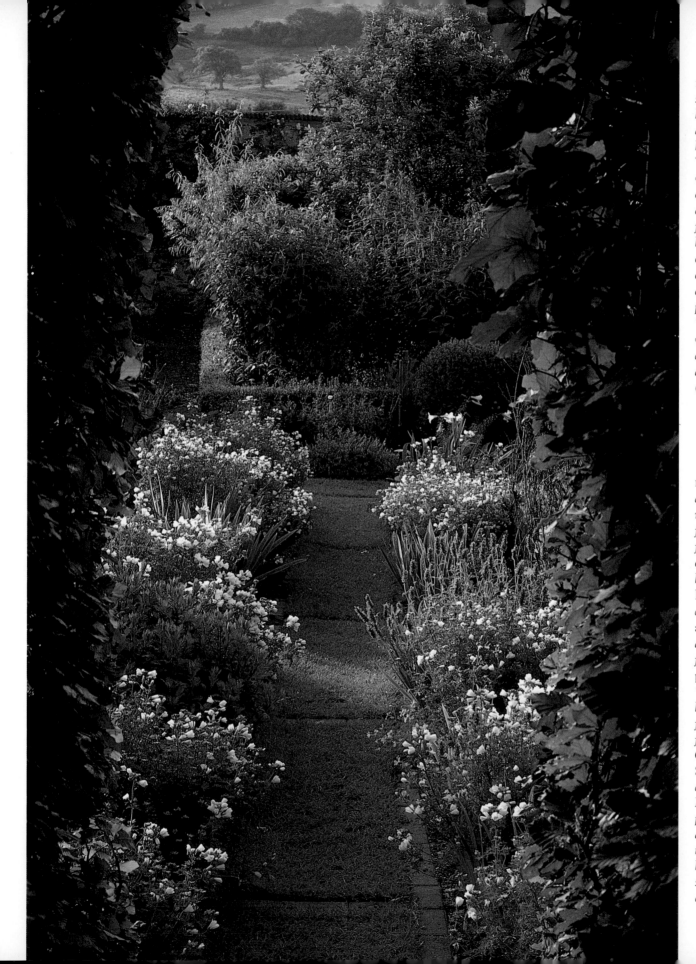

LEFT *Looking from shade into sunlight. A mixed tapestry hedge, clipped to form an archway, frames a broad lawn walk at Chilcombe. This is one of my favourite views, allowing just a hint of open sky beyond. In this tight enclosed garden most of the framed vistas are inward-looking, giving a strong sense of security but potentially claustrophobic in effect. The elegant stone edging and cross pattern is another instance of 'framing'; this time the grass walk is panelled to give definition. The white flowers are self-seeded mallow (Malva moschata alba).*

RIGHT *In the lower garden another hedged enclosure with newly laid paths was for flowers and vegetables. The flowers seem to be taking over: penstemons, silvery-leaved* Lotus hirsutus *(syn.* Dorycnium hirsutum), *daisy-flowered* Felicia amelloides *and F. amoena, and cotton lavender – my favourite one,* Santolina pinnata neapolitana *'Sulphurea', with feathery leaves and pale lime-green flowers, which is not grown frequently enough in gardens. On the corner a clump of* Salvia sclarea turkestanica *dominates the scene. Normally biennial, it can be perennial in a climate as mild as that of Chilcombe. With intensely musk-like aromatic leaves and pinkish-grey flower spires, this salvia is a must for every garden.*

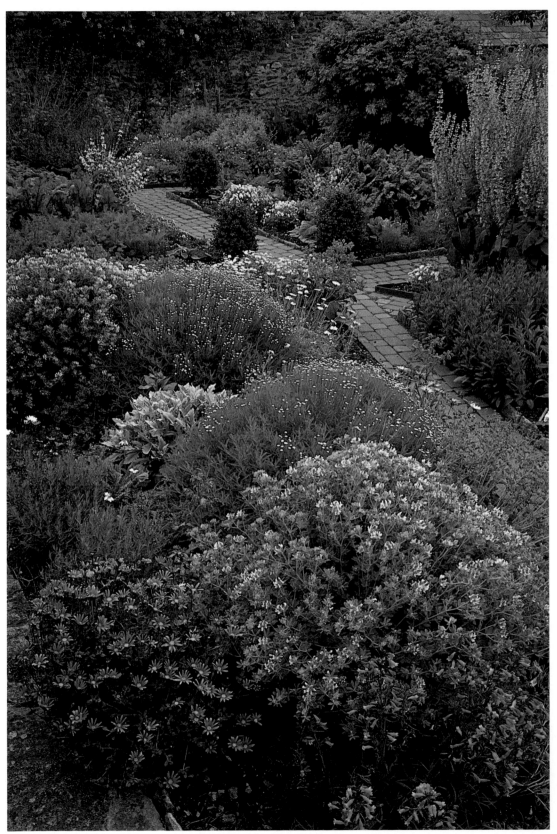

ABOVE *A view of planting on one side of the main borders where the vista terminated by the tapestry hedge is framed by a pair of Irish yews. Shrub roses, tall silvery thistles* (Onopordum nervosum) *and artichokes* (Cynara scolymus), *acanthus with pink spikes, lavender and the double-flowered* Geranium pratense 'Plenum Violaceum' *all grow gloriously together. The almost white leaves of* Stachys byzantina *beside the white violets* (Viola cornuta alba) *make an extra focal point. Backed by the dark yew, the herbaceous* Clematis heracleifolia *is about to open its blue flowers.*

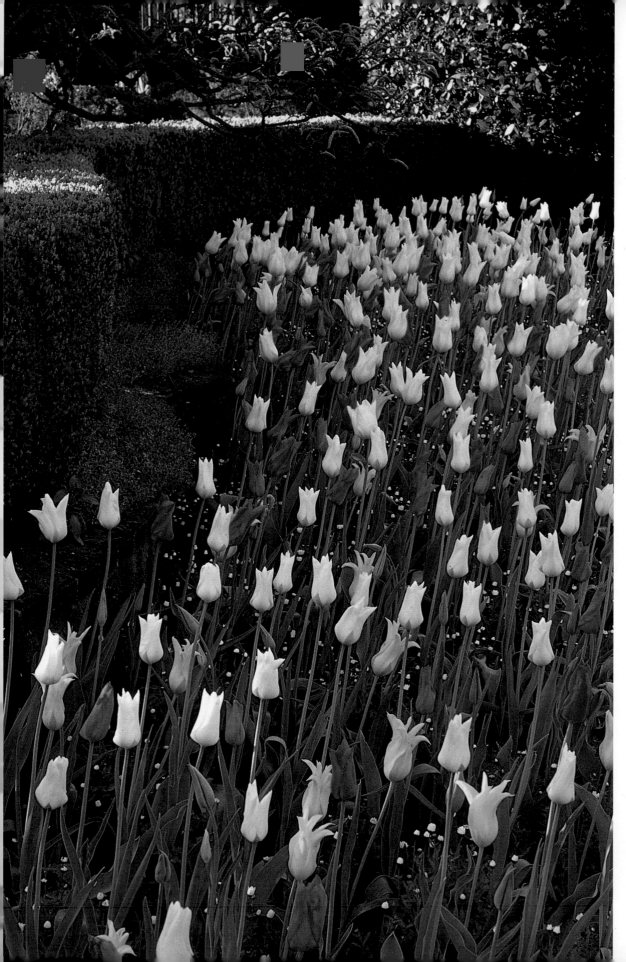

FILOLI IN CALIFORNIA

The gardens of Filoli, an hour's drive south of San Francisco, are very formal and impeccably kept, a deliberate contrast to the rugged countryside where beautiful Californian live oaks (*Quercus agrifolia*) provide almost the only vegetation in the burnt ochre-coloured earth. The gardens, now in the charge of the National Trust for Historic Preservation, are nearly 16 acres in extent. Designed by Bruce Porter for William Bowers Bourne II between 1915 and 1919, they are almost Italian in concept, with each area enclosed by hedges. Tall Irish yews (*Taxus baccata* 'Fastigiata') define alleys to resemble the cypress-lined *viales* of Tuscany and grey-leaved olive trees are clipped into cylinder shapes. Espaliered fruit trees accentuate the formal lines.

Each inner garden has a distinct theme. In one, pink flowers and silvery foliage make the pattern of stained glass of a window of

In a tulip bed framed by high box hedges colours are mixed to give an embroidered look. The lily-flowered tulip 'White Triumphator', pink 'Mariette' and golden-yellow 'West Point' are underplanted with a fine stitching of white daisies (Bellis perennis). At first glance effects seem casual, but the bulbs are very carefully planted to make a uniform pattern. At Filoli all planting schemes are as exact and each bed is repeated with mirror-image planting to complete the symmetry of the layout. In this part of the garden one of the beds frames a circular pool and a standard wisteria, while another surrounds a sundial.

Chartres cathedral; in another a maze is laid out in boxwood; another is Dutch in conception; yet another is an Elizabethan knot. Colour schemes used in the annual beds are as originally planned. Fine collections of trees and superb roses, magnolias, azaleas, rhododendrons and camellias are all grown with consummate skill. To some the geometry and precision is overpowering, but I find it completely satisfying, and a fine reminder of how background framing and symmetry of effects can make an incomparable setting for flowers. Filoli may represent an extreme in manicured perfection, but it sets a fine standard which other gardens could mould and alter to a more relaxed approach and a smaller scale. Inside each scheme trees give an extra dimension: honey locusts, Japanese maples, dawn redwoods, standard wisterias as well as more tender shrubs such as New Zealand tea trees (forms of *Leptospermum*) and *Luma apiculata* with peeling brown bark.

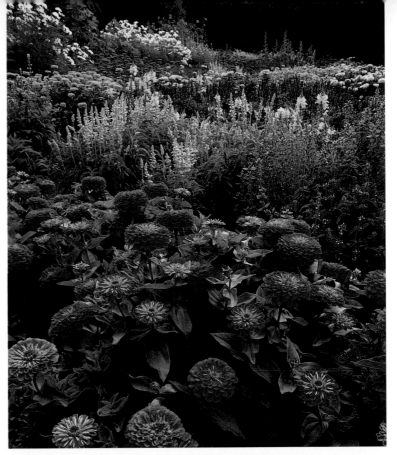

In the annual borders beyond the knot gardens scarlet zinnias (Z. 'Dreamland'), blue- and white-flowered salvias (including the blue Salvia farinacea 'Victoria') and clary (Salvia viridis 'Claryssa') with a distant view of white cosmos, have a more relaxed air. They appear as pleasantly jumbled drifts and blocks of rich colour and reduce the tension in the garden. The scale and ebullient style of these annuals contrasts with the more obviously controlled areas of planting, but the containing frame is none the less present.

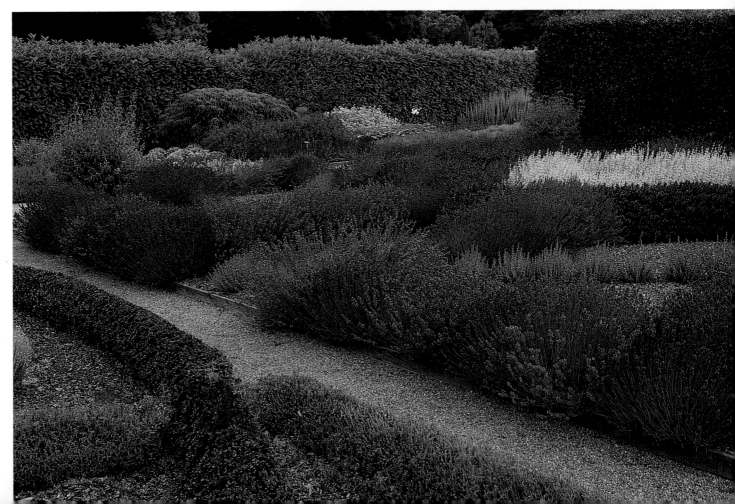

In the Elizabethan knot garden, dwarf berberis and germander (Teucrium chamaedrys) are clipped tightly into low hedges to mark out a formal pattern beside beds of lavender cultivars which, as they grow older, make broader sweeps of mauve and blue flower colour. Everywhere at Filoli, inside each enclosure containing different plant themes or colour schemes, linear hedges define the planting within the beds. As lavender bushes mature and develop a pleasantly gnarled woody appearance, they give the whole garden a feeling of age without detracting from their structural role as low hedging plants.

ABELIA
(Caprifoliaceae)
A. × *grandiflora* is a graceful arching semi-evergreen shrub of garden origin with glossy purplish leaves. Pink tubular flowers, slightly scented, are borne for a long period in late summer. Sun; protect from cold wind.
MEDIUM SHRUB H: 1.5–1.8m/5–6ft
s: 90–120cm/36–48in z: 6[6–10]

ABUTILON
(Malvaceae)
A. *vitifolium* (Chile) is a pyramidal semi-evergreen shrub with soft vine-like grey-green leaves; bell- or saucer-shaped flowers of pale mauve or lilac in early summer. Fast growing; best planted against a sheltering wall. Cut back hard after flowering. A. × *suntense*, its hybrid with A. *ochsenii*, bears smaller deep violet flowers slightly earlier.
MEDIUM SHRUB H: 2.4m/8ft or more s: 1.5m/5ft or more z: 9[9–10]

ACAENA
(Rosaceae) New Zealand burr New Zealand
Evergreen perennials making dense low ground cover of attractive pinnate leaves, grey-green in A. *buchananii* and intense blue-green in A. *adscendens* 'Glauca'. Full sun and well-drained soil. Good for paths and paving, especially for disguising ugly pavement joints.
H: 2.5–5cm/1–2in s: 25–50cm/10–20in z: 6[6–9]

ACANTHUS
(Acanthaceae) bear's breeches
southern Europe
Semi-evergreen or herbaceous perennials with sculptural deeply cut foliage. Well-drained soil; in cold regions mulch in winter.
A. *mollis* (Latifolius group; from Portugal) has large glossy green arching leaves and handsome 45cm/18in spikes of pink/white foxglove-like flowers in summer. Hardier than the species.
H: 90–120cm/36–48in s: 90cm/36in z: 8[6–10] or colder if mulched

ACHILLEA
(Compositae) yarrow Europe, western Asia
Herbaceous perennials whose flower-heads are dense corymbs of crowded daisies. Sun and well-drained soil; tolerates drought.
A. 'Coronation Gold' has ferny green leaves and vivid yellow flowers in summer. Needs staking.
H: 90cm/36in s: 30cm/12in z: 3[3–10]
A. *grandifolia* with grey-green dissected leaves, has dull white flowers in early summer. Needs staking.
H: 75cm/30in s: 30cm/12in z: 3[3–10]
A. *ptarmica* 'Boule de Neige' (syn. A.*p.* 'The Pearl'), with bright white double flowers in summer, is clump-forming and invasive.
H: 45cm/18in s: 60cm/24in z: 3[3–10]

A. × *taygetea* has lemon-yellow flowers in summer above finely dissected grey leaves. Needs good drainage.
H: 45cm/18in s: 15cm/6in z: 3[3–10]

ACONITUM
(Ranunculaceae) Europe, Asia
A. *napellus* (common monkshood, helmet flower) is a deciduous perennial. A. 'Bressingham Spire', another perennial, has indigo-blue flower-spikes above deeply cut dark green leaves in late summer. A. 'Ivorine' is a perennial with hooded creamy-white flowers in early summer. Sun or part shade and moist rich soil.
H: 90cm/36in s: 30cm/12in z: 6[6–9]

AGAPANTHUS
(Liliaceae/Alliaceae) blue African lily
S. Africa
Sun-loving deciduous perennials with strap-shaped leaves and rounded umbels of mainly blue flowers in late summer. Fertile moist but well-drained soil.
A. *campanulatus albus* (bell agapanthus) has flattish heads of white flowers that blend to a creamy-green effect. Best tightly massed. Mulch in winter.
H: 75–100cm/30–40in s: 35–45cm/14–18in z: 8[8–10]
A. Headbourne Hybrids bear rounded umbels

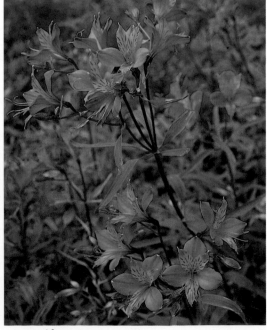

ABOVE *Alstroemeria aurea*
LEFT *Abutilon* × *suntense*

ranging from dark blue through violet and pale blue to white: choose plants when in flower. Reliably hardy, but mulch in very cold regions.
H: 60–120cm/24–48in s: 35–45cm/14–18in
z: 8[8-10]

AJUGA
(Labiatae) bugle, bugleweed Europe
A. *reptans* forms are vigorous spreading evergreen perennials making carpeting ground cover on ordinary moist soil in part shade. Ovate leaves may be green, purple-bronze, cream-variegated or tricolour – bronze, pink and green. Blue flower-spikes enrich the colour scheme in summer.
H: 10cm/4in s: 15cm/6in z: 3[3–10]

ALCEA
(Malvaceae) hollyhock
A. *rosea* (China) provides a colourful backdrop to a late summer border, but the beautiful mallow-flowers on immensely tall spikes are worth appreciating close to. Single and double forms are available, as well as single or mixed coloured flowers in reds, pinks, yellows and white. A.r. 'Nigra' has maroon flowers that are so dark they are almost black. Grow as a perennial or biennial in sun and rich, well-drained soil.
H: 1.5–3m/5–10ft s: 90cm/36in z: 2[2–10]

ALCHEMILLA
(Rosaceae) lady's mantle eastern Europe to Asia Minor
A. *mollis* is a deciduous perennial making a mound of light green umbrella-shaped leaves: serrated leaf edges sparkle with droplets of rain or dew. Carries clouds of soft lime-green flowers in summer. Seeds freely in full sun or part shade, and may be invasive.
H: 30cm/12in s: 35cm/14in z: 3[3–8]

ALLIUM
(Liliaceae/Alliaceae)
Different allium species flower all through the summer months, mostly with flower-heads in shades of pinkish-mauve, though others are yellow or white. These bulbous perennials are useful for interplanting in herbaceous beds – the flower-spikes and onion-leaves providing contrast of form and texture. All need good drainage and most prefer sun.
A. *cernuum* (N. America) has drooping heads of lilac-pink in summer. Colonizes rapidly but is still small enough to grow under shrub roses.
H: 45cm/18in s: 15cm/6in z: 5[3–8]

A. *christophii* (Turkestan) has huge but delicate spherical heads composed of a web of pale amethyst-coloured stars; they rise on stout stems above untidy leaves to make statuesque accents between groups of perennials in early summer.
H: 60cm/24in s: 45cm/18in z: 5[5–10]
A. *schubertii* (eastern regions of Mediterranean, central Asia) is a version of A. *christophii* with irregular-shaped flower-heads of lilac-pink in spring. Although the bulb is hardy, the leaves and flower stem are frost tender.
H: 60cm/24in s: 45cm/18in z: 5[5–10]
A. *tuberosum* (Far East) has flat heads of dark-eyed white flowers in summer. Grow in sun or shade at the front of a border.
H: 45cm/18in s: 23cm/9in z: 5[4–10]

ALONSOA
(Scrophulariaceae) mask flower Peru
Half-hardy perennials often grown as annuals in sunny site on rich well-drained soil.
A. *warscewiczii* makes a compact bush, with deep green leaves and reddish stems. Has bright orange-scarlet spurred flowers in late summer.
H: 30–60cm/12–24in s: 35cm/14in z: 9[9–10]

ALOYSIA
(Verbenaceae)
A. *triphylla* (syn. *Lippia citriodora*; lemon verbena from Chile) has lemon-scented leaves and panicles of tiny pale mauve flowers in late summer. This tender deciduous shrub, for a container or sheltered wall in temperate climates, may be trained into a formal shape.
MEDIUM SHRUB H: 1.5m/5ft s: 1.2m/4ft
z: 9[8–10]

ALSTROEMERIA
(Liliaceae/Alstroemeriaceae) Peruvian lily
Chile
Tuberous-rooted herbaceous perennials with strap-shaped leaves making spring ground cover. Clusters of attractively marked lily-flowers appear in summer. Stake unobtrusively with twigs. Slow to establish (most are best grown from seed), but eventually invasive; mulch for frost protection until settled. Sun or part shade.
A. *aurantiaca* (now correctly A. *aurea*) has flowers in varying yellows and oranges. Hardy, vigorous and relatively easy to transplant after flowering.
H: 90cm/36in s: 30cm/12in z: 7[7–10]
A. Ligtu Hybrids are grey-leaved, with flowers in blush pinks, brighter coral tones and soft yellows.
H: 60cm/24in s: 30cm/12in z: 7[7–10]

AMSONIA
(Apocynaceae) blue dogbane, bluestar
N. America
A. *tabernaemontana* is a deciduous perennial with erect willowy stems clad in long narrow leaves.

Amsonia tabernaemontana

Both stems and leaves turn golden in late summer. Terminal clusters of starry pale blue flowers are borne in summer. Sun and moist fertile soil.
H & S: 60–90cm/24–36in z: 3[3–9]

ANAPHALIS
(Compositae) pearl or pearly everlasting
A. *margaritacea* (N. America, eastern Asia) is a deciduous perennial with downy grey leaves and large heads of pearly-white everlasting flowers with yellow eyes in late summer. Sun or part shade and well-drained soil.
H & S: 30–45cm/12–18in z: 3[3–9]

ANEMONE
(Ranunculaceae) windflower
The spring-flowering European species are compact deciduous perennials with tuberous roots. Summer-flowering Japanese anemones are larger, fibrous-rooted border plants.
A. *apennina* (Europe) has carpeting ferny leaves and blue daisy-flowers in spring. Rich soil and part shade; loves to naturalize through borders under deciduous shrubs.
H & S: 10–15cm/4–6in z: 6[6–10]
Japanese anemones are low-maintenance plants with clumps of palmate dark green leaves, for sun or part shade and fertile, well-drained but moisture-retentive soil. Slow to establish and eventually invasive, but worth having for the leaves and the display of late-summer flowers. Most garden plants are hybrids: A. × *hybrida* 'Honorine Jobert' has long-lasting pure white flowers with conspicuous yellow stamens. A. × *h.* 'Prince Henry' ('Prinz Heinrich') has deep rose double flowers.
H: 60–90cm/24–36in s: 45–60/18–24in
z: 6[6–10]
A. *nemorosa* (European wood anemone) has simple flowers – usually creamy-white – in spring, though some forms are pink or blue. Naturalizes in part shade under shrubs in soil rich in leaf-mould.
H & S: 15–20cm/6–8in z: 3[3–9]

ANGELICA
(Umbelliferae) archangel, wild parsnip
Europe, Asia
A. *archangelica* is a dramatic biennial or perennial with deeply dissected fresh green leaves. Large greenish-yellow flower umbels top 1.8–2.4m/6–8ft stems in summer. Sun or part shade and rich soil.
H: 60–150cm/24–60in s: 90cm/36in
z: 4[4–9]

ANISODONTEA
(Malvaceae)
A. *capensis* (S. Africa) is a tender evergreen shrub with attractive green leaves and pink flowers from spring through to autumn, perfect for growing as a centrepiece in an ornamental pot. Root cuttings in late summer and keep frost free.
SMALL SHRUB H & S: 90cm/36in z: 10[9–10]

ANTHEMIS
(Compositae) Europe
A. *tinctoria* 'E. C. Buxton' is a variety of ox-eye chamomile or golden marguerite with cool lemon-yellow daisy-flowers in summer above attractive deeply cut mid-green leaves. Cut back this deciduous perennial after flowering. Sun and well-drained soil.
H: 75cm/30in s: 45cm/18in z: 3[3–10]

ANTHERICUM
(Liliaceae/Anthericaceae) southern Europe
A. *liliago* (St Bernard's lily) is an herbaceous perennial with slender spikes of delicate trumpet-shaped white flowers in early summer above clumps of grass-like leaves. Cut back after flowering unless seed-heads are wanted. Sun or part shade and good soil, preferably acid.
H: 45–60cm/18–24in s: 30–38cm/12–15in
z: 8[8–10]

AQUILEGIA
(Ranunculaceae) columbine
Herbaceous perennials for moist, well-drained soil in sun or part shade. Divided foliage resembles large-scale maidenhair fern; in early summer funnel-shaped flowers have spurred petals.
A. *canadensis* (N. America) has dainty red-spurred lemon-yellow flowers and light green leaves. Grow in naturalized drifts.
H: 45–60cm/18–24in s: 30cm/12in z: 3[3–10]
A. *vulgaris* 'Nora Barlow' is an old variety of the European granny's bonnet – with spurless pink/red/green/blue double flowers and glaucous leaves. Seeds true.
H: 90cm/36in s: 45cm/18in z: 3[3–10]

ARBUTUS
(Ericaceae) strawberry tree southern Europe, Asia Minor
A. *unedo* (Killarney strawberry tree) is evergreen with glossy dark green leaves. Dangling panicles of white pitcher-shaped flowers in late summer intermingle with strawberry-like fruit. Can be a lawn specimen or part of a border scheme. Sun or

Asphodeline liburnica

Anemone apennina

Aquilegia vulgaris 'Nora Barlow'

part shade; protect from cold winds. Ericaceous, but lime-tolerant.
SMALL TREE/LARGE SHRUB H: 5–6m/15–20ft
s: 3–4m/10–12ft z: 8[8–10]

ARGYRANTHEMUM
(Compositae)
These tender chrysanthemums, which are easy to overwinter from cuttings taken in late summer, grow into attractive shrubby plants that flower prolifically. Ideal as focal points in large pots on a wall or terrace in full sun.
A. foeniculaceum (formerly *Chrysanthemum foeniculaceum*; marguerite, Paris daisy from the Canary Islands) is an evergreen perennial with deeply divided silvery-grey almost glaucous foliage and white daisy-flowers in summer. *A.* 'Jamaica Primrose' bears lovely pale yellow single flowers, complemented by deeply cut green leaves.
H & s: 60–90cm/24–36in z: 9[9–10]

ARTEMISIA
(Compositae)
Shrubs and perennials grown for grey and silver leaves that make an attractive foil for other plantings. Survive low temperatures in full sun and well-drained soil.
A. absinthium 'Lambrook Silver', a cultivar of the European absinthe or common wormwood, is a semi-evergreen sub-shrub with woody stems bearing silver-grey dissected leaves. Pale yellow flowers appear in summer.
H & s: 90cm/36in z: 4[4–10]

A. ludoviciana (white sage from N. America) is an herbaceous perennial with silvery-white felty leaves and silvery-grey flowers in summer. Suckers freely and may be invasive.
H: 120cm/48in s: 60cm/24in z: 5[5–10]
A. pontica (south-eastern and central Europe) is a suckering perennial that has smoky-grey feathery foliage and makes good ground cover or pathway edging in sun.
H: 45–75cm/18–30in s: 45cm/18in z: 5[5–10]
A. 'Powis Castle' is an evergreen sub-shrub, making a sturdy pewter-toned cushion of fine-cut leaves.
H: 60cm/24in s: 45cm/18in z: 8[8–10]
A. schmidtiana 'Silver Mound' is a perennial that makes low mounds of silvery grass-like silky foliage.
H: 10cm/4in s: 25cm/10in z: 4[4–10]

ARUM
(Araceae) south-eastern Europe
A. italicum pictum (correctly *A.i. marmoratum*) has leaves that unfurl in autumn and grow to full lushness in spring – glossy arrow-shapes veined in creamy-white. Spikes of red berries take the place of leaves in late summer. Seeds true. This tuberous perennial makes attractive ground cover in sun or part shade.
H: 38cm/15in s: 30cm/12in z: 6[6–10]

ARUNCUS
(Rosaceae) goatsbeard northern hemisphere
A. dioicus is a deciduous perennial that makes an attractive clump of elegant fern-like foliage.

Creamy-white plumes of astilbe-like flowers rise 2.1m/7ft tall in summer. An essential border companion plant for making bold groups. Sun or part shade and rich moist soil.
H: 120cm/48in s: 90cm/36in z: 3[3–9]

ASARUM
(Aristolochiaceae) wild ginger
A. europaeum (Europe) is an evergreen rhizomatous perennial that makes creeping ground cover in moist shade or part shade. Handsome dark green glossy leaves, shaped like a rounded heart, hide inconspicuous greenish-brown flowers in spring. Attractive to slugs.
H: 12–15cm/5–6in s: 20–30cm/8–12in
z: 4[4–8]

ASPHODELINE
(Liliaceae/Asphodelaceae) Jacob's rod
Mediterranean
A. lutea (king's spear, yellow asphodel) makes architectural perennial clumps of stiff stems clad in semi-evergreen grey-green grassy leaves. Tall racemes of shiny yellow starry flowers in early summer are followed by attractive seed-heads. *A. liburnica* is a shorter form. Rhizomatous rootstock increases slowly. Sun or part shade and well-drained soil.
H: 90–120cm/36–48in s: 30cm/12in z: 6[6–10]

ASTER
(Compositae) N. America
Herbaceous perennials grown for daisy-like flowers. Sun or part shade and rich but well-drained soil.
A. divaricatus (white wood aster) has sprawling wiry black stems that bear a profusion of little white starry flower-heads in late summer to autumn. Tolerates dry shade.
H & s: 45–60cm/18–24in z: 3[3–9]
A. × frikartii is one of the best later-flowering plants, with freely borne yellow-centred lavender-blue flowers from late summer onwards. *A. × f.* 'Mönch' is the best.
H: 60–90cm/24–36in s: 38–45cm/15–18in
z: 5[5–10]
A. lateriflorus 'Horizontalis' has compact twiggy stems that bear small dark green leaves with distinctive horizontal habit. Is crowned with a hedge-like mass of tiny palest silvery-lilac flowers with browny-pink centres in autumn.
H: 60–90cm/24–36in s: 30cm/12in z: 3[3–10]
A. novae-angliae 'Andenken an Alma Pötschke' (Michaelmas daisy, New England aster) bears

heads of long-lasting rich cherry-red flowers in late summer to autumn. Tolerates moister soils.
H: 90–150cm/36–60in s: 45–60cm/18–24in
z: 4[4–9]

ASTILBE
(Saxifragaceae) eastern Asia
Deciduous perennials with handsome ferny foliage and long-lasting plumes of flowers. Moist or even boggy soil. Sun (in Europe) or part shade in the hotter zones of N. America.
A. rivularis has elegant leaves, very deeply divided and luxuriant. Tall plumed panicles of long-lasting creamy-green flowers, which appear in summer, are attractive even when fading to buff.
A. × arendsii hybrids in white, pinks and reds all have attractive sometimes bronze leaves: choose flower tones to suit individual schemes.
H: 1.8m/6ft s: 1.2m/4ft z: 4[4–9]

ASTRANTIA
(Umbelliferae) masterwort
Deciduous perennials with attractive palmate leaves and dainty flowers in summer, each one a miniature posy of florets in a circle of pointed bracts. Moist rich soil in sun or part shade.
A. major (Europe) has flowers that look greeny-

white. A.m. 'Sunningdale Variegated' has young leaves extensively splashed with cream – one of the best variegated perennials. Needs shade to retain this colouring.
H: 60–90cm/24–36in s: 38cm/15in z: 4[4–9]
A. maxima (Europe, eastern Caucasus) has three-lobed leaves and shell-pink flower-heads, surrounded by a deeper pink frill of bracts.
H: 45–75cm/18–30in s: 30–45cm/12–18in
z: 4[4–9]

BALLOTA
(Labiatae) Crete
B. pseudodictamnus has pale woolly-textured rounded leaves. Cut back this evergreen sub-shrub in spring to keep a compact shape and to encourage new growth of silvery-green foliage. Full sun in front of border and good drainage.
H: 30–60cm/12–24in s: 45–60cm/18–24in
z: 8[8–10]

BAPTISIA
(Leguminosae) false indigo
eastern N. America
B. australis is a handsome border perennial with blue-green trifoliate leaves and spikes of indigo-blue pea-flowers in early summer. Dark grey

almost black seed-pods are attractive later. Allow to establish in rich moist acid or neutral soil in sun. Tolerates heat and humidity.
H: 60–120cm/24–48in s: 60cm/24in z: 3[3–9]

BERGENIA
(Saxifragaceae)
Large rounded leathery green leaves spread slowly to make substantial evergreen perennial ground cover, good for anchoring front-of-border planting. Full sun or shade; happy in most conditions. Some hybrids carry particularly attractive leaves or flowers: B. purpurascens has purple-flushed leaves in winter. B. × schmidtii has 30cm/12in sprays of clear pink flowers in early spring. B. 'Silberlicht' ('Silver Light') produces pure white flowers slightly later; these become pinkish as they mature.
H: 30cm/12in s: 45–60cm/18–24in z: 4[4–10]

BOLTONIA
(Compositae) N. America
B. asteroides is a perennial that bears masses of pale lilac Michaelmas-daisy flowers above grey foliage in late summer to autumn, making pretty back-of-border infill to complement hydrangeas and other perennials. Easy to grow in sun or part shade and any fertile soil; tolerates heat and humidity.
H: 1.2–2.1m/4–7ft s: 1.2m/4ft z: 3[3–10]

BRUNNERA
(Boraginaceae) western Caucasus
B. macrophylla (Siberian bugloss) makes effective late-spring perennial ground cover, with intensely blue forget-me-not flowers in early summer glowing among heart-shaped hairy dark foliage. As leaves gradually darken and coarsen, allow neighbouring plants to eclipse them with summer flowers. Sun or shade and moist soil; does not tolerate humid heat. B.m. 'Hadspen Cream' is an elegant variegated form that needs protection from drying winds and sun.
H: 45cm/18in s: 60cm/2ft z: 3[3–10]

BUDDLEJA
(Loganiaceae)
Buddlejas like full sun and good loamy soil. Lime-tolerant.
B. alternifolia (China) can grow as a spreading deciduous shrub or be trained as an elegant small tree. Lanceolate leaves are a dark grey-green. Rounded clusters of very fragrant pale lilac flowers appear in summer on the previous year's growth.

Astrantia major

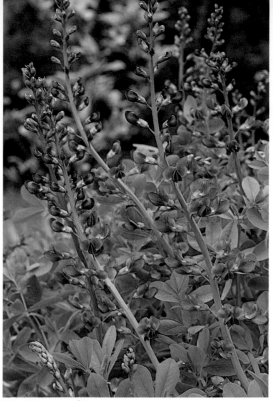

Baptisia australis

B.a. 'Argentea' is a less vigorous silver-leaved form for a small garden.
LARGE SHRUB H & S: 4–6m/12–20ft z: 6[6–9]
B. crispa (syn. *B. paniculata*; from northern India) is a beautiful semi-evergreen shrub for a warm wall in sun. Deeply toothed white-felted leaves make a shimmering dusty-silvery-grey mass, the perfect background for terminal clusters of fragrant lilac-pink flowers with orange throats, which appear in summer on the current year's growth.
MEDIUM SHRUB H: 1.8–3m/6–10ft
s: 1.2–2.4m/4–8ft. z: 9[8–10]
B. davidii (butterfly bush from China) is a decid-uous shrub with terminal trusses of fragrant lilac-purple flowers in late summer on new season's growth. Garden forms offer a colour range from warm red-purple through violet to blue. *B.* 'Lochinch', its hybrid with *B. fallowiana*, has violet-blue flowers and grey woolly leaves with paler undersides. Its misty colouring and graceful habit suit mixed pastel-toned plantings.
MEDIUM SHRUB H & S: 2.7m/9ft z: 6[6–10]

BUGLOSSOIDES
(Boraginaceae)
B. purpurocaerulea is an attractive and useful perennial carpeter, with purplish-blue flowers in late spring to early summer. Vigorous and lime- and shade-tolerant.
H: 40cm/16in s: 90cm/36in z: 4[4–10]

BUPLEURUM
(Umbelliferae) thoroughwax central and southern Europe to Asia
B. fruticosum (shrubby hare's ear), an evergreen shrub of attractive bushy habit, is quick-growing. Subtle colourings of shiny blue-green young foliage and, from midsummer onwards, greenish-yellow flower- and seed-umbels are an effective foil for neighbouring planting. Full sun or part shade. Provide wind shelter and frost drainage.
MEDIUM SHRUB H: 1.8m/6ft s: 3m/10ft
z: 8[8–10]

CALENDULA
(Compositae) marigold
C. officinalis (pot marigold from southern Europe) has large, cheerful daisy-flowers in yellows and oranges; named varieties may offer double flowers, more compact habit and pinkish or pastel tones. Undemanding annuals with a long summer flowering period, thriving in sun and poor soils. Often self-seeds.
H: 30–60cm/12–24in s: 23–45cm/9–18in
ANNUAL

CALLICARPA
(Verbenaceae)
C. bodinieri (China) is a deciduous shrub grown principally for its clusters of deep lilac-coloured fruit carried among rose-tinted autumn foliage. Both male and female shrubs are necessary for fruiting. Insignificant lilac-coloured flowers appear in midsummer. Sunny sheltered position and good garden soil.
MEDIUM SHRUB H & S: 1.5–1.8m/5–6ft z: 5[5–9]

CALTHA
(Ranunculaceae) marsh marigold
Europe, N. America
C. palustris bears numerous rich yellow 25mm/1in flowers in spring above mounded perennial clumps of shiny rounded green leaves. Thrives in damp soil near water, but will flourish in drier shaded sites provided the soil is rich and moist.
H: 30–60cm/12–24in s: 45cm/18in z: 3[3–10]

CAMPANULA
(Campanulaceae)
Border campanulas are easy to grow in good well-drained soil in sun or shade. Flowers in summer. Perennial species make useful colonizers, but tall flower-spikes often need staking.
C. lactiflora (Caucasus) is a perennial with open branching stems clothed in lanceolate leaves, and panicles of bell-shaped flowers in attractive 'washed-out' shades of blue.
H: 90–150cm/36–60in s: 38–45cm/15–18in
z: 6[6–10]
C. latifolia 'Brantwood' is a cultivar of the peren-nial giant bellflower (Europe, Asia). Produces long tubular flowers, in rich violet-purple, above a handsome rosette of rounded leaves.
H: 120–150cm/48–60in s: 38–45cm/15–18in
z: 3[3–10]
C. medium (Canterbury bell from southern Europe) carries large showy bell-shaped flowers in blues, whites and pastels over a long period.
H: 38–90cm/15–36in s: 30cm/12in z: 8[8–10]
or grow as ANNUAL/BIENNIAL
C. persicifolia (peach-leaved or willow bellflower from Europe, northern Africa, Asia) is a peren-nial with blue or white saucer-shaped flowers that stud tall stems clothed with narrow leaves.
H: 30–90cm/12–36in s: 30–45cm/12–18in
z: 3[3–10]
C. pyramidalis (chimney bellflower, steeple bells; from southern Europe) is a short-lived perennial, often grown as a biennial. Tall spires clad in cool blue or white bell-shaped flowers make an arrest-ing pillar of colour above a pyramid of heart-shaped basal leaves.
H: 120–180cm/48–72in s: 45–60cm/18–24in
z: 8[8–10]
C. takesimana (Korea) is a superlative perennial that should be better known. Tubular bell-shaped white flowers, borne on stems arching upwards from a rosette of large leaves, are lilac-mottled outside, maroon-spotted inside.
H: 60cm/24in s: 45cm/18in z: 5[5–10]

CAMPSIS
(Bignoniaceae) trumpet creeper, trumpet vine
Deciduous climbing shrubs that make a dense curtain of attractive pinnate foliage and produce huge drooping clusters of 75mm/3in orange-scarlet tubular flowers in late summer. Full sun, well-drained rich soil and a sheltered site.
C. grandiflora from Asia has wider flowers and is more tender than *C. radicans* from N. America, which is hardy to zone 5.
CLIMBER H: 9–12m/28–40ft z: 7[7–10]

CARDIOCRINUM
(Liliaceae) giant lily
C. giganteum (Himalaya, Tibet) is a dramatic cli-max plant for the light shade of a shrubbery or woodland glade. In summer a spectacular spire of 15cm/6in greenish-white trumpet-flowers emerges

Centranthus ruber

Cestrum parqui

from a deep whorl of glossy heart-shaped leaves. Bulb dies after flowering, but produces offsets that take 3–5 years to mature. A good flowering group is slow to establish but well worth the nurturing and waiting. Moisture-retentive but well-drained soil enriched with plenty of humus is vital.
H: 1.8–3m/6–10ft   s: 0.9–1.2m/3–4ft   z: 6[6–9]

CAREX
(Cyperaceae)   sedge
Grass-like perennials with arching leaves that thrive in sun where soil is cool and moist.
C. *elata* 'Aurea' (Bowles's golden sedge) has leaves striped in green and yellow, turning to gold in summer and then buff.
H: 60cm/24in   s: 45cm/18in   z: 5[5–9]
C. *oshimensis* 'Evergold' (syn. C. *morrowii* 'Evergold') makes shaggy rounded clumps of foliage that remain effective all year, the leaves brightly variegated in green and yellow.
H: 20–30cm/8–12in   s: 15–20cm/6–8in
z: 8[8–10]

CARYOPTERIS
(Verbenaceae)   eastern Asia
C. × *clandonensis* is a small deciduous shrub with narrow grey-green aromatic leaves that make a smoky background to clusters of lavender-blue tubular flowers that appear in late summer: several

darker blue forms exist. Sun and well-drained soil.
SMALL SHRUB H & S: 60–120cm/24–48in
z: 7[6–10] (may be cut to ground below zone 7)

CEANOTHUS
(Rhamnaceae)   Californian lilac   N. America
Evergreen species are tender, wall-loving shrubs, needing favourable sites, though many hybrids are hardier. Deciduous ceanothus are even hardier. Plant in good garden soil.
C. *arboreus* 'Trewithen Blue' grows fast to become a tree-like evergreen shrub in warm gardens, spectacular in late spring and early summer with long panicles of deep blue scented flowers. Its relatively large soft leaves make its hardiness unreliable.
LARGE SHRUB H: 5m/15ft   s: 6–8m/20–25ft
z: 9[9–10]
C. 'Burkwoodii', also evergreen, has shiny green leaves with grey undersides and bright blue flowers from midsummer through to autumn.
MEDIUM SHRUB H: 1.8–3m/6–10ft
s: 1.8–2.4m/6–8ft   z: 8[8–10]
C. 'Cascade' has arching branches making an elegant weeping evergreen shrub. Small intensely blue flowers appear in early summer.
LARGE SHRUB H & S: 3m/10ft   z: 9[8–10]
C. × *delileanus* hybrids are deciduous and hardy enough for open borders, contributing useful flower colour at the end of the season. Prune hard

in spring. C. 'Gloire de Versailles' has a strong open habit and long panicles of pale blue flowers that fit beautifully into misty schemes.
MEDIUM SHRUB H & S: 1.8–2.4m/6–8ft   z: 6[6–10]

CELASTRUS
(Celastraceae)   climbing staff vine, bittersweet
C. *orbiculatus* (north-eastern Asia) is a strong-growing deciduous climber that will twine over walls, fences, tree stumps etc. Inconspicuous summer flowers are of less interest than the pea-sized bright orange-scarlet fruits, freely borne in autumn against a background of yellowing foliage.
CLIMBER H: to 10m/30ft   z: 5[5–10]

CENTRANTHUS
(Valerianaceae)   valerian
C. *ruber* (Jupiter's beard, red valerian, fox's brush; from Europe and other Mediterranean regions) is a short-lived perennial with panicles of tiny rosy-red flowers (white in the form C.*r. albus*) from summer onwards above fleshy grey-green leaves. Discard leggy plants after flowering. Tolerates poor, well-drained soils, and is happy to seed and naturalize in walls and paving.
H: 45–90cm/18–36in   s: 30–45cm/12–18in
z: 4[4–10]

CERASTIUM
(Caryophyllaceae)
C. *tomentosum* (snow-in-summer from southern Europe) is an evergreen perennial that makes a silvery foliage mat covered in early summer by starry saucer-shaped white flowers. Quickly spreads to soften paving and masonry. Sun and well-drained soil.
H: 15cm/6in   s: 60cm/24in   z: 3[3–10]

CESTRUM
(Solanaceae)   S. America
C. *parqui* is a half-hardy narrow-leaved deciduous willowy shrub bearing plumes of small greeny-yellow tubular flowers – musk-scented at night – in late summer. Sunny, sheltered site and good loamy soil. Prone to frost damage, but if cut back hard sends out new flowering shoots.
MEDIUM SHRUB H & S: 1.2–1.5m/4–5ft   z: 8[7–10]

CHELONE
(Scrophulariaceae)   turtlehead   N. America
C. *obliqua* forms perennial clumps of stiff leafy stems and flowers in late summer to autumn, with deep rosy-purple spikes of curious snapdragon-shape flowers to augment a border scheme. Sun or

part shade and deep light soil or near water.
H: 60–90cm/24–36in   s: 45–60cm/18–24in
z: 3[3–9]

CHIASTOPHYLLUM
(Crassulaceae)   Caucasus
C. oppositifolium resembles a miniature bergenia,
its small succulent dark green leaves making it a
useful edging or carpeting evergreen perennial in
sun or part shade. Small golden-yellow flowers
appear in sprays on 20cm/8in reddish stalks in late
summer. Spreads quickly by stem-rooting, and
tolerates poor conditions.
H: 10cm/4in   s: 30cm/12in   z: 6[6–10]

CHIONANTHUS
(Oleaceae)   fringe tree
C. virginicus (N. America) is a large deciduous
tree-like shrub with fragrant white flowers con-
sisting of strap-like petals. Flowers in midsummer.
LARGE SHRUB H: 7m/22ft   s: 3m/10ft   z: 5[5–9]

CHIONODOXA
(Liliaceae/Hyacinthaceae)   glory of the snow
Turkey
C. forbesii (syn. *C. luciliae*) has short racemes of
intensely blue white-eyed flowers that appear with
blunt strap-shaped leaves in early spring. In
autumn plant groups of bulbs in well-drained soil
in short grass or borders, in sun or part shade.
H: 15cm/6in   z: 4[4–10]

CHOISYA
(Rutaceae)   Mexican orange   Mexico
C. ternata is a handsome evergreen shrub with
aromatic glossy leaves and sweet-scented orange-
blossom flowers in spring. May be massed in part
shade or planted more architecturally in formal
areas. Shelter by a wall in a cold site, and protect
from full sun in hotter areas. Well-drained soil.
Look for the new compact form if space is limited.
MEDIUM SHRUB H: 1.5–1.8m/5–6ft
s: 1.8–2.4m/6–8ft   z: 8[8–10]

CIMICIFUGA
(Ranunculaceae)   bugbane
Graceful perennials for the back of a border or
informal planting among shrubs. Tall wands
of bottlebrush-flowers appear above clumps of
elegant ferny leaves. Prefer cool moist places;
intolerant of high humidity.

Cimicifuga racemosa

C. racemosa (black cohosh, black snakeroot; from eastern N. America) has fragrant feathery white flowers on 2.4m/8ft branching stems in summer.
H: 1.2–1.5m/4–5ft s: 0.6m/2ft z: 3[3–10]
C. ramosa (China) produces 30cm/12in spires of white flowers from late summer into autumn. *C.r.* 'Atropurpurea' is a purple-leaved form.
H: 1.5–2.1m/5–7ft s: 0.9–1.2m/3–4ft z: 3[3–9]

CIRSIUM
(Compositae) thistle central Europe
C. rivulare atropurpureum is a deciduous perennial grown for the sculptural shape of its bristly pinnate leaves as well as for the deep wine-red pincushion-flowers that appear in summer. Sun and damp soil.
H: 60–120cm/24–48in s: 60cm/24in
z: 4[4–10]

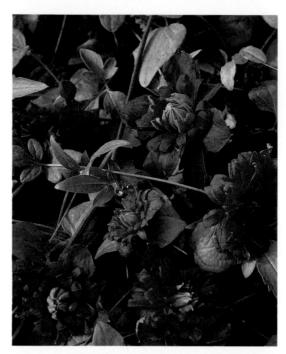

RIGHT *Clematis viticella* 'Purpurea Plena Elegans'
BELOW *Clematis recta*

CISTUS
(Cistaceae) rock rose, sun rose
Mediterranean
Sun-loving evergreen shrubs massed with white or pale pink flowers like single roses in early summer. Flowers last only a day, but are borne in long succession. Not reliably hardy; suitable for dry rocky banks or sheltered corners. Prefer poor well-drained soils.
C. × cyprius, *C. ladanifer*'s hybrid with *C. laurifolius*, has sticky olive-green leaves and papery white flowers, 75mm/3in wide, with a crimson blotch. Vigorous and one of the hardiest cistus.
MEDIUM SHRUB H: 1.8–2.4m/6–8ft
s: 2.1–2.7m/7–9ft z: 8[8–10]
C. ladanifer (gum cistus) is a stiff upright bush with dull green leaves. The 60mm/2½in flowers have a chocolate blotch at each petal base and yellow centres.
MEDIUM SHRUB H: 1.8m/6ft s: 1.2m/4ft
z: 8[8–10]
C. 'Silver Pink' is an attractive compact hardy shrub. Clusters of clear pink yellow-centred flowers are freely carried above leathery dark green leaves with grey undersides.
SMALL SHRUB H & s: 60–90cm/24–36in
z: 8[8–10]

CLEMATIS
(Ranunculaceae)
The climbing species and hybrids are indispensable for curtaining walls, garlanding pergolas, decorating plain evergreens and leafy shrubs, and disguising stumps. Full sun, roots in shade. All like well-drained fertile soil with some lime. Choose from wide range available, selecting flowers in the colouring, scale and season that suit your situation.
C. alpina (southern and central Europe) and *C. macropetala* (Siberia, northern China) are both scrambling spring-flowering deciduous species, typically blue and not too vigorous.
CLIMBER H: 1.8–4m/6–12ft z: 2–6[2–9]
C. armandii (China) is a vigorous evergreen, with long leathery dark green leaves and creamy-white clustered flowers in spring. Feed generously. Not reliably hardy.
CLIMBER H: to 10m/30ft z: 8[8–10]
C. cirrhosa (Balearic Islands) has ferny evergreen leaves. Drooping creamy flowers with purple-spotted insides appear in spring. Not reliably hardy.
CLIMBER H: 3m/10ft z: 8[8–10]
C. flammula (fragrant virgin's bower from southern Europe) has bushy deciduous growth. Panicles

of small pure white fragrant flowers appear in late summer. Grow through trellis or low spring-flowering shrubs of open habit.
CLIMBER H: 3m/10ft   z: 7[7–10]
C. heracleifolia 'Wyevale' is a perennial that forms a leafy shrub-like mound, with clusters of deep blue hyacinth-flowers in late summer.
H: 60–90cm/24–36in   z: 3[3–9]
C. 'Huldine' has almost translucent white petals, palest mauve outside and with greenish stamens. Cut back this deciduous climber hard in winter to encourage summer flowering on young wood.
CLIMBER H: 4m/12ft   z: 5[5–10]
C. × *jackmanii* is a large-flowered deciduous clematis hybrid (*C. viticella* is one parent) producing violet-purple flowers for many weeks from midsummer. Prune in late winter and train into shape during spring. A wonderful companion for bronze foliage and deep red flowers.
CLIMBER H: 4m/12ft   z: 5[5–10]
C. montana (central and western China, Himalayas) is rampant, a beautiful deciduous backdrop in a big enough garden. The species has white flowers in early summer; many varieties have pink or lilac tints and are slightly less vigorous. Prune after flowering if necessary to control spread.
CLIMBER H: to 12m/40ft   s: 5–6m/15–20ft   z: 5[5–10]
C. recta (ground clematis from southern Europe) is a perennial with a tendency to sprawl. Makes superb clumps with 180cm/6ft stems carrying starry white flowers to produce a cloud effect in early summer. A companion to early-flowering thalictrums and crambes.
H: 60–150cm/24–60cm.   z: 3[3–10]
C. viticella types are moderately vigorous deciduous climbers, with nodding bell-shaped flowers in shades of blue and purple in summer. *C.v.* 'Purpurea Plena Elegans' is rose-purple, a densely packed rosette of sepals. *C.* 'Abundance' has soft purple flowers. Grow on walls and through neighbouring shrubs, and prune hard in early spring.
CLIMBER H: 2.7–4m/9–12ft   z: 5[5–10]

CLEOME
(Capparidaceae)   spider flower
tropical America
C. hassleriana (syn. *C. spinosa* of gardens) is a late-summer flowering annual with clusters of pink and white or violet flowers that appear at the tips of hairy stalks. Plant seed in late spring. Group in sunny beds and borders for a pretty weaving mass of pastel colour.
H: 90cm/36in   s: 45cm/18in   ANNUAL

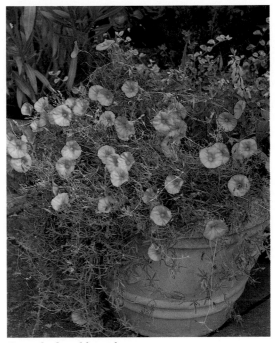
Convolvulus althaeoides

CLERODENDRUM
(Verbenaceae)   Far East
C. trichotomum makes a strong-growing deciduous shrub, best as a lawn specimen in a sunny sheltered site, where suckers may be controlled. Very fragrant white star-shaped flowers with persistent maroon calyces appear in late summer, followed by turquoise berries. Those of *C.t. fargesii* are a lighter blue.
SMALL TREE H & S: 3–5m/10–15ft   z: 6[6–10]

COLCHICUM
(Liliaceae/Colchicaceae)   autumn crocus
C. speciosum (Turkey, Caucasus) has large crocus-like flowers 15cm/6in high in shades of pinkish mauve; *C.s.* 'Album' is white. Plant in drifts in sun or shade for an autumn carpet in grass or at the edge of a shrubbery, where there is space for the dense spring foliage. Allow corms to naturalize and increase.
H: 30–40cm/12–16in   s: 23–30cm/9–12in   z: 4[4–10]

CONVALLARIA
(Liliaceae/Convallariaceae)   lily-of-the-valley
Europe, Asia, N. America
C. majalis 'Fortin's Giant' is a perennial that is larger and later-flowering than the species: dainty waxy white flowers in late spring are bell-shaped and very sweetly scented. The mid-green leaf-spikes make good summer ground cover in shade and humus-rich soil. Creeping rhizomes colonize quickly once established, becoming invasive in favourable conditions.
H: 20cm/8in   s: 30cm/12in   z: 3[3–9]

CONVOLVULUS
(Convolvulaceae)
All like light well-drained soil and full sun, and need frost protection in exposed sites.
C. althaeoides (southern Europe) is a deciduous semi-climber with silvery grey-green dissected foliage and trailing stems. Funnel-shaped shell-pink flowers in summer open wide in sun. Grow in a container or over a wall where the root-run is contained but the plant can sprawl in charming abandon.
H: 15cm/6in   s: 45–60cm/18–24in   z: 8[7–10]
C. cneorum (evergreen silverbush from southern Europe) is an evergreen shrub. Its small narrow leaves have a silky silvery sheen. White funnel-flowers open from pinkish buds in early summer.
SMALL SHRUB H: 45cm/18in   s: 60cm/24in   z: 8[8–10]
C. sabatius (syn. *C. mauritanicus*; ground morning glory from northern Africa) also forms a sprawling perennial mat of grey-green ovate leaves. In early summer twisted flower-buds open to wide funnel-flowers of deep lavender blue. Cut back hard to encourage spring growth.
H: 15cm/6in   s: 60cm/24in   z: 9[8–10]

CORDYLINE
(Liliaceae/Agavaceae)   evergreen cabbage palm
New Zealand
Evergreen trees and shrubs grown for handsome palm-like foliage. Cordylines are tender or half-hardy; in cold districts, grow as pot plants about 90cm/36in tall for architectural emphasis and shelter in winter.
C. australis (cabbage tree) has branches bearing dense clusters of sword-like leaves atop an erect stem. Produces huge drooping panicles of fragrant creamy flowers in summer in a favourable site.
SMALL TREE H: 8m/25ft   s: 1.8–3m/6–10ft   z: 9[9–10]

COREOPSIS
(Compositae)   tickseed   N. America
C. verticillata (thread-leaf tickseed or coreopsis) is an erect bushy perennial with very fine hair-like foliage and loose corymbs of rather brassy yellow daisy-flowers in late summer. *C.v.* 'Moonbeam', which has paler flowers to associate in a cooler

Cosmos atrosanguineus

scheme, flowers for longer, enduring intense summer heat. Dead-head to prolong flowering. Sun and well-drained soil. Slow to establish.
H: 45–60cm/18–24in s: 30–45cm/12–18in
z: 3[3–10]

CORNUS
(Cornaceae) dogwood
The dogwoods described are graceful middle-storey deciduous trees or shrubs with flower interest in spring and attractive autumn leaves.
C. alternifolia 'Argentea' (N. America) is a handsome small tree with tiered branches of delicate silver and green foliage. Flat corymbs of small flowers appear in late spring.
SMALL TREE H: 4m/12ft s: 3m/10ft z: 4[4–9]
C. controversa 'Variegata' (China, Japan) also has horizontal branches in wedding-cake tiers, and the alternate leaves are cream-edged. Like *C. alternifolia* 'Argentea', on a larger scale, it is elegantly architectural even when leafless in winter.
MEDIUM TREE H & s: 8m/25ft z: 6[6–10]
C. florida (flowering dogwood from eastern USA) is an elegant spreading shrub or small tree. Four petal-like white bracts surround tiny green flowers in late spring. Susceptible to late frosts.
LARGE SHRUB/SMALL TREE H: 3–5m/10–15ft
s: 6m/20ft z: 5[5–9]
C. kousa chinensis (China) is a small upright tree with spreading branches and inconspicuous flowers set in showy white bracts in early summer. Lime-tolerant. Plant in woodland with some shade from fierce summer sun.
LARGE SHRUB/SMALL TREE H: 3m/10ft
s: 2.4–3m/8–10ft z: 5[5-9]

C. nuttallii (Nuttall's West Coast dogwood from western N. America) has conspicuous white bracts in late spring, which take on a pink tinge in sun. Leaves colour in autumn. Acid soil essential.
LARGE SHRUB H: 5–6m/15–20ft
s: 2.4–3m/8–10ft z: 8[8–10]

CORONILLA
(Leguminosae)
C. glauca (southern Europe) has delicate grey-green evergreen leaves. Its delightful pale yellow pea-flowers, borne intermittently all winter, are at their best in spring. Grow as a wall shrub or as a sprawling bush in full sun to accompany violet-flowered abutilons.
MEDIUM SHRUB H & s: 2.1m/7ft z: 9[9–10]

CORYDALIS
(Papaveraceae)
C. cheilanthifolia (China) makes neat evergreen perennial clumps of fresh green ferny leaves and bears little spikes of yellow miniature snapdragon-flowers all summer. Self-seeds and spreads in a cool site. Good for interplanting with bulbs.
H & s: 25–30cm/10–12in z: 5[5–10]

CORYLOPSIS
(Hamamelidaceae)
C. pauciflora (Japan) is a pretty deciduous shrub of open habit for a shady mixed border or a woodland glade. Drooping pale yellow cup-shaped cowslip-scented flowers are carried in spring, just before the leaves open. Grow above blue-flowered scillas or anemones.
MEDIUM SHRUB H & s: 1.8m/6ft z: 6[6–9]

COSMOS
(Compositae) Mexico
C. atrosanguineus (black cosmos) is an unusual dahlia-related perennial with long-lasting chocolate-scented velvety-maroon flowers in late summer. The slightly tender tubers may be lifted in winter or protected with a thick mulch. Sun and deep moisture-retentive soil. Striking grown in a container.
H: 75cm/30in s: 30cm/12in z: 9[7–10]

COTINUS
(Anacardiaceae) smoke tree
C. coggygria (smoke bush, Venetian sumach; from Europe to Caucasus) is a deciduous shrub with bronzy-green ovate leaves that give good autumn colour. Panicles of tiny purple flowers in summer create a smoky hazy texture amid the foliage. Named forms have purple leaves.
MEDIUM SHRUB H & s: 2.4m/8ft z: 5[5–10]
C. obovatus (syn. *C. americanus*; chittam wood from south-eastern USA) is more upright deciduous shrub with purplish-pink leaves that shade in summer to glaucous-green and colour brilliantly in autumn.
LARGE SHRUB H: 3m/10ft s: 1.8–2.4m/6–8ft
z: 6[6–9]

COTONEASTER
(Rosaceae)
Low-growing cotoneasters are architectural shrubs and make shapely ground covers. Taller ones offer good back-of-border furnishing or screening.
C. conspicuus (Tibet) is semi-evergreen, its branches clothed with pink buds opening to white flowers in summer. Soft red berries are carried in autumn. Its arching mound-like habit is attractive on a dry bank.
MEDIUM SHRUB H: 1.8–2.1m/6–7ft
s: 1.5–1.8m/5–6ft z: 6[6–9]
C. 'Cornubia' is semi-evergreen, with long dark green leaves and creamy flowers in early summer. Large red fruits are prolific and long-lasting.
LARGE SHRUB/SMALL TREE H & s: 6m/20ft
z: 7[7–9]
C. horizontalis (herringbone cotoneaster from China) has stiffly spreading fan-like branches that provide a useful base to anchor upright forms. Foliage colour and dark red berries glow in autumn. Use this deciduous shrub to spread over neighbouring pavements or against walls.
SMALL SHRUB H: 0.6m/2ft s: 1.8–2.1m/6–7ft
z: 6[6–9]

C. lacteus (China) is evergreen, with large oval leaves, grey beneath. Milky-white flowers in summer are followed by late-ripening red fruits. Good for hedging.
LARGE SHRUB H: 3–5m/10–15ft
s: 2.4–4m/8–12ft z: 7[7–9]
C. 'Rothschildianus' is evergreen, with a more spreading habit and light green leaves. Fruit is creamy-yellow.
MEDIUM SHRUB H: 1.8–3m/6–10ft
s: 3–5m/10–15ft z: 7[7–9]

CRAMBE
(Cruciferae) kale
C. cordifolia (colewort, giant kale; from the Caucasus) is a dramatic perennial with large rough heart-shaped leaves and tall stems bearing a cloud of tiny white flowers in early summer. Stalks need firm staking. Trim off any damaged leaves as they appear during summer. A statuesque back-of-border or cornerstone plant for sun and deep well-drained soil.
H: 1.8m/6ft s: 1.2m/4ft z: 6[6–9]

CRATAEGUS
(Rosaceae) thorn
C. × lavallei is a dense-headed deciduous tree with long glossy leaves. Clusters of white single flowers appear in early summer, and orange-red fruits in autumn. Drought- and wind-resistant.
SMALL TREE H: 5–6m/15–20ft s: 3–5m/10–15ft
z: 5[5–9]

CRINUM
(Liliaceae/Amaryllidaceae) S. Africa
C. × powellii is free-flowering and relatively hardy. Bright green strap-shaped leaves emerge from the enormous bulb in spring, followed by stout stems bearing umbels of fragrant pink or white trumpet-shaped flowers in late summer. Sun and rich deep soil; in cold districts protect by a heat-reflecting wall and with a winter mulch.
H: 45cm/18in s: 30–45cm/12–18in
z: 9[7–10 when mulched]

CROCOSMIA
(Iridaceae) montbretia S. Africa
Sheaves of sword-like leaves from corms provide useful textural contrast in borders, with elegant branching spikes of tubular flowers contributing eye-catching colour in summer; the related montbretia colonizes and may be invasive. Sunny well-drained site. Named hybrids are hardier and make important contributions to border colour schemes:
C. 'Lucifer' is robust but elegant, with brilliant flame-red flowers in midsummer.
H: 120cm/48in s: 23cm/9in z: 7[5–10 when mulched]
C. 'Solfaterre' has bronze-tinged leaves and pale apricot-yellow flowers, together creating an understated smoky tone.
H: 60cm/24in s: 15cm/6in
z: 8[7–10 when mulched]

Cyclamen repandum

CROCUS
(Iridaceae) Levant, southern Europe
C. sativus (saffron crocus) is a cormous perennial with large rich purple dark-veined flowers opening to reveal red stigma and orange anthers. Flowers appear with the leaves in late summer to autumn. Plant in drifts in sun and rich soil; needs a warm site to thrive.
H: 10cm/4in z: 4[4–10]
C. tommasinianus (Yugoslavia) flowers in spring, in a range of shades from lavender-blue to deep reddish-purple, and there is a white form. This sturdy hardy corm happily colonizes in short grass.
H: 75mm/3in z: 4[4–10]

CYCLAMEN
(Primulaceae) Mediterranean
Hardy species of cyclamen make attractive carpets of subtly patterned foliage and pinkish-toned flowers in partly shaded sites. Well-drained soil, rich in humus.
C. hederifolium (sowbread) is a tuberous perennial with marbled ivy-like leaves in winter and early spring. These disappear and are succeeded by flowers in shades of mauve to pale pink and white in late summer and autumn.
H: 10cm/4in s: 10–15cm/4–6in z: 5[5–10]
C. repandum is a tuberous perennial with arrow-shaped leaves. Scented flowers with twisted petals in pale pinks, whites and deep carmine appear in spring. Sheltered site.
H: 15cm/6in s: 15–20cm/6–8in z: 8[8–10]

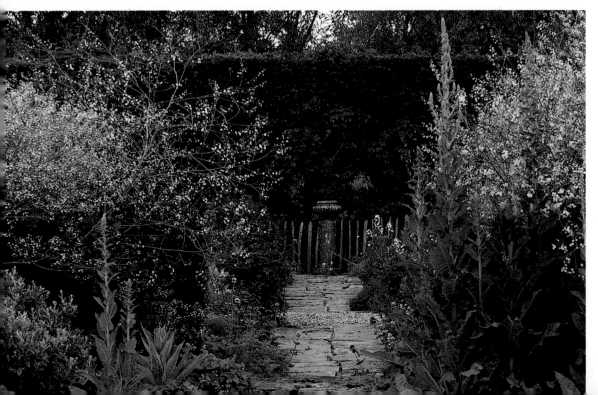

Crambe cordifolia

CYNARA

(Compositae)   Europe

C. cardunculus (cardoon) is a striking architectural perennial. Its bold clumps of deeply divided silvery-grey leaves are effective punctuating a design as well as massed in large-scale textural groups. Stout branching stems bear large violet thistle-flowers in summer. Sun, with some shade in hot climates, and well-drained fertile soil; winter mulch in cold areas.

H: 1.8m/6ft   s: 0.9m/3ft   z: 8[6–10 when mulched]

CYTISUS

(Leguminosae)   broom

C. battandieri (Moroccan broom, Pineapple broom) is a slightly tender semi-evergreen shrub with silvery trifoliate leaves and racemes of pineapple-scented pea-flowers in summer. Protect near a sunny wall. May be pruned and tied back.

LARGE SHRUB H: 5m/15ft   s: 2.4–4m/8–12ft z: 8[8–10]

C. × praecox 'Warminster' (Warminster broom) is a hardier deciduous shrub. The sprays of flat stem-like leaves are insignificant until covered with a profusion of creamy-coloured flowers in early summer. Full sun and well-drained soil.

MEDIUM SHRUB H & s: 1.5–1.8m/5–6ft z: 7[7–9]

DAHLIA

(Compositae)   Mexico

Dahlia hybrids offer a wide spectrum of long-lasting colour for late summer. Many of the more extravagant forms are best massed (and carefully staked) in grandiose bedding schemes; the following have enough character to make eloquent contributions to mixed plantings. Most tubers are tender but if thickly mulched will survive low temperatures.

D. 'Bishop of Llandaff' has elegant pinnate foliage of a metallic bronze-purple colour, which sets off the bright scarlet of the peony-flowers and adds its richness to border schemes of glowing or sombre reds.

H: 120cm/48in   s: 60cm/24in   z: 9[8–10 when mulched]

D. merckii (bedding dahlia from Mexico) is a slender elegant hardy species bearing simple single pink to lavender flowers. Planted in a block, it seldom requires staking.

H: 1.8m/6ft   s: 0.9m/3ft
z: 9[8–10 when mulched]

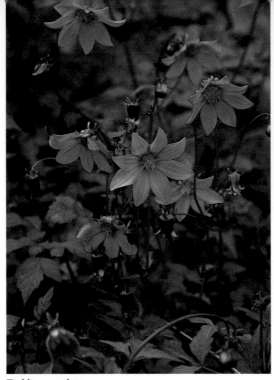

Dahlia merckii

DAPHNE

(Thymelaeaceae)

D. × burkwoodii 'Somerset' is semi-evergreen and one of the faster-growing daphnes, with very fragrant pink flowers in early summer. Sun or part shade and well-drained site.

SMALL SHRUB H & s: 90–120cm/36–48in z: 6[6–9]

D. odora 'Aureomarginata' (China, Japan) with a spreading habit has variegated glossy evergreen leaves and fragrant pink flowers in spring. Is more vigorous and hardier than its green-leaved type.

MEDIUM SHRUB H & s: 1.5–1.8m/5–6ft   z: 8[8–10]

DARMERA

(Saxifragaceae)

D. peltata (formerly *Peltiphyllum peltatum*; umbrella plant from California and Oregon) has round heads of starry pinkish-white flowers carried on tall stems in spring, before the shield-shaped leaves emerge to make a dense low perennial mound of handsome rounded foliage. Good for autumn colour. Sun or shade, but likes moist soil: plant in a bog-garden or at the waterside with primulas and other moisture-loving perennials.

H: 60–120cm/24–48in   s: 60–90cm/24–36in
z: 6[6–9]

DATURA

(Solanaceae)

D. inoxia (formerly *D. meteloides*; from Texas) is an exotic shrubby perennial with hairy greyish

Dierama pulcherrimum

leaves and fragrant creamy-white trumpet-flowers 15cm/6in long borne in summer. Likes hot sun. Usually grown as an annual border plant in rich soil; also good in containers.

H: 90cm/36in   s: 75cm/30in   ANNUAL

DELPHINIUM

(Ranunculaceae)

Tall spires of large-flowered hybrids are a classic ingredient in traditional herbaceous borders. Sun and richly fed well-drained soil.

D. × belladonna hybrids are compact perennials producing graceful loose flower-spikes from mid-summer. The branching stems may not need staking. Flowers are white, and blue from palest to navy. *D.b.* 'Lamartine' is a deep violet-blue.

H: 90–135cm/36–54in   s: 60cm/24in
z: 3[3–10]

D. elatum hybrids are perennials producing stately erect spikes crowded in summer with flowers in every gradation of blue, plus white, pinkish-lavenders, mauves and violets, some with contrasting eyes. Choose from named colour forms. Stake stems individually in early summer.

H: 0.9–2.4m/3–8ft   s: 0.6–0.9m/2–3ft
z: 3[3–10]

DEUTZIA

(Hydrangeaceae)

D. × rosea is a compact deciduous shrub with gracefully arching branches bearing clusters of wide bell-shaped pink flowers in summer. Sun

and well-drained soil, with plenty of moisture-retentive compost to encourage flowering.
SMALL SHRUB H & S: 90cm/36in Z: 6[6–9]

DIANTHUS
(Caryophyllaceae) pink
Pinks make sprawling tufts of grey-green spiky grass-like leaves that are often evergreen. Fragrant flowers in shades of pinks and white, single or double, and often marked or zoned in a deeper tone, appear in summer; modern hybrids often flower again in late summer. Full sun or part shade and gritty well-drained soil.
H: 25–38cm/10–15in s: 30cm/12in z: 4[4–10]
D. barbatus (sweet William from eastern Europe, Asia) is a cottage-garden perennial often grown as a biennial. Crowded flattened flower-heads range

in colour from white through pinks to carmine and crimson-purple, and are often zoned in two tones. Is often sold as a mixture of colours; a mass in a bed or border front makes a mosaic pattern of harmonizing colours. Single colours are sometimes available. *D.b.* 'Niger' has dusky purple-tinged foliage and dark red almost black flowers. Sun and rich moist well-drained alkaline soil. Sow seed outdoors for summer transplanting to next year's site.
H & S: 30–60cm/12–24in z: 4[4–10]

DIASCIA
(Scrophulariaceae) twinspur S. Africa
D. vigilis (syn. *D. elegans*) makes a loose perennial mound of erect and sprawling leaf-clad stems, tipped throughout the summer months with

racemes of pale pink-lipped flowers. Makes an attractive bedding or container plant for temperate regions: overwinter cuttings. Sun or part shade and rich well-drained but moisture-retentive soil. *D.* 'Ruby Field' is a relatively hardy hybrid with deep coral-pink flowers.
H: 30–45cm/12–18in s: 45cm/18in
z: 8–9[8–10]

DICENTRA
(Fumariaceae) bleeding heart
D. formosa (N. America) has pretty lacy grey-green leaves. Drooping heart-shaped flowers borne in early summer are pinky-mauve. Low clumps of foliage make good perennial ground cover in the part shade of shrub roses of the same classic 'rose' tones. *D.f.* 'Stuart Boothman' produces a subtle combination of pink flowers and smoky-grey foliage.
H & S: 30–45cm/12–18in z: 3[3–10]

DICTAMNUS
(Rutaceae) burning bush, gas plant
southern Europe, Asia
D. albus (dittany, fraxinella) is a handsome long-lived perennial with aromatic leaves. White flowers with long stamens emit volatile oil and are carried in erect spikes for a short period in early summer. They are followed by attractive star-shaped seed-pods. Sun or part shade. *D.a. purpureus* has mauve flowers with darker veining.
H: 60–90cm/24–36in s: 75cm/30in z: 3[3–10]

DIERAMA
(Iridaceae) angel's fishing rod, wandflower
S. Africa
D. pulcherrimum has a corm that forms tufts of grass-like evergreen leaves that anchor long arching 'wands' of flowers in summer – silvery calyces opening to hanging bell-flowers of pale to deep rose-pink. Looks lovely reflected in water. Well-drained soil, preferably in sun, though part shade is tolerated. Self-seeds in unexpected corners.
H: 180cm/72in s: 30–60cm/12–24in z: 9[8–10]

DIGITALIS
(Scrophulariaceae) foxglove
Tall spikes of thimble-shaped flowers in early summer make charming vertical emphasis in informal plantings. Part shade or sun, but not too hot, and ordinary humus-rich soil.

Dictamnus albus and *D.a. purpureus*

Eryngium giganteum

D. ferruginea (rusty foxglove from southern Europe, central Asia) is a perennial best treated as a biennial. Has tall stems of fine small coppery-yellow flower-trumpets with rust-coloured veining.
H: 90–120cm/36–48in   S: 30–45cm/12–18in
Z: 4[4–10]

D. grandiflora (yellow foxglove from Europe, Caucasus, Siberia) is a stockier clump-forming evergreen perennial with large creamy-yellow flowers and slightly shiny leaves.
H: 60–90cm/24–36in   S: 30cm/12in   Z: 4[4–10]

D. lutea (small yellow foxglove from south-western Europe, north-western Africa) is a graceful perennial with slender tapering spires of slim pale yellow tubular flowers. Self-seeds freely.
H: 60–90cm/24–36in   S: 30cm/12in   Z: 4[4–10]

D. purpurea alba (western Europe) is the lovely white form of the common biennial or perennial foxglove. Allow to naturalize in woodland and 'wild' areas. Weed out seedlings with reddish leaf-stems, which produce pink flowers.
H: 90–150cm/36–60in   S: 45–60cm/18–24in
Z: 3[3–10]

DODECATHEON
(Primulaceae)   American cowslip, shooting star
N. America
D. meadia is a perennial with a rosette of long smooth leaves, reddish at the base, that die away after flowering. In early summer stout 60cm/24in stems bear loose umbels of nodding cyclamen-like flowers with reflexed petals, in shades from palest pinky-white to purplish-rose. Shade or part shade and damp humus-rich soil.
H: 30–45cm/12–18in   S: 30cm/12in   Z: 4[4–9]

ECCREMOCARPUS
(Bignoniaceae)   Chilean glory flower   Chile
E. scaber is a perennial climber that seeds freely and may be grown as an annual against a warm wall or curtaining shrubs in colder areas. Has attractive pinnate leaves and racemes of tubular orange-scarlet flowers from midsummer onwards. Crimson-red, yellow and orange forms are available and usually come true from seed. The fire colours are lovely in 'hot' schemes, brightening dark green neighbouring foliage like lamps.
CLIMBER H: 2.4–3m/8–10ft   Z: 9[9–10] or grow as ANNUAL

ECHINOPS
(Compositae)   globe thistle
Imposing perennials with divided thistle-like leaves and spherical flower-heads on wiry stems in late summer. Sun and ordinary garden soil.
E. 'Nivalis' is a splendid, elegant foliage plant, with grey spiky leaves and greyish-white drumstick flowers.
H: 180cm/72in   S: 60cm/24in   Z: 3[3–10]
E. ritro (eastern Europe, western Asia) is compact, with jagged green leaves, grey beneath, and grey stems bearing deep steel-blue globular flower-heads.
H: 60–120cm/24–48in   S: 60cm/24in   Z: 3[3–10]

EPILOBIUM
(Onagraceae)   fireweed
E. angustifolium album (northern hemisphere), a white form of the very invasive rose-bay, French or great willow herb, is sufficiently well-behaved to allow in the garden, where it makes a superlative perennial in sun or shade. Tall spires of ethereal white flowers, giving a ghostly effect, top stems clothed in narrow green leaves in summer. Seed capsules open to reveal glistening seeds resembling feathery hairs.
H: 90–150cm/36–60in   S: 60cm/24in
Z: 3[3–9]

EPIMEDIUM
(Berberidaceae)   barrenwort, bishop's hat
Once established, these perennials spread to make attractive weed-suppressing ground cover in sun or shade. Prefer a cool position and tolerate root competition under shrubs. Roughly heart-shaped veined leaves colour to pink and bronze in winter, and in some species almost hide the sprays of small flowers in spring.
E. grandiflorum 'Rose Queen' has loose spikes of deep pink white-spurred flowers held above the leaves.
H: 23–30cm/9–12in   S: 30cm/12in   Z: 5[5–9]
E. pinnatum colchicum (Caucasus, Iran) is almost evergreen and has bright yellow short-spurred flowers.
H: 23–30cm/9–12in   S: 30cm/12in   Z: 5[5–9]

ERANTHIS
(Ranunculaceae)
E. hyemalis (winter aconite from Europe) is a perennial with a ruff of bright green leaf-like bracts around the single buttercup-flower in mid-winter, massed flowers forming a glowing carpet of golden-green under deciduous shrubs and trees. Clumps of its deeply cut leaves may be mown with the grass in spring.
H & S: 75–100mm/3–4in   Z: 5[5–9]

EREMURUS
(Liliaceae/Asphodelaceae)   foxtail lily
E. robustus (giant desert candle from Turkestan) has immensely tall flower-spikes of peachy-pink, soaring from a perennial clump of lax strap-shaped leaves in summer. Grow in sun and rich well-drained soil at the back of a border where bushy neighbours can spread to fill the vacuum left when the leaves die away untidily after flowering.
H: 1.8–2.7m/6–9ft   S: 0.9m/3ft   Z: 6[6–9]
E. Shelford Hybrids are more compact perennials,

with grass-like foliage and, in summer, flowers from palest pink and yellow to rich coppery-orange.
H: 180cm/72in s: 75cm/30in z: 6[6–9]

ERIGERON
(Compositae) fleabane
E. karvinskianus (bonytip fleabane, Mexican daisy; from central America) is a sprawling slightly shrubby perennial with wiry stems bearing a mass of white daisy-flowers later tinged with pink. In a warm climate it flowers from spring to autumn, colonizing well-drained spots such as drystone walls and paving.
H: 15–45cm/6–18in s: 60cm/24in z: 9[9–10]

ERYNGIUM
(Umbelliferae)
Handsome plants with steel-blue, silvery or marbled white leaves.
E. giganteum (Miss Willmott's ghost from Cauca-

Digitalis ferruginea

sus, Iran) is a biennial: grow in sun to encourage the leaves to fade from green in spring to shimmering almost translucent grey, a beautiful foil for the pale blue-grey thistle-heads at midsummer. Well-drained soil. Freely self-seeds.
H: 90–120cm/36–48in s: 60cm/24in z: 5[5–10]
E. × zabelii 'Violetta' is of more compact stature and perennial. Large flower-heads and ruffs of delicate bracts borne in summer are violet-blue.
H: 60–75cm/24–30in s: 45cm/18in z: 5[5–10]

ERYSIMUM
(Cruciferae)
E. 'Bowles' Mauve' (also listed as *E. linifolium* 'E. A. Bowles' and *Cheiranthus* 'Bowles' Mauve') is a short-lived woody perennial. Clear pale magenta spikes of wallflower-like blooms are borne above bushy mounds of grey-green leaves for many weeks in early summer. Take cuttings each spring and plant out in late summer. Sun; dislikes high humidity.
H: 60cm/24in s: 45cm/18in z: 8[8–10]

ERYTHRONIUM
(Liliaceae) dog's-tooth violet, dog tooth violet
Thriving in rich woodland soil, clumps of these small hardy tuberous perennials grouped around shrubs and trees are among the most desirable early-summer flowerers. *E. grandiflorum* and *E.* 'Pagoda' are both slow spreaders.
E. grandiflorum has plain green leaves and bright yellow flowers.
H: 30–45cm/12–18in s: 15cm/6in z: 4[4–9]
E. 'Pagoda' has luminous yellow flowers with reflexed turk's-cap petals above marbled leaves.
H: 30–45cm/12–18in s: 15cm/6in z: 4[4–9]

ESCALLONIA
(Escalloniaceae) S. America
These glossy-leaved evergreen shrubs that flower in summer make attractive hedges, specimens and wall plants for sheltered sunny gardens in temperate zones. Choose one of appropriate size, habit and flower colour for your garden layout.
E. 'Apple Blossom' is one of the more compact, with pinky-white flowers. Its regular form makes it a useful anchor plant in borders.
MEDIUM SHRUB H & S: 1.5m/5ft z: 8[8–10]
E. 'Donard Seedling' has a weeping habit that makes an attractive cascading hedge, the dark green leaves softened with pinkish-white flowers in summer.
MEDIUM SHRUB H: 1.8–2.4m/6–8ft
s: 1.5–1.8m/5–6ft z: 8[8–10]

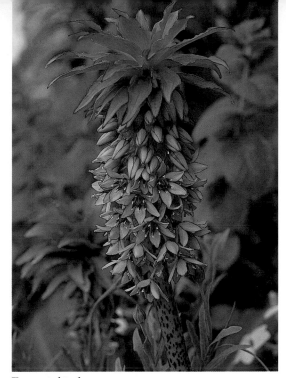

Eucomis bicolor

E. 'Iveyi' has a regular pyramidal shape that makes a solid buttress-like mass against a sunny wall. Erect panicles of white flowers cover the shrub in late summer.
LARGE SHRUB H: 3m/10ft s: 1.8–2.4m/6–8ft
z: 8[8–10]

ESCHSCHOLZIA
(Papaveraceae)
E. californica (California poppy) is usually grown as an annual, though in warm regions it is a short-lived perennial. Orange poppy-flowers appear above ferny blue-green foliage in long succession from early summer if dead-heads are removed regularly. Cultivar flowers range from cream through yellows and oranges to pinks and reds. Plant a whole bed in a bright mix, sowing seed *in situ* in poor soil in a sunny site.
H: 20–45cm/8–18in s: 30cm/12in z: 9[9–10]
or grow as ANNUAL

EUCOMIS
(Liliaceae/Hyacinthaceae) pineapple flower
S. Africa
Large bulbs produce rosettes of lax fleshy leaves in spring and eye-catching flower-spikes in late summer. Each pineapple-cluster of starry flowers is topped by a tuft of leaf-like bracts. Grow in a sunny sheltered spot or in a container, and protect with thick mulch or in a greenhouse during winter dormancy.
E. bicolor has pale green flowers, edged with

purple, and brownish-maroon spotting on the stem.
h: 45cm/18in s: 30cm/12in z: 9[8–10]
E. comosa is elegant and more colourful, with a slight pinkish-lilac tinge to flowers, which have conspicuous dark centres.
h: 75cm/30in s: 30cm/12in z: 9[8–10]

EUCRYPHIA
(Eucryphiaceae)   Australasia, S. America
These shrubs have glossy leaves and creamy-white cup-shaped flowers that open to reveal central yellow stamens. Most are acid-loving.
E. × *intermedia* 'Rostrevor' is a quick-growing evergreen with an erect habit. Flowers in late summer. Grow behind kirengeshomas and toad lilies. Relatively lime-tolerant.
LARGE SHRUB h: 3m/10ft s: 1.8–2.4m/6–8ft
z: 9[9–10]

EUPATORIUM
(Compositae)   boneset, hemp agrimony
E. coelestinum (southern USA, W. Indies) is a hardy perennial form of the annual ageratum with bright blue clustered flowers from late summer. Thrives in hot sun.
h: 30–90cm/12–36in s: 30–45cm/12–18in
z: 6[6–10]
E. ligustrinum (Mexico) is an evergreen shrub that grows upwards against a warm wall or forms a rounded free-standing bush. Shiny elliptical slightly serrated leaves are attractive all year. In late summer clouds of small pinky-white flowers create a gypsophila effect.
MEDIUM SHRUB h & s: 1.2–2.4m/4–8ft z: 9[9–10]
E. maculatum atropurpureum (Joe Pye weed from N. America) is a clump-forming deciduous perennial. Whorls of pointed purple-veined leaves on purple stems provide a fine feature through summer months for the back of a border. Late-season large flat flower-heads are deep rosy-purple. Sun or part shade and rich moist soil.
h: 1.2–1.8m/4–6ft s: 0.9–1.2m/3–4ft z: 3[3–10]

EUPHORBIA
(Euphorbiaceae)   spurge
Representatives of this richly varied genus with attractive foliage and conspicuous petal-like bracts play important roles in different areas of the flower garden.
E. amygdaloides robbiae (Mrs Robb's bonnet from Asia Minor) is a suckering perennial spreader, useful for making evergreen ground cover in poor soil or woodland. Produces dark green rosettes of leathery foliage. Thrives and spreads in shade, but the long-lasting pale yellow bracts in spring perform best in full sun. Purple-leaved forms are stunning in lightly shaded beds between erythroniums and trilliums.
h: 30–60cm/12–24in s: 30–45cm/12–18in
z: 8[8–10]
E. characias and *E.c. wulfenii* (Mediterranean regions) are similar, forming rounded clumps of erect stems clothed in linear glaucous blue-green leaves. Evergreen foliage is architectural and remains handsome all year, and the flower-spikes curve over attractively in the months before flowering, in early summer. *E. characias* has black-eyed bracts; those of *E.c. wulfenii* and its numerous cultivars are pure greenish-yellow with a yellow centre. Dead-head when flower-heads become unsightly, but avoid skin contact with the milky sap. Sun or part shade and well-drained site.
SMALL SHRUB h: 90–150cm/36–60in
s: 90cm/36in z: 8[8–10]
E. cyparissias (cypress spurge from Europe) has delicate light green deciduous foliage that resembles a mass of miniature conifer seedlings and bright lime-yellow flowers in early summer. Spreads by underground runners to make weed-suppressing perennial ground cover in sun or part shade. Though invasive, it is not a strangler and so can underplant shrub roses.
h: 30cm/12in s: 30–45cm/12–18in z: 3[3–9]
E. griffithii 'Fireglow' has vibrant tomato-red bracts in early summer. The red and orange tones of its good-looking foliage enrich 'hot' colour schemes all season. More tolerant than *E. cyparissias* of shade and of moisture, it spreads to form perennial clumps but is not unduly invasive. *E.g.* 'Dixter' is more compact, with slightly less vivid bracts.
h: 90cm/36in s: 60cm/24in z: 5[5–9]
E. myrsinites (southern Europe, Asia Minor) is a fleshy-leaved evergreen perennial with trailing stems clothed in ice-grey leaves bearing lime-yellow bracts in spring. Needing sun and good drainage, it is best allowed to sprawl in a rockery or over the low wall of a raised bed.
h: 15cm/6in s: 30–38cm/12–15in z: 5[5–10]

EURYOPS
(Compositae)   Africa
E. acraeus (formerly *E. evansii*) is an evergreen shrub with erect stiff stems clothed in linear leaves of an intense silvery-grey. Take cuttings in late summer. A good furnishing plant for the front of a sunny well-drained border.
SMALL SHRUB h: 45–60cm/18–30in
s: 45cm/18in z: 9[9–10]

Exochorda × *macrantha* 'The Bride'

EXOCHORDA
(Rosaceae) pearlbush Asia
E. × macrantha 'The Bride' is a compact deciduous shrub, suitable as a lawn specimen or to grow in mixed border schemes. Its graceful arching branches are wreathed with masses of delicate white flowers in early summer. Sun or part shade.
SMALL SHRUB H: 0.9–1.5m/3–5ft
s: 1.2–1.8m/4–6ft z: 5[5–9]

FELICIA
(Compositae) blue daisy, blue marguerite
S. Africa
F. amelloides is a half-hardy semi-woody perennial of upright habit with pale blue daisy flowers in summer. Dead-head to ensure continuous flowering. Can be grown in a container as well as a sunny border.
H: 45cm/18in s: 30cm/12in z: 9[9–10] or grow as
ANNUAL

FERULA
(Umbelliferae) giant fennel southern Europe
F. communis is an herbaceous perennial making a mound of finely dissected leaves, a soft glinting green texture that is an excellent foil for more defined flower and leaf shapes near by. When well-established, large stout stems bearing wide heads of greenish-yellow cow-parsley flowers soar to 2.4m/8ft in summer. Sun and deep well-drained soil.
H: 60cm/24in s: 90cm/36in z: 6[6–10]

FESTUCA
(Gramineae) fescue
F. glauca (blue fescue from central and south-western Europe) is a tufted perennial grass with fine grey-blue leaves and compact habit. Straw-coloured flowers in summer and dead leaves mute the somewhat luminous blueness. Good for edging and front-of-border groups. Sun and well-drained soil.
H: 30cm/12in s: 45cm/18in z: 4[4–8]

FILIPENDULA
(Rosaceae) meadowsweet Japan
F. purpurea forms handsome clumps of divided foliage from which rise flattish heads of tiny deep pink flowers towards the end of summer. Best in part shade, but tolerates sun provided the soil is deep and moist. A good back-of-border or water-side perennial.
H: 90–120cm/36–48in s: 60cm/24in
z: 6[6–9]

FOENICULUM
(Umbelliferae) fennel Europe
F. vulgare purpureum (bronze or copper fennel) is a form of the edible herb with a mahogany tinge to the young feathery thread-like leaves; these become a softer bronze later in the season. In a border the smoky effect of the foliage relieves a mass of more solid 'leafy' foliage. Flat umbels of tiny yellowish flowers of this short-lived perennial appear atop tall stems in late summer: remove them if you want to prevent a rash of seedlings. Sun and poor or ordinary well-drained soil.
H: 0.9–1.8m/3–6ft s: 0.6m/2ft z: 4[4–10]

FRANCOA
(Saxifragaceae) Chile
F. sonchifolia (bridal wreath) makes a perennial clump of hairy deeply lobed leaves; graceful wands of small deep pink flowers appear to make a long-lasting 'wreath' in summer. Seed-heads remain attractive for many weeks. Good evergreen ground cover in warm climates; in colder areas it may be container-grown, wintered under glass.
H: 60–90cm/24–36in s: 45–60cm/18–24in
z: 8[8–10]

FRITILLARIA
(Liliaceae) fritillary
F. imperialis (crown imperial from Persia) is a majestic plant known in gardens since the late sixteenth century. A ruff of bright green glossy leaves surrounds the stout stem. In spring the stem top bears a hanging cluster of large bell-shaped flowers beneath a tuft of leaf-like bracts: choose clear yellow, burnt orange or red flowers to complement neighbouring colours. Bulbs increase slowly in fertile well-drained soil, preferably where they can bake in summer sun. Good for a spring border.
H: 90–120cm/36–48in s: 30cm/12in z: 5[5–10]
F. meleagris (snakeshead from northern Europe) bears bell-shaped flowers dangling singly or in pairs from a grass-like stalk in spring. Flowers have chequered markings – white faintly mottled with green, or pale and deep tones of purplish-pink. A native of damp meadows, this bulbous perennial is lovely naturalized in grass, but also thrives in dry borders.
H: 30cm/12in s: 10–15cm/4–6in z: 5[5–9]
F. persica 'Adiyaman' from the Middle East is similar to the crown imperial in habit and needs. Its racemes of more slender dangling conical flowers are in shades of remarkably murky blackish-purple.
H: 100cm/40in s: 30cm/12in z: 6[6–9]

Fritillaria persica

FUCHSIA
(Onagraceae)
Fuchsias hardy to your region make useful border plants: from innumerable hybrids and cultivars choose fuchsias to suit climate and colour schemes or grow selected favourites as annuals and in pots, taking cuttings each autumn.
F. magellanica molinae (syn. F.m. 'Alba') is a deciduous shrub that has pale pink flowers in summer and autumn.
LARGE SHRUB H: 3–4m/10–12ft s: 1.8m/6ft
z: 7[7–10]
F. 'Thalia' is a good variety for bedding in a 'red' scheme: its deciduous dark green leaves are shadowed beneath with red, and the clusters of graceful long trumpet-flowers in summer are a soft orange-scarlet.
SMALL SHRUB H: 90cm/36in s: 60cm/24in
z: 9[9–10]

GALANTHUS
(Liliaceae/Amaryllidaceae) snowdrop
G. elwesii (giant snowdrop from Asia Minor) flowers slightly later than G. nivalis.
H: 10–30cm/4–12in s: 5–7.5cm/2–3in
G. nivalis (common snowdrop from Europe) is an indispensable early-spring carpeting bulb. Its pendent white flowers and grey-green leaves relish the light and air beneath leafless deciduous shrubs, and equally appreciate shade in summer.
H: 7.5–20cm/3–8in s: 7.5–15cm/3–6in
z: 2[2–9]

Galega × hartlandii

Gentiana asclepiadea

GALEGA
(Leguminosae)   goat's rue
G. *officinalis* (southern Europe, Asia Minor) is an old cottage-garden perennial with tall bushy clumps of light green pinnate leaves. Pea-flowers in summer are white or a pale washed-out blue, but there are good garden forms such as G. × *hartlandii* which have warmer tones of lilac, lavender or pinky-mauve. Good 'fillers' for borders in sun or part shade.
H: 90–150cm/36–60in   s: 75–90cm/30–36in
z: 4[4–9]
G. *orientalis* (Caucasus) is similar except the erect flower-spikes are violet-tinted blue and carried for many weeks in late spring. A rampant but valuable spreader.
H: 90–120cm/36–48in   s: 60cm/24in
z: 5[5–9]

GALIUM
(Rubiaceae)
G. *odoratum* (sweet woodruff from Europe, Siberia) may be invasive but its whorls of narrow green leaves make attractive perennial ground cover in shady sites. Clusters of white starry flowers appear in early summer.
H: 15–25cm/6–10in   s: 30cm/12in   z: 3[3–9]

GALTONIA
(Liliaceae/Hyacinthaceae)   summer hyacinth
S. Africa
G. *candicans*, a useful late-flowering summer bulb, has erect stems bearing elegant loose spires of bell-shaped scented white flowers, shaded or marked with green, above long lax greyish leaves. Interplant in borders among earlier performers. Sun and rich well-drained soil. Unless drainage is excellent, treat as an annual, lifting bulb in autumn for frost-free overwintering.
H: 120cm/48in   s: 30cm/12in   z: 8[7–10]

GAURA
(Onagraceae)   south-eastern USA
G. *lindheimeri* is a perennial that forms an open bush of willow-like foliage. Wiry stems bear tall spikes delicately set with small pinkish-white flowers from summer to autumn. Not vigorous enough for border competition, but worth finding a special place for: a clump is an eye-catcher in late summer. Sun and well-drained soil.
H: 90–120cm/36–48in   s: 60–90cm/24–36in
z: 6[6–10]

GAZANIA
(Compositae)   S. Africa
Gazanias form compact grey-leaved clumps of daisy-flowers – mainly orange and centrally zoned with brown. Named hybrids come in a wide range of yellows, browns, pinks and warm reds, often with vivid zoning. Flowering from summer onwards, they are useful as colour-grouped bedding in the front of a border. Perennials usually grown as annuals from overwintered cuttings.
H: 15–30cm/6–12in   s: 30cm/12in   z: 9[9–10]
or grow as ANNUAL

GENISTA
(Leguminoseae)   broom
G. *aetnensis* (Mount Etna broom from Sardinia, Sicily) is an almost leafless shrub with a cloud of golden-yellow flowers carried in midsummer on arching rush-like branches that give a graceful appearance all season. Grow next to more 'solid' bush-like shrubs and underplant with lower-growing flowerers. Sun and ordinary or poor well-drained soil.
LARGE SHRUB H: 5–6m/15–20ft
s: 5–5.5m/15–18ft   z: 8[8–10]

GENTIANA

(Gentianaceae)   gentian

G. *acaulis* (trumpet gentian from Europe) is a prostrate-growing evergreen perennial, with brilliant blue trumpet-flowers in early summer above mats of glossy leaves. Flower performance may be unpredictable. Sunny open site and moist humus-rich soil.

H: 7.5cm/3in   s: to 45cm/18in   z: 5[5–9]

G. *asclepiadea* (willow gentian from Europe) is a graceful perennial for a shady border. Arching leafy stems bear clusters of flowers in various shades of blue in late summer. Deep moist humus-rich soil, preferably (but not necessarily) acid. A valuable specimen plant for sun or shade, when not jostled by competitive neighbours.

H: 90cm/36in   s: 60cm/24in   z: 5[5–9]

G. *sino-ornata* (western China, Tibet) is an autumn-flowering and acid-loving prostrate evergreen perennial. Glowing blue flowers above leafy mats are streaked with deep blue and green.

H: 15cm/6in   s: 30–38cm/12–15in   z: 5[5–9]

GERANIUM

(Geraniaceae)   cranesbill

Most of the hardy cranesbills have a fine early flowering period. Cut back stems and leaves as flowers fade to produce new leafy growth attractive for the rest of the season. Some cranesbills are best in ground-covering masses; others are more distinguished and merit places in a border.

G. 'Ann Folkard' is a perennial with yellow-green leaves like those of its parent, G. *psilostemon*. Large purplish-magenta flowers, in summer, are black-veined and black-centred.

H & s: 45cm/18in   z: 5[5–10]

G. *clarkei* 'Kashmir Purple' has large saucer-shaped flowers, with thin red veining on purple petals, in summer. Deeply dissected foliage of this perennial is upright and branching. Sun.

H & s: 45cm/18in   z: 4[4–10]

G. 'Johnson's Blue' makes a sprawling mass of elegant delicately lobed leaves; violet-blue flowers appear over a long period from early summer.

H: 30–60cm/12–24in   s: 60cm/24in
z: 5[5–10]

G. × *magnificum* has dark-veined violet-blue flowers in early summer above an upright perennial clump of handsome lobed mid-green leaves that tint to red in autumn. A good front-of-border companion to pale yellows and pinks.

H: 45–60cm/18–24in   s: 60cm/24in   z: 3[3–10]

G. *maderense* (Madeira) is a striking semi-evergreen perennial with large ferny leaves and, in early summer, purplish-pink flowers dark-veined at centre and with petal edges white-veined. Seeds prolifically: overwinter seedlings under glass in cold areas. Sunny sheltered site.

H: 90–120cm/36–48in   s: 60–90cm/24–36in
z: 10

G. *nodosum* (Europe) is one of the more compact perennial species that revels in shade: give it a corner to itself where it will self-seed and colonize vigorously. Flowers – which appear throughout the summer – are pinkish-lilac and the leaves are shiny and attractive.

H & s: 45cm/18in   z: 5[5–9]

G. *palmatum* (Canary Islands) has divided anemone-like leaves and purplish-red flowers in late summer. The foliage, tinged with pink or red, of this semi-evergreen perennial is good underplanted with *Viola riviana purpurea* (formerly known as *V. labradorica purpurea*). Seeds prolifically: overwinter seedlings under glass in cold areas. Sunny, sheltered site.

H: 45cm/18in   s: 60cm/24in   z: 8[8–10]

G. *psilostemon* (Armenia) has striking magenta flowers with black eyes and veins in summer, beautifully echoing the tones of purple-bronze foliage such as that of *Rosa glauca* and wonderful with dark pink shrub roses. Its lax perennial clump of elegant leaves may need some support. Leaves colour well in late summer.

H: 75–120cm/30–48in   s: 90–120cm/36–48in
z: 5[5–10]

G. *renardii* (Caucasus) forms neat perennial clumps of velvet grey-green leaves and has starry white flowers veined with maroon in early summer. Open situation.

H & s: 30cm/12in   z: 4[4–10]

Geranium clarkei 'Kashmir Purple'

Geranium maderense

Geranium renardii

GILLENIA

(Rosaceae)   bowman's root, Indian physic
eastern N. America
G. trifoliata is a tough wiry but graceful perennial
with reddish stems and trifoliate leaves, resembling an arching spiraea. Loose clusters of dainty
starry white or pink-tinged flowers in summer are
succeeded by attractive red calyces. Slight preference for acid soil, and part shade in hot areas.
H: 60–120cm/24–48in s: 60cm/24in
z: 4[4–9]

GLADIOLUS

(Iridaceae)
G. callianthus (formerly *Acidanthera bicolor*; from
eastern Africa) is a graceful species with grassy
leaves and fragrant dark-blotched white flowers
that appear in late summer. Grow as a hybrid gladioli, lifting corm In autumn and planting out in a
sunny position in late spring.
H: 90cm/36in s: 30cm/12in z: 9[8–10]
G. communis byzantinus (Byzantine gladiolus from
Europe) is an early-flowering species with typical
sword-like gladiolus leaves and vivid reddish-
purple flowers in early summer. Seeds and
colonizes readily in light soils: keep this cormous
perennial in an emphatic clump, to harmonize
with *Geranium psilostemon*, Rugosa rose R. 'Ros-
eraie de l'Haÿ' or a purple cotinus. Sun or part
shade.
H: 90cm/36in z: 7[7–10]

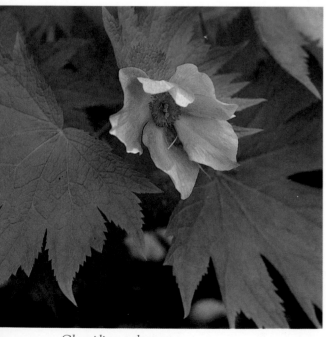

Glaucidium palmatum

GLAUCIDIUM

(Paeoniaceae)   Japan
G. palmatum is a handsome-leaved perennial
woodlander bearing large delicate poppy-flowers
of pale lavender (or white, in the form *G.p. leu-
canthum*) in late spring. Retentive humus-rich
acid soil; protect from sun and wind.
H: 60–120cm/24–48in s: 60cm/24in z: 6[6–9]

GLAUCIUM

(Papaveraceae)   horned poppy, sea poppy
Europe, other regions of Mediterranean
G. flavum is a sprawling unruly perennial bearing
bright yellow cup-shaped papery flowers in late
summer above very attractive pale grey-green
lobed leaves. It can be perennial given sun and
poor well-drained soil; otherwise grow as an
annual or biennial and allow to self-seed.
H: 25–60cm/10–24in s: 45cm/18in z: 5[5–10]
or grow as ANNUAL/BIENNIAL

GOMPHRENA

(Amaranthaceae)
G. globosa (globe amaranth from India) is a bushy
half-hardy annual with clover-like 'everlasting'
flower-heads, in white, yellow, orange or pinkish-
purples, which appear in late summer. Good for
bedding or growing in a pot. Hot sun and well-
drained soil.
H: 30cm/12in s: 15–25cm/6–10in   ANNUAL

GUNNERA

(Gunneraceae)
G. manicata (Brazil), with its giant umbrella-like
leaves, adds a dramatic element to a large garden.
Furrowed and puckered kidney-shaped leaves, up
to 3m/10ft across, are brown-tinged and, in summer, almost hide exotic club-shaped flower-buds.
This herbaceous perennial prefers marshy ground,
providing scale and substance to waterside drifts
of pink and red primulas and astilbes. Feed well;
protect crown from frost.
H: 1.8–3m/6–10ft s: 2.4–3m/8–10ft
z: 7[7–10]

GYPSOPHILA

(Caryophyllaceae)   baby's breath
G. paniculata (eastern Europe, Siberia) is a perennial making a long-lasting froth of tiny white
flowers in summer. Perfect for infilling gaps between pastel- or strong-coloured neighbours, and
for concealing withering stalks and heads of
earlier-flowering perennials. Avoid disturbing
deep fleshy roots of established plants. Grow from

cuttings, which root quickly as shoots appear in
late spring. Sun and well-drained deep and preferably limy soil. Pinkish and double forms are
also grown. *G.p.* 'Bristol Fairy' with double white
flowers is often temperamental, but well worth
trying.
H & s: 90–120cm/36–48in z: 3[3–10]

HALIMIUM

(Cistaceae)   Mediterranean
H. lasianthum is a half-hardy cistus-like evergreen
shrub with grey-green leaves and, in late spring
and early summer, rock-rose flowers whose
golden-yellow petals have mahogany basal
blotches. Sun and well-drained soil: a rock garden
or raised bed suits perfectly.
SMALL SHRUB H: 45–90cm/18–36in
s: 60–120cm/24–48in z: 9[9–10]

HEBE

(Scrophulariaceae)   shrubby speedwell,
shrubby veronica   New Zealand
Hebes are invaluable furnishing shrubs for foliage
texture and flower colour. Hardiness varies
according to species, but all like sun, well-drained
soil and plenty of moisture – none tolerates a cold
climate.
H. albicans is a dense compact evergreen shrub
with rounded glaucous leaves and short white
flower-spikes in spring. Good for low ground
cover and front of a border.
SMALL SHRUB H & s: 60cm/24in z: 8[8–10]
H. buchananii is a dwarf evergreen that makes a
spreading cushion of little rounded leaves,
sprinkled with white flowers in summer.
DWARF SHRUB H: 5cm/2in s: 15cm/6in
z: 7[7–10]
H. hulkeana is untypical: its attractive evergreen
leaves are glossy green, toothed and ovate. Delicate
lavender flowers in large loose panicles are borne
in early summer. In cold regions grow in a pot.
SMALL SHRUB H: 90–120cm/36–48in
s: 60–120cm/24–48in z: 9[9–10]
H. 'Midsummer Beauty' is evergreen and has pur-
plish-tinged leaves and long lavender racemes
throughout summer.
MEDIUM SHRUB H: 1.8m/6ft s: 1.5m/5ft
z: 8[8–10]
H. pinguifolia 'Pagei' is a prostrate evergreen shrub
with small blue-grey leaves and short white
flower-spikes in early summer. Good for ground
cover under roses and open shrubs.
SMALL SHRUB H: 15–25cm/6–10in s: 90cm/36in
z: 6[6–10]

Hebe hulkeana

Hebe albicans

H. rakaiensis is one of the hardier evergreen hebes with dense pale green foliage and white flower racemes in summer.
SMALL SHRUB H: 50cm/20in S: 70cm/28in
z: 6[6–10]

HEDERA
(Araliaceae) ivy
Best in part shade and moisture-retentive soil, ivies are indispensable both as an evergreen backdrop and as ground cover. Scale, shape and colour of leaves all contribute to a wide range of overall textures.
H. canariensis 'Gloire de Marengo' has wide triangular leaves on long pink leaf-stalks. Cream margins, wider at the base, surround dark and grey-green central markings.
CLIMBER H: 5–6m/15–20ft z: 8[8–10]
H. colchica (Persian ivy) has heart-shaped leaves, the largest of the genus. It climbs rapidly but does not make dense cover. *H.c.* 'Sulphur Heart' leaves have central splashes of yellow.
CLIMBER H: 6–10m/20–30ft z: 8[8–10]
H. helix (common ivy from Europe) has a wide range of useful named varieties. *H.h.* 'Angularis Aurea' has leaves shaded in gold while *H.h.* 'Digitata' (finger-leaved ivy) has leaves divided into five narrow lobes, making a dark lacy curtain of foliage. *H.h. hibernica* has distinctive large leaves.
CLIMBER H or S: 4m/12ft z: 5[5–9]

HEDYCHIUM
(Zingiberaceae) ginger lily, gingerwort
India
Hedychiums are spectacular evergreen perennials in warm situations; in temperate zones, given a sunny sheltered position, they survive some frost, the canna-like leaves dying down in winter. Plant fleshy rhizomes shallowly in organically rich moist soil. Good in pots if generously watered. Cut down spent flower-spikes and mulch well after flowering.
H. gardnerianum (kahili ginger) produces a spike of clear yellow orchid-like heavily scented flowers, with prominent red stamens, in late summer and early autumn. Broad glaucous leaves add to this tropical effect in late borders.
H: 1.5–1.8m/5–6ft S: 0.9m/3ft
z: 9[9–10]

HEDYSARUM
(Leguminosae)
H. coronarium (French honeysuckle, sukka sweet-vetch from Europe) is a vigorous shrubby biennial or short-lived perennial with lax stems, pale green-grey pinnate leaves and spikes of small fragrant subtle red pea-flowers borne in summer. Suits both pale-flowered and brighter colour schemes. Sun and well-drained soil.
H: 75–120cm/30–48in S: 45–60cm/18–24in
z: 5[5–9] or grow as ANNUAL

HELENIUM
(Compositae) sneezeweed
eastern N. America
These clump-forming perennials are good for late-summer borders. Hybrids of *H. autumnale* have daisy-like flowers, each with a prominent central boss, in a wide range of yellows and coppery-reds. Sun and moisture-retentive soil.
H. 'Moerheim Beauty' is compact and has rich bronze-red flowers from late summer to autumn.
H: 90cm/36in S: 30–45cm/12–18in
z: 3[3–10]

HELIANTHEMUM
(Cistaceae) rock rose, sun rose
Spreading evergreen foliage of small dull green leaves provides good front-of-border furnishing all year. Short-lived papery flowers open with the sun in summer. Very well-drained and slightly alkaline soil. Choose named varieties for leaf and flower colour. Two attractive grey-leaved cultivars are *H.* 'Wisley Pink', with soft pink flowers, and *H.* 'Wisley Primrose', a delicate yellow, both of which are a foil to pale border schemes.
DWARF SHRUB H: 15–25cm/6–10in S: 60cm/24in
z: 5[5–10]

needs a warm sunny position in neutral or alkaline soil in a container or in front of a heat-reflecting wall. Several fragrant pure white open trumpet-flowers are borne in summer.
H: 120–150cm/48–60in S: 23cm/9in
Z: 4[4–9]
L. lancifolium (syn. *L. tigrinum*; tiger lily from Far East) is good for a late-summer border in sun. Orange turk's-cap flowers are spotted and flecked with black and purple. Prefers acid soil.
H: 90–180cm/36–72in S: 23cm/9in
Z: 3[3–9]
L. regale (regal lily from China) has loose clusters of funnel-shaped creamy-white blooms with yellow centres, shaded with purple on outside, in summer. Easy to grow in a pot or clump in an herbaceous border where perennials protect emergent shoots from late frosts. Sun or part shade, e.g. light woodland. Acid or alkaline soil, enriched with loam, leaf-mould and compost.
H: 90–180cm/36–72in S: 30cm/12in
Z: 4[4–9]

LINUM
(Linaceae)   flax
L. grandiflorum (Algeria) is an annual flax with saucer-shaped red flowers in summer; *L. g.* 'Rubrum' is brighter crimson-red. Grow in a pot or make drifts in a flower bed.
H: 30–50cm/12–20in S: 15cm/6in ANNUAL

LIRIOPE
(Liliaceae/Convallariaceae)   lilyturf
L. muscari (big blue lilyturf from eastern Asia) makes compact evergreen perennial clumps of grassy dark green foliage; excellent for edging or ground cover in sun or shade. Whorls of deep purple flowers are a bonus in late summer.
H: 30cm/12in S: 45cm/18in Z: 6[6–10]

LOBELIA
(Campanulaceae)
L. cardinalis (cardinal flower from USA) is a perennial with a basal rosette of green or bronze leaves above which spikes of lipped scarlet flowers make a splendid display in late summer. Hybrids (often with *L. fulgens*) offer subtly different leaf and flower colour tones: *L.* 'Queen Victoria' has deep red flowers and beetroot-coloured foliage; *L.* 'Dark Crusader' has flowers of even deeper red, with coppery-green foliage; *L.* 'Cherry Ripe' is a brighter cerise-scarlet. Sun and rich damp soil. Give winter protection in cold areas.
H: 90cm/36in S: 30cm/12in Z: 4[4–9]
L. tupa (Chile) is an attractive tender sub-shrubby perennial with dark erect stems bearing long downy pale green leaves. Curious red-brown flowers are borne in tapering racemes in summer. Sun and good moist soil; shelter from wind.
H: 1.5–2.1m/5–7ft S: 0.9m/3ft
Z: 9[9–10]

LONICERA
(Caprifoliaceae)   honeysuckle
Climbing and twining honeysuckles make attractive leafy backdrops or vertical accents; choose from the range of flower colour and season to suit adjacent planting and the sun/shade aspect of the site.
L. × *brownii* (scarlet trumpet honeysuckle) is semi-evergreen, with long glaucous downy leaves and whorls of orange-scarlet flowers in spring and again in late summer. Its exotic colouring looks good as a background to other tender sun-loving plants, and it is not too vigorous for such mixed planting. *L.* × *b.* 'Dropmore Scarlet' is a good form.
CLIMBER H: 3–5m/10–15ft Z: 3[3–9]
L. etrusca (Mediterranean regions) is semi-evergreen and bears fragrant large cream to yellow showy flowers in midsummer. Sun.
CLIMBER H: 4m/12ft S: 1.8m/6ft Z: 8[8–10]
L. × *heckrottii* is deciduous and has long fragrant flowers, pinkish-purple opening to yellow, throughout summer.
CLIMBER H: 4m/12ft S: 1.8m/6ft Z: 6[6–9]
L. japonica 'Halliana' is semi-evergreen (deciduous in zones 5-6) and vigorous, bearing scented flowers, white fading to yellow, in sun or shade all summer.
CLIMBER H: 4m/12ft Z: 5[5–9]
L. × *tellmanniana*, a hybrid of the following species, is tender with bronze-yellow flowers, reddish in bud, in summer. Produces handsome bronze deciduous foliage, but no fragrance. Thrives in shade.
CLIMBER H: 5m/15ft Z: 8[8–10]
L. tragophylla (Chinese woodbine) is deciduous shade-tolerant and vigorous; its flowers in summer are a beautiful pure yellow, but unscented.
CLIMBER H: 6m/20ft Z: 6[6–9]

LOTUS
(Leguminosae)
L. hirsutus (syn. *Dorycnium hirsutum*; from southern Europe) is a spreading evergreen sub-shrub with downy grey-green leaves, making a soft mound of grey to spill over walls or on to paths. Pink and white clover-like flowers are borne in summer, and attractive reddish-brown seed-pods are carried all winter. Prune back half the branches each spring to encourage new shoots with fresh young foliage. Sun and poor well-drained soil.
H: 30–60cm/12–24in S: 60cm/24in
Z: 8[8–10]

Matteuccia struthiopteris

Linum grandiflorum 'Rubrum'

LUNARIA

(Cruciferae) honesty Europe

L. annua (silver dollar plant) is a biennial, self-seeding to make useful background colour in spring and early summer. Flowers are mauve to purplish-crimson and look less garish when in shade; white-flowered and variegated-leaved forms come true when grown separately. Has attractive papery seed-heads. *L. rediviva* is its perennial cousin, with fragrant lavender-white flowers; good for shade.

H: 60–90cm/24–36in s: 60cm/24in z: 6[6–10]

LUPINUS

(Leguminosae) lupin

L. arboreus (tree lupin from California) is a quick-growing sprawling semi-evergreen shrub with attractive digitate lupin leaves and little spikes of scented pea-flowers in cool yellow or tones of purple and blue, borne in summer. Sun and well-drained soil.

SMALL SHRUB H: 120cm/48in s: 90cm/36in z: 8[8–10]

LUZULA

(Juncaceae)

L. sylvatica (great woodrush from south-western Europe) is an evergreen rhizomatous perennial making handsome tufts of grassy leaves in damp shade. Loose clusters of brownish flowers appear in early summer. Spreads slowly to make rough ground cover, ideal for woodland edges; small groups provide contrast of form.

H: 45cm/18in s: 30cm/12in z: 5[5–9]

LYSICHITON

(Araceae)

Both species of this genus of deciduous, perennial bog plants thrive in moist soil near water. In spring striking arum-like spathes emerge, followed by massive smooth ovate leaves.

L. americanus (yellow skunk cabbage, bog arum; from Canada, northern USA) has clear yellow green-tipped spathes. Seeds freely once established.

H & s: 60–120cm/24–48in z: 7[7–9]

L. camtschatcensis (white skunk cabbage from Siberia, Japan) has pure white spathes.

H & s: 45–90cm/18–36in z: 7[7–9]

LYSIMACHIA

(Primulaceae) loosestrife

L. clethroides (gooseneck loosestrife, shepherd's crook; from China, Japan) has starry grey-white flowers carried in gently arching spikes in late summer. May sucker and be invasive in damp soils, but fortunately this herbaceous perennial thrives in drier sites.

H: 90cm/36in s: 60cm/24in z: 3[3–10]

L. ephemerum (south-western Europe) makes a lovely perennial clump within a grey/white garden. Glaucous-grey leaves in spring later turn green. Tall slender spikes of delicate greyish-white flowers appear in summer. Sun (but not too hot) or shade and preferably moist soil.

H: 90cm/36in s: 30cm/12in z: 6[6–9]

LYTHRUM

(Lythraceae) loosestrife

Lythrums grow in any reasonable soil and freely provide spires of late-summer flower colour in shade. Good garden forms are derived from two perennial species.

L. salicaria (purple loosestrife from northern temperate zones) has grey-green willow-like leaves and tall magenta flower-spikes. *L.s.* 'Feuerkerze' is an intense rosy-red.

H: 60–90cm/24–36in s: 45–60cm/18–24in z: 3[3–10]

L. virgatum (wand loosestrife from eastern Europe) is similar, but more delicate. Flowers are in warm pink tones.

H: 60–90cm/24–36in s: 45–60cm/18–24in z: 3[3–10]

MACLEAYA

(Papaveraceae) plume poppy Far East

M. microcarpa is a strikingly architectural back-of-border perennial, with large deeply lobed leaves, bronzy-green above and felted greyish beneath. *M.m.* 'Kelway's Coral Plume' has tall fluffy plume-like panicles of tiny pink-tinted flowers in summer. Sun and well-drained deep loamy soil. May be invasive.

H: 1.5–2.4m/5–8ft s: 0.9–1.2m/3–4ft z: 4[4–10]

MALVA

(Malvaceae) mallow

M. moschata (musk mallow from Europe) is a perennial, but not long-lived. In summer spikes of open funnel-shaped rose-pink flowers (or white in *M.m. alba*) cover bushy foliage of soft green leaves, deeply lobed and cut. Full sun and ordinary garden soil; tolerates poor dry soil. Allow to seed *in situ*.

H: 60–75cm/24–30in s: 60cm/24in z: 3[3–10]

Malva moschata alba

MATTEUCCIA

(Aspleniaceae)

M. struthiopteris (ostrich plume fern, shuttlecock fern; from the northern hemisphere) is a moisture-loving rhizomatous perennial; suitable for a bog-garden or waterside site. Its 'shuttlecock' of bright spring greenery makes a perfect backdrop for primulas or blue poppies. Part shade, but tolerates sun; avoid drying winds.

H: 90–150cm/36–60in s: 60–90cm/24–36in z: 2[2–9]

MATTHIOLA

(Cruciferae) stock

M. bicornis (night-scented stock from Greece) is an annual grown for its vespertine scent. Trivial lilac flowers, opening at night in summer, are scattered over untidy bushes of grey-green leaves. Plant in drifts between more striking neighbours.

H: 38cm/15in s: 23cm/9in ANNUAL

M. incana (southern Europe) is the parent of many of the richly scented garden hybrids with dense

Meconopsis × *sheldonii*

Monarda 'Cambridge Scarlet'

flower spikes, including the Brompton and Ten-week Stocks. The species is a short-lived perennial with narrow felty grey-green leaves and spikes of mauve flowers in summer.
H: 30–60cm/12–24in   s: 30cm/12in
z: 8[8–10]

MECONOPSIS
(Papaveraceae)   poppy
M. *betonicifolia* (Himalayan blue poppy from Asia) is an herbaceous perennial bearing pale blue papery-textured flowers 55–75mm/2¼–3in across, which open in summer on slender stems above grey-green leaves. The larger deeper blue flowers of M. *grandis* appear slightly earlier. M. × *sheldonii* is a desirable hybrid of the two preceding species, with large nodding pure blue flowers. All these Asian poppies need relatively mild winters and like rich deep lime-free soil in a sheltered site with humidity and part shade – a woodland glade is ideal.
H: 90–120cm/36–48in   s: 45cm/18in
z: 7[7–9]
M. *cambrica* (Welsh poppy from western Europe) is a perennial best treated as annual, since tap roots are difficult to eradicate. Clear yellow flowers are borne all summer above fresh green ferny leaves. Flourishes in any soil and position, seeding freely.
H: 30–60cm/12–24in   s: 30cm/12in
z: 6[6–9] or grow as ANNUAL

MELIANTHUS
(Melianthaceae)
M. *major* (India, S. Africa) is a beautiful exotic-looking foliage evergreen sub-shrub, with large deeply serrated grey-green pinnate leaves. In warm areas brownish-maroon flowers appear in spring, but the plant is often grown only for its striking architectural foliage. Leaves cut down by frost shoot again in spring. Full sun and well-drained soil.
H: 1.5–3m/5–10ft   s: 1.2m/4ft   z: 9[8–10]

MERTENSIA
(Boraginaceae)
M. *pulmonarioides* (syn. M. *virginica*; Virginia cowslip from eastern USA) has blue-grey foliage and leafy stems bearing drooping clusters of fragrant lavender-blue bell-like flowers in late spring to early summer. Disappears in midsummer: grow ferns to take its place. A perennial woodlander for acid loam in shade or part shade.
H: 30–60cm/12–24in   s: 45cm/18in   z: 3[3–10]

MIMULUS

(Scrophulariaceae)   monkey flower

M. *aurantiacus* (monkey musk from western N. America) is an evergreen shrubby perennial of sprawling habit, with sticky mid-green leaves on brittle stems. Pale translucent yellow-orange 50mm/2in trumpet-flowers appear all summer. Give cuttings winter protection in cold areas. Prefers dry sunny position, but tolerates shade.
H & S: 30cm/12in   z: 9[9–10]

MIRABILIS

(Nyctaginaceae)

M. *jalapa* (four o'clock plant, marvel of Peru; from tropical America) flowers prolifically in summer. Fragrant 30mm/1¼in trumpet-flowers, ranging from crimson through pink to white and yellow, open mid-afternoon and fade next morning. Dahlia-like tubers may be lifted for overwintering indoors in cold areas, or raise plants annually from seed. Sun and moderately rich soil.
H: 60–90cm/24–36in   s: 60cm/24in
z: 10[9–10]

MISCANTHUS

(Gramineae)   Far East

M. *sinensis* is a giant ornamental perennial grass with blue-green white-ribbed leaves. Is clump-forming but not invasive, making an excellent windbreaking backdrop. Sun and rich moist soil; tolerates sandy soils given sufficient rainfall.
H: to 1.8m/6ft   s: 0.9m/3ft   z: 5[5–10]
M.s. 'Gracillimus' is more compact. Its narrow sage-green leaves fade in winter to straw-colour.
H: 30–75cm/12–30in   s: 45–60cm/18–24in
z: 5[5–10]

MONARDA

(Labiatae)   bergamot

M. *didyma* (bee balm, Oswego tea; from N. America) is a tall summer-flowering border perennial for sun or part shade and enriched moist soil; may be invasive. 'Cambridge Scarlet' bears rich scarlet flowers with deep crimson calyces in dense whorled heads up to 75mm/3in across.
H: 75–90cm/30–36in   s: 45cm/18in
z: 4[4–10]

MYOSOTIS

(Boraginaceae)   forget-me-not   Europe

M. *alpestris* has clusters of fragrant azure flowers with yellow centres in early summer. Allow this short-lived perennial to naturalize, but replace every few years with new plants grown from seed

Mirabilis jalapa

sown the previous summer. Part shade and well-drained soil with organic matter, or a rock garden.
H: 7.5–20cm/3–8in   s: 15cm/6in   z: 5[5–9]
M. *sylvatica* is a similar but larger plant: named forms of this biennial have deeper blue flowers, in early summer. Self-seeds readily in a shady border.
H & S: 30cm/12in   z: 5[5–9]

NANDINA

(Nandinaceae)   sacred bamboo   China

N. *domestica* is an elegant evergreen shrub that grows like a bamboo with unbranched stems. Very large delicate pinnate leaves are usually tinged with pink. Large terminal panicles of small white flowers in summer ripen to scarlet or white fruits. Rich moist well-drained soil; shelter in cold areas.
MEDIUM SHRUB H: 1.2–1.8m/4–6ft
s: 0.6–0.9m/2–3ft   z: 8[8–10]

NARCISSUS

(Liliaceae/Amaryllidaceae)   daffodil

Most narcissi will happily naturalize in grassy glades or under deciduous trees. To make bright focal points early in the year plant these bulbous perennials in containers.

N. *cyclamineus* (Iberian Peninsula) has solitary flowers of rich yellow with cyclamen-like swept-back petals and long trumpets in late winter and early spring. A dainty species for fine grass or a peaty pocket in a rock garden or even a border. Enjoys dampish soil. Cyclamineus hybrids are taller and more resilient.
H: 15–20cm/6–8in   z: 5[5–10]
N. *pseudonarcissus* (Lent lily, wild daffodil; from Europe) has pale almost white petals with lemon-yellow trumpets in spring. Native to damp meadows.
H: 20–35cm/8–14in   z: 3[3–10]
N. *tazetta* (Mediterranean regions, Asia Minor, Far East) is for a frost-free area, preferably where its bulb can be sun-baked in summer, or for forcing for a pot display. Clustered heads of small fragrant cream and papery-white flowers appear from late autumn to mid-spring.
H: 30–45cm/12–18in   z: 9[9–10]
N. 'Tresamble' has the swept-back petals and pendent flower-heads of the Triandrus group. Clusters of two or three creamy-white flowers, each with an open cup, appear in early spring.
H: 20–35cm/8–14in   z: 3[3–10]

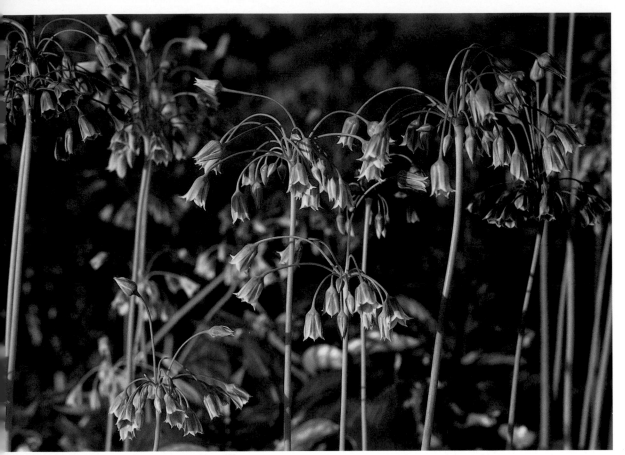

Nectaroscordum siculum bulgaricum

NECTAROSCORDUM
(Liliaceae/Alliaceae)

N. siculum bulgaricum (sometimes known as *Allium bulgaricum*; from southern Europe) has leaves and bulb with the characteristic onion smell of allium when bruised. Leaves are long mid-green and keeled. In early summer umbels of pendent bell-shaped greeny-white flowers, marked with dull purple, are carried on tall wiry stems. Seeds in unexpected places. Useful shape and texture for mixed borders. Vigorous enough to naturalize in grass or to form colonies between shrubs.
H: 60–120cm/24–48in s: 25cm/10in z: 5[5–9]

NEPETA
(Labiatae) catmint

Catmints are hardy perennials that like well-drained soil and sun.

N. × *faassenii* has soft grey-green leaves and a profusion of arching spikes of lavender-coloured flowers in early summer. Cut back after flowering to encourage a crop of late-summer flowers. Useful for edging, making a billowing low hedge, or

for ground cover.
H: 30–60cm/12–24in s: 45cm/18in z: 3[3–10]

N. nervosa (Kashmir) makes a good-looking rounded bush of long narrow green leaves with pronounced veining. Bears bright blue flowers all through late summer.
H: 30–60cm/12–24in s: 30cm/12in z: 4[4–9]

N. 'Souvenir d'André Chaudron' (syn. *N.* 'Blue Beauty') has almost bronze leaves and long-lasting pale blue flowers in summer. Useful for a border.
H: 45cm/18in s: 25cm/10in z: 5[5–10]

NERINE
(Liliaceae/Amaryllidaceae) S. Africa

N. bowdenii provides valuable colour at the end of summer. Umbels of fine lily-like pink flowers are borne on strong bare stems just before the strap-shaped leaves re-emerge after dying down in early summer. Hardy, but bulb appreciates a sunny site with warmth reflected by a wall in marginal districts. Well-drained soil.
H: 45–60cm/18–24in s: 15–20cm/6–8in z: 8[8–10]

NICOTIANA
(Solanaceae) tobacco plant

N. alata (flowering tobacco, jasmine tobacco; from S. America) is a perennial often grown as an annual. Tubular flowers, ranging from white (often tinted yellow or green) to red and purple, offer scent as well as colour throughout summer. Sticky green leaves are good weed-smotherers. Sun and well-drained rich soil.
H: 60–90cm/24–36in s: 30cm/12in
z: 9[9–10] or grow as ANNUAL

N. glauca (southern Bolivia, northern Argentina) is a sprawling tender semi-evergreen shrub with lax branches bearing smooth grey-green leaves. Only its tubular flowers in summer and early autumn betray the family resemblance. Worth coaxing as a desirable foliage perennial or annual; may be invasive in warm areas.
LARGE SHRUB H: 3m/10ft z: 9[9–10] or grow as ANNUAL

N. langsdorfii (Brazil, Chile) is a perennial grown as an annual. Strange pendent sulphur-yellow flowers appear in early summer.
H: 75cm/30in s: 30cm/12in z: 9[9–10] or grow as ANNUAL

N. sylvestris (Argentina) is a majestic perennial, but grow as annual in cold areas. Pendent clusters of almost lily-like long white flower-tubes are borne above large leaves in late summer. Good grouped at the back of a border. Sun or light shade. Self-seeds *in situ*.
H: 150cm/60in s: 30cm/12in z: 9[9–10] or grow as ANNUAL

NIGELLA
(Ranunculaceae) love-in-a-mist

N. damascena 'Miss Jekyll' has clear blue corn-flower-heads in a halo of thread-like bracts amid delicate grassy foliage. Sow seed *in situ* in spring for summer flowering. Self-seeds readily to make a flowery carpet in summer – between iris rhizomes, for example, its flower-heads disguise unsightly iris leaves.
H: 45–60cm/18–24in s: 25cm/10in ANNUAL

NYMPHAEA
(Nymphaeaceae) waterlily

Waterlily hybrids, chosen for their colour, may charmingly continue a flower theme into formal or informal ponds. Available water depth, plant hardiness, size and vigour are all factors to consider when selecting these perennial water plants, as well as flower colour and form. The hardy *N.* 'James Brydon', for example, has 10cm/4in flowers of rose-crimson, which tone with its maroon-splashed leaves and might echo a planting of deep-coloured astilbes and bronze rodgersias at the water's edge or, in more formal schemes, might complement near-by borders of hot strong colours. Free-flowering and compact; suitable for water depths to 45cm/18in.

OENOTHERA
(Onagraceae)   evening primrose
O. biennis (biennial evening primrose from N. America) is a biennial that has rosettes of long green leaves from which arise erect stems bearing clusters of pale yellow flowers from midsummer onwards. Delicate colour of newly opened flowers gleams at twilight and perfectly complements blues and murky purples. Readily self-seeds in weed-like numbers. Sun and well-drained soil.
H: 50–100cm/20–40in   s: 30cm/12in
O. speciosa (showy primrose from southern USA) is a compact but invasive perennial. Bowl-shaped flowers in delicate faded pinks and whites appear in summer during the daytime.
H: 15–60cm/6–24in   s: 60cm/24in   z: 5[5–10]

OMPHALODES
(Boraginaceae)   navelwort
O. cappadocica (Turkey) forms perennial clumps of long-stalked green leaves. Sprays of azure-blue flowers, reminiscent of a distinguished forget-me-not, are produced in spring. Grow in drifts at the edge of a woodland or under shrubs. Part shade and peaty soil.
H & s: 15–23cm/6–9in   z: 6[6–10]
O. linifolia (Greek forget-me-not, Venus's navelwort; from Greece) is a biennial best grown as an annual. Charming almost bluish-white flowers are produced in summer above pale silvery leaves. Sow seed in early spring; overwintered plants can damp off and young plants are vulnerable to slugs. Can be grown in a container in sun for a froth of blossom.
H & s: 30cm/12in   z: 6[6–9] or grow as ANNUAL
O. verna (blue-eyed Mary from Europe) is a semi-evergreen perennial using rooting runners to spread more quickly into a carpet of heart-shaped foliage decorated with sprays of small blue flowers in spring. Evergreen in frost-free areas.
H: 15–20cm/6–8in   s: 30cm/12in   z: 5[5–9]

ONOPORDUM
(Compositae)
O. acanthium (cotton thistle, Scotch thistle; from UK) is a statuesque biennial foliage plant, beauti-

ful at the back of a border, with purple flowers at midsummer. Ethereal silvery-grey leaves and branching stems look ghostly at twilight and are a mainstay in 'white' gardens – but spines armouring the entire plant are painful to hands of weeders and to soft leaves of neighbouring plants. Allow to self-seed and remove young plants in the wrong place, or dead-head. In cold areas grow seed in individual pots and overwinter. Sun or part shade and rich soil.
H: 180cm/72in   s: 75cm/30in   z: 6[6–10]

OSMANTHUS
(Oleaceae)
Hardy evergreen shrubs for any situation, making dense bushy shapes of dark and glossy green, with fragrant flowers in spring.
O. decorus (Asia) has hard smooth oblong leaves forming a dense graceful domed shape, ideal for introducing a touch of formality. Slow-growing. Sun or part shade.
LARGE SHRUB H: 3m/10ft   s: 1.8m/6ft   z: 8[8–10]
O. delavayi (China) has handsome dark green toothed leaves. Showy white flowers in axillary clusters, rather like those of a jasmine, smother this shrub in late spring. Clip into shape after flowering: may be used for hedging. Prefers an open site in sun.
MEDIUM SHRUB H & s: 1.8–2.4m/6–8ft   z: 8[8–10]

OSMUNDA
(Osmundaceae)
O. regalis (royal fern; world-wide except Australasia) is a handsome deciduous perennial with pinnate leaves, resembling those of *Dryopteris filix-mas* (male fern), that unfurl from copper-toned crosiers in spring. Moist humus-rich soil.
H & s: 90–120cm/36–48in   z: 3[3–9]

OSTEOSPERMUM
(Compositae)
O. ecklonis (S. Africa) is a slightly tender sprawling evergreen sub-shrub with a profusion of blue-centred white daisy-flowers all summer. Sun and fairly fertile well-drained soil. Drought-tolerant.
H: 60–90cm/24–36in   s: 30–60cm/12–24in
z: 9[9–10]

PACHYSANDRA
(Buxaceae)
P. procumbens (N. America) is a semi-evergreen perennial – less vigorous than *P. terminalis* – which is lovely in a woodland setting. Spikes of white or purplish flowers are borne in spring.

Nigella damascena 'Miss Jekyll'

P. terminalis (Japanese spurge) is a creeping shrubby evergreen perennial that can be massed to make ground cover under deciduous and evergreen trees and shrubs. Clusters of diamond-shaped smooth leaves with toothed edges make a handsome contrast to both grass and rougher foliage. Spikes of inconspicuous whitish flowers appear in spring. Acid-loving, but shallow roots tolerate lime provided they have plenty of leafmould.
H: 30cm/12in   s: 45cm/18in   z: 5[5–9]

PAEONIA
(Paeoniaceae)   peony
This decorative genus includes a wide range of shrubby and herbaceous plants with gorgeous showy flowers framed by architectural divided foliage. Leaves make good ground cover and often colour well in spring and autumn. Rich well-drained soil. Disturb roots as little as possible.
P. cambessedesii (Balearic Islands) is a slightly

Papaver somniferum

tender perennial that needs a special site in sun where thrusting neighbours will not overwhelm it. Late-spring flowers are deep rose-pink with darker centres, and the foliage is particularly handsome, exotically tinted with deep red stalks and undersides.
H & S: 45cm/18in z: 9[9–10]
P. lactiflora (Mongolia, Siberia) garden hybrids are numerous, with attractive mid- to deep green foliage and large flowers in all shades of pinks and whites from early summer. Varieties of these perennials include singles, doubles, semi-doubles and so on, but the single forms, often with conspicuous yellow stamens, are the most elegant. A valuable border plant.
H: 45–105cm/18–42in s: 60–90cm/24–36in
z: 2[2–10]
P. mlokosewitschii (Caucasus) is a perennial and earliest to flower. Fat cherry-buds herald spring and open to clear lemon-yellow globular flowers with golden anthers clustered among blue-green leaves. By midsummer pods open to reveal shining black seeds nestling in a crimson lining.
H & S: 60cm/24in z: 5[5–10]

P. officinalis (common peony from southern Europe and Asia) is a tuberous perennial with flowers in late spring. Single and double forms are available, in whites, pinks and reds. Fresh green foliage lasts well all summer. Good under and with shrub roses.
H: 75cm/30in s: 90cm/36in z: 2[2–10]
P. suffruticosa (moutan from China, Tibet) is a deciduous shrub with single white flowers, blotched with crimson to maroon at the petal base, in a framework of pale green leaves. There are many wonderful cultivars with pink or yellow flowers, usually grafted.
MEDIUM SHRUB H & S: 1.5–1.8m/5–6ft z: 5[5–9]
P. wittmanniana (Caucasus) is a handsome perennial with rather coarser leaves. In late spring produces pale single flowers, from white to yellow, with crimson filaments in centre.
H: 90cm/36in s: 60cm/24in z: 5[5–10]

PAPAVER
(Papaveraceae) poppy
P. orientale (oriental poppy from Armenia) is a perennial with flamboyant tissue-paper flowers in white, pink, scarlet and vermilion amid pale bristly deeply cut leaves. Makes an exciting early-summer climax in a border. After flowering the plants sprawl untidily and are best veiled by later-flowering neighbours. Sun and deep well-drained soil.
H: 60–120cm/24–48in s: 60–90cm/24–36in
z: 3[3–9]
P. rhoeas (field poppy from Europe) with papery scarlet petals on delicate stalks colours wildflower meadows in summer. Garden varieties, the Shirley poppies, make useful annual front-of-border fillers in drifts of pinks, whites and reds.
H: 60cm/24in s: 20cm/8in ANNUAL
P. somniferum (opium poppy from Greece and the Orient) is an annual with smooth pale grey-green leaves. Peony-flowered varieties have double flowers in white, pink, red and purple in summer. Endures very high temperatures.
H: 75cm/30in s: 30cm/12in ANNUAL

PARAHEBE
(Scrophulariaceae)
P. catarractae is a neat little evergreen sub-shrub. A mound of mid-green leaves is covered by a mass of pale whitish-mauve speedwell-flowers in summer. Sun and well-drained soil.
H: 15–20cm/6–8in s: 30–45cm/12–18in
z: 9[9–10]
P. perfoliata (often listed as *Veronica perfoliata*; digger's speedwell from Australia) is an unusual distinctive evergreen sub-shrub with waxy-grey oval leaves clasping and encircling long arching stems. Elegant racemes of lavender-blue flowers in late summer will trail gracefully over the edge of a low sunny wall.
H: 60cm/24in s: 45cm/18in z: 8[8–10]

PARTHENOCISSUS
(Vitaceae)
These self-clinging deciduous creepers clothe walls to make rich foliage backdrops to borders, and are particularly dramatic with vivid autumn colouring.
P. henryana (Chinese Virginia creeper) has attractive palmate leaves of velvety dark green variegated with white and pink along midribs and veins. Variegation persists after the dark green leaves have turned to fiery red in autumn. Shade.
CLIMBER H: 8–10m/25–30ft z: 8[8–10]
P. quinquefolia (Virginia creeper from N. America) has serrated five-leaflet leaves that turn a brilliant crimson in autumn.
CLIMBER H: 20m/70ft z: 3[3–9]

P. tricuspidata 'Veitchii' (Boston ivy from China, Japan) has variable leaves, often with three leaflets or three lobes.
CLIMBER H: 15m/50ft z: 4[4–9]

PELARGONIUM
(Geraniaceae) geranium
Pelargoniums are invaluable for their colour: dense rounded flower-heads bloom all summer if dead-heads are removed. Grow named forms from seed or choose colours carefully to fit in with orchestrated schemes of summer bedding.
P. 'The Boar' has pretty salmon-pink flowers and dark foliage. Perennial, but grow as annual from seed or as cutting.
H & S: 90cm/36in z: 10 or grow as ANNUAL

PENNISETUM
(Gramineae)
P. alopecuroides (Argentina, eastern Asia, eastern Australia) is a perennial grass with narrow grey-green leaves forming a dense clump. Bottle-brush flower-spikes appear in autumn. Sun; protect from frost.
H: 90cm/36in s: 45–60cm/18–24in z: 5[5–10]

PENSTEMON
(Scrophulariaceae)
northern and central America
Penstemons make a valuable contribution to summer and autumn borders with freely produced loose spikes of tubular flowers in lovely rich colours. Border varieties are often only half-hardy but root easily from cuttings to be grown as annual bedding (left *in situ* they become unsightly in winter and succumb to cold spring wind). Keep dead-headed. Sun and well-drained fertile soil.
P. 'Garnet' (correctly *P.* 'Andenken an Friedrich Hahn') is a semi-evergreen perennial with flowers of deep purple-red from midsummer to autumn. Flowers tone particularly well when planted under pink shrub roses.
H: 75cm/30in s: 60cm/24in z: 8[8–10]
P. heterophyllus is a semi-evergreen alpine variety with narrow grey-green leaves and spikes of blue flowers in summer.
SMALL SHRUB H & S: 45cm/18in z: 5[5–10]
P. 'Schoenholzeri' has scarlet flowers that glow beside other 'hot' colours from midsummer to autumn. Vigorous bushy semi-evergreen perennial.
H: 90cm/36in s: 60cm/24in z: 8[8–10]

PERILLA
(Labiatae)
P. frutescens (China) is an annual needing hot sun to ripen the seed. Has handsome red-purple leaves, ovate and pointed and attractively textured with veining. Spikes of white flowers appear in late summer.
H: 60cm/24in s: 30cm/12in ANNUAL

PEROVSKIA
(Labiatae)
P. atriplicifolia (Russian sage from Afghanistan to Tibet) is a graceful deciduous sub-shrub with grey-blue leaves and open panicles of violet-blue tubular flowers throughout late summer: the effect of the whole plant in a border amounts to more than the sum of its parts. Named forms have bluer flowers. Is generally cut to the ground each winter and shoots again from the base. Suckers may be invasive. Sun and good drainage.
H: 90–150cm/36–60in s: 45–60cm/18–24in z: 6[6–10]

PERSICARIA
(Polygonaceae) knotweed
P. campanulata (formerly *Polygonum campanulatum*; from the Himalayas) has attractively veined and brown-marked leaves that appear in early spring. Wide branching flower-heads of tiny shell-pink bells last for many weeks from midsummer to early autumn. Colonizes moist or cool soil to make perennial ground cover in part shade or non-scorching sun, but its easily controlled shallow roots make it less alarmingly invasive than other knotweeds.
H & S: 90cm/36in z: 6[6–9]
P. capitata (formerly *Polygonum capitatum*; from the Himalayas) makes charming low ground cover for mild areas, with dark green brown-marked foliage and a long succession of little rounded pink flower-heads throughout summer. Perennial in its native habitat; in cold zones overwinter indoors and grow as an annual, or allow to self-seed.
H: 10–15cm/4–6in s: 30–45cm/12–18in z: 9[9–10] or grow as ANNUAL

PHILADELPHUS
(Philadelphaceae) mock orange
A range of species and hybrids of deciduous shrubs varying in size and flowering time provide scented white flowers for many weeks in shrub borders and woodland.
P. 'Belle Etoile' is a compact shrub with single white flowers opening wide to display maroon-blotched petal bases in summer.
MEDIUM SHRUB H & S: 2.4m/8ft z: 5[5–9]

Perovskia atriplicifolia 'Blue Spire'

Philadelphus coronarius

Philadelphus 'Innocence'

P. coronarius (southern Europe) has richly scented creamy-white flowers in early summer, and is not fussy about soil or site. Its golden-leaved and variegated forms need part shade.
MEDIUM SHRUB H & S: 1.8–3m/6–10ft   Z: 5[5–9]
P. 'Innocence' bears single pure white flowers in summer. Leaves have distinctive cream and white variegation.
MEDIUM SHRUB H: 2.4m/8ft   S: 1.8m–2.4m/6–8ft
Z: 5[5–9]
P. 'Virginal' has wide-opening double white flowers in summer on upright branches.
MEDIUM SHRUB H: 2.4–3m/8–10ft
S: 1.8–2.4m/6–8ft   Z: 5[5–9]

PHILLYREA
(Oleaceae)   southern Europe, northern Africa, Middle East
Phillyreas are slow-growing evergreens with a dense mass of glistening foliage to clip into formal shapes as emphatic foils for exuberant flowering companions.
P. angustifolia rosmarinifolia makes a compact dome-shaped bush, with narrow plain dark green leaves.
SMALL SHRUB H & S: 60cm/24in   Z: 8[8–10]
P. latifolia is an elegant tree similar to an olive, its small leaves revealing pale undersides and fluttering attractively in a breeze.
SMALL TREE H & S: to 5m/15ft   Z: 8[8–10]

PHLOMIS
(Labiatae)
P. fruticosa (Jerusalem sage from the Mediterranean) is a sprawling bushy evergreen shrub with hairy grey-green foliage and whorls of bright yellow flowers carried in leaf axils in summer.
SMALL SHRUB H: 90–120cm/36–48in
S: 60–90cm/24–36in   Z: 8[8–10]
P. italica (Balearic Islands) is, in summer, a beautiful combination of silver-grey felted leaves and palest dusty-pink flowers. Prune hard, if necessary to ground level, in early summer to make a shapely upright evergreen bush. Slightly tender until well-established. Sunny sheltered site and well-drained soil.
SMALL SHRUB H: 30–45cm/12–18in   S: 30cm/12in
Z: 8[8–10]

PHLOX
(Polemoniaceae)
The *Phlox* genus provides flower colour for almost every season and section of the garden.
P. 'Chattahoochee', a trailing woodland-type short-lived perennial, is a valuable early-flowering front-of-border plant. In summer and autumn purple-eyed flowers of a rich soft blue fade to pale lavender-blue in a lovely blended mixture. Leaves are dark, hairy and rather pointed. Part shade and cool soil.
H: 25cm/10in   S: 30cm/12in   Z: 4[4–9]
P. divaricata (wild blue phlox from north-eastern USA) – a probable parent of *P.* 'Chattahoochee' – forms an open perennial mat of semi-evergreen foliage. Bears loose clusters of light blue or lavender flowers in spring. Needs woodland conditions of part shade and moist humus-rich soil.
H & S: 30cm/12in   Z: 4[4–9]
P. douglasii (western N. America) is an evergreen perennial forming a dense sub-shrubby mat of mid-green leaves. Garden forms have flowers in tones of pink, mauve and white in early summer. Good for front of a sunny border.
H: 7.5cm/3in   S: 45cm/18in   Z: 5[5–8]
P. drummondii (Texas) is a half-hardy annual, flowering from midsummer onwards with dense flower-heads in shades of reds, pinks, lavender and white. There are garden varieties of more compact habit with various flower shapes and colours.
H: 38cm/15in   S: 23cm/9in   ANNUAL
P. maculata (wild sweet William, meadow phlox; from eastern USA), a perennial, freely produces tall cylindrical spikes of fragrant mauvish flowers from late summer on. Feed richly and divide periodically for best results. Useful late-flowering plant for an open border or part shade. Feed richly and divide periodically for best results. Rich moisture-retentive well-drained soil. *P.m.* 'Alpha' has dark-eyed flowers of soft lilac-pink. *P.m.* 'Omega' is white with a slight lilac tinge and a violet eye.
H: 60–120cm/24–48in   S: 45–60cm/18–24in
Z: 3[3–9]
P. paniculata (border phlox, garden phlox; from north-eastern USA) is a perennial with, in summer, many good named varieties in a wide spectrum ranging from violet-blues to reds, sometimes with a darker eye. If possible choose from a flowering plant rather than a catalogue description to ensure the right tone for a scheme. Heavy pyramidal flower panicles may need staking. Feed richly and divide periodically for best results. Good for open border. Part shade and rich moisture-retentive well-drained soil.
H: 45–150cm/18–60in   S: 45–60cm/18–24in
Z: 3[3–9]

Phygelius × rectus 'African Queen'

P. stolonifera (creeping phlox from south-eastern USA) makes a low evergreen mat of oval leaves with loose clusters of rose-purple flowers in late spring; named forms come in pink, white and blue. Makes good perennial ground cover in part shade. Tolerates sun that is not too intense.
H: 15–20cm/6–8in s: 30cm/12in z: 3[3–9]
P. subulata (moss phlox from eastern USA) makes a dense perennial mass of thin evergreen leaves with pink or mauve flowers in late spring. Named forms include good tones of pink, red and lavender. Good for front of a sunny border.
H: 7.5cm/3in s: 45cm/18in z: 3[3–8]

PHORMIUM
(Agavaceae/Phormiaceae)
P. tenax (New Zealand flax) is an evergreen perennial with tough sword-like leaves rising from the ground in a huge fan, making a striking architectural focal point and a valuable contrast with most other foliage shapes and textures. Panicles of dark brownish-red flowers tower above the leaves in summer. Sun and moist but well-drained fertile soil. Withstands salt, drought and city atmosphere. Provide winter protection in cold areas. *P.t. purpureum* has grey-green leaves with a purplish sheen. There are many tender cultivars and hybrids with variegated and purple leaf tones.
H: 1.8–3m/6–10ft s: 1.2m/4ft z: 8[8–10]

PHYGELIUS
(Scrophulariaceae)   S. Africa
These sub-shrubby plants are evergreen in warm areas, but may be grown as herbaceous perennials in colder gardens in sunny sheltered well-drained sites.
P. aequalis is a spreading sub-shrub with salmon-buff flowers from midsummer to autumn. *P.a.* 'Yellow Trumpet', a compact form, has spikes of palest yellow slender tubular flowers.
H: 75cm/30in s: 50cm/20in z: 8[8–10]
P. × rectus are hybrids between *P. aequalis* and *P. capensis* (Cape fuchsia). *P. × r.* 'African Queen' has light red flowers with yellow throats from midsummer to autumn. *P. × r.* 'Winchester Fanfare' bears pendulous flowers of dusky red lined with yellow from midsummer to early autumn.
H: 75cm/30in s: 50cm/20in z: 8[8–10]

PILEOSTEGIA
(Hydrangeaceae)
P. viburnoides (China) is a good self-clinging evergreen climber with dull green leaves and creamy flowers in terminal panicles in late summer and

autumn. Ideal for lighting a dark corner or shady wall. Slow-growing, it takes time to establish.
CLIMBER H & S: 6m/20ft z: 9[9–10]

PIPTANTHUS
(Leguminosae)
P. nepalensis (evergreen laburnum from the Himalayas) is a short-lived semi-evergreen shrub. Racemes of bright yellow pea-flowers in late spring are set amid silver-haired young leaves, which later turn into elegant long leaflets, dark green above and greyish below. Sun; plant by warm wall and shelter from cold wind.
LARGE SHRUB H & S: 2.4–4m/8–12ft z: 8[8–10]

PLUMBAGO
(Plumbaginaceae)
P. auriculata (syn. *P. capensis*; from S. Africa) is an evergreen climber with lovely panicles of ice-blue primrose-like flowers for many months in summer, amid soft green elliptical leaves. Tie its lax stems to a wall or allow to sprawl over neighbouring plants. Cut back after flowering and water sparingly in winter. Overwinter in a frost-free greenhouse and in spring put out in its pot, or plant out, to transform a sunny corner with its flowers.
CLIMBER H: 5m/15ft s: 3m/10ft z: 9[9–10]

PODOPHYLLUM
(Podophyllaceae)
P. hexandrum (syn. *P. emodi*; from India) is a rhizomatous perennial colonizing slowly in a moist shady border. Deeply lobed leaves emerge folded downwards like a furled umbrella and open to show coppery-brown markings. Saucer-shaped pink or white flowers in early summer are followed by egg-shaped red fruits, which are edible, though the plant is poisonous.
H: 30cm/12in s: 45cm/18in z: 5[5–9]

POLEMONIUM
(Polemoniaceae)   Jacob's ladder
Polemoniums are pretty border perennials for sun or part shade and ordinary garden soil. Cut back spent flower stems to freshen up ferny foliage.
P. caeruleum (Asia, Europe) makes a basal clump of bright green pinnate leaves and produces loose clusters of bell-shaped lavender-blue flowers with orange stamens in early summer.
H: 60–90cm/24–36in s: 30–60cm/12–24in z: 3[3–9]
P. foliosissimum (western N. America) has erect stems carrying dark green pinnate leaves and ter-

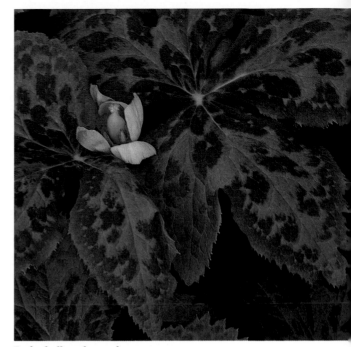
Podophyllum hexandrum

minating in dense clusters of cup-shaped flowers of rich lilac-blue, produced in long succession throughout summer.
H: 75–90cm/30–36in s: 60cm/24in z: 4[4–9]

POLYGONATUM
(Liliaceae/Convallariaceae)
P. × hybridum (David's harp, Solomon's harp) is an elegant shade-loving spreading perennial for a border. Long arching stems bear horizontally held elliptical leaves all along their length, and green-tinged white bells hang downwards in clusters during early summer. Pale green leaves emerge to camouflage anemone and fritillary flowers as they fade in late spring, and their simple lines become the perfect foil for shapely ferns and acanthus and for massed darker small-leaved foliage.
H: 90–120cm/36–48in s: 60cm/24in z: 4[4–10]

POLYSTICHUM
(Aspleniaceae)
P. setiferum (soft shield fern from Europe) has dainty elegant fronds and thrives in most conditions. This evergreen or semi-evergreen perennial tolerates drought, but is most luxuriant in a cool shady site.
H: 60–120cm/24–48in s: 90–150cm/36–60in z: 5[5–9]

POTENTILLA

(Rosaceae)   cinquefoil

These useful hardy deciduous shrubs have a long flowering period. Their brown stems and seed-heads are attractive all winter.

P. fruticosa 'Abbotswood' has abundant white flowers against a mass of greyish leaves throughout summer and autumn.

SMALL SHRUB H: 90cm/36in   s: 120cm/48in z: 2[2–9]

P. f. arbuscula (Himalayas, northern China) has sage-green leaves and brown shaggy stems in winter. Clusters of large rich yellow flowers are borne from early summer to autumn.

SMALL SHRUB H: 60cm/24in   s: 150cm/60in z: 2[2–9]

P. f. 'Elizabeth' is dome-shaped and has rich canary-flowers, freely produced late spring to early autumn. Good for hedging or in groups.

SMALL SHRUB H: 90cm/36in   s: 120cm/48in z: 2[2–9]

P. f. 'Vilmoriniana' has intense silver leaves prim-rose-flowers from late spring to early autumn, and a more upright habit than *P. f.* 'Elizabeth'

SMALL SHRUB H: 120cm/48in   s: 90cm/36in z: 2[2–9]

PRIMULA

(Primulaceae)   primrose

Asian species prefer part shade in cool humus-rich soil – moist or well-mulched, but not waterlogged in winter. Given a suitable site, their contribution of flower colour and form is stunning.

P. florindae (giant cowslip, Tibetan primrose; from western China, Tibet) is a handsome vigorous perennial for a moist site, with long-lasting summer flowers. Several tall stems bearing fragrant drooping sulphur-yellow flowers powdered with white rise from a clump of large rounded leaves.

H: 60–90cm/24–36in   s: 60cm/24in z: 6[6–9]

P. pulverulenta (western China) is a candelabra-type perennial, with wrinkled green leaves and tiered flowers carried on stems covered in floury meal in early summer. Garden cultivars have tones from almost crimson with a darker red or purple eye to softer pink tints. Plant in drifts at a pond's edge, with bronze rodgersia foliage or gunnera leaves as a background.

H: 60–90cm/24–36in   s: 45cm/18in z: 6[6–9]

P. sikkimensis (Himalayan cowslip) is a slighter version of *P. florindae*, with narrower leaves and pale yellow flowers in summer. This perennial is less easily grown.

H: 45cm/18in   s: 23–30cm/9–12in z: 6[6–9]

P. vulgaris (common primrose from Europe) is a perennial that should be encouraged to colonize shrubberies and woodland areas, the simple pale yellow flowers evoking the arrival of spring.

H: 15cm/6in   s: 23cm/9in   z: 5[5–9]

PRUNUS

(Rosaceae)   flowering cherry

P. maackii (Manchurian cherry from China) is deciduous and has outstanding golden-brown bark that flakes as it ages. Shows up best in a group planting, glowing against a plain background, a carpet of yellow aconites reflecting its brightness.

MEDIUM TREE H: 12m/40ft   s: 6m/20ft   z: 2[2–9]

P. 'Ukon' (Japanese cherry) is deciduous and has long-lasting green-tinged creamy double flowers in midspring set amid bronze young leaves, a beautiful combination against a dark backdrop.

SMALL TREE H: 5–6m/15–20ft   s: 5.5–8m/18–25ft z: 6[6–9]

PULMONARIA

(Boraginaceae)   lungwort

Pulmonarias make useful perennial ground cover in moist shady sites, but two species with shapely leaves offer more textural interest than most.

P. angustifolia (blue cowslip from central Europe) has elliptical leaves of plain dark green. These emerge in spring with the flowers – sprays of pink buds unfurling to blue cowslip-flowers.

H: 23–30cm/9–12in   s: 30–45cm/12–18in z: 3[3–9]

LEFT *Primula florindae*   ABOVE Candelabra primulas

P. longifolia (western Europe) has long narrow pointed leaves spotted with white, and the dense clusters of blue spring flowers last into summer, later than most of the genus.
H: 30cm/12in s: 45cm/18in z: 5[5–9]

PULSATILLA
(Ranunculaceae)
P. vulgaris (pasque flower from Europe) has purple flowers that appear in spring before the delicate finely cut foliage has fully emerged. Silky hairs give this perennial a silvery sheen. Full sun and well-drained dryish chalky soil.
H & s: 23–30cm/9–12in z: 3[3–9]

PYRUS
(Rosaceae)   pear
P. calleryana 'Chanticleer' (Bradford pear), a cultivar of the Chinese wild pear, is deciduous and has a graceful pyramidal habit. Carries a mass of white blossom in spring and good rich leaf colouring in autumn.
MEDIUM TREE H: 15m/50ft s: 6m/20ft
z: 5[5–9]
P. salicifolia 'Pendula' (weeping silver pear) has gracefully drooping dark stems and willow-like silver leaves. Its colour shimmers against a dark backdrop, but also contributes well to beds of mixed planting. Prune lower branches to keep a graceful shape to this deciduous tree.
SMALL TREE H: 8m/25ft s: 6m/20ft
z: 6[6–9]

RANUNCULUS
(Ranunculaceae)   buttercup
R. aconitifolius (Europe) makes strong leafy perennial clumps of dark green buttercup-foliage. Wiry branching stems bear loose clusters of dainty white flowers in early summer. Beautiful white button-flowers of double-flowered *R. a.* 'Flore Pleno' (fair maids of France) make elegant contrast with the dark foliage. Sun or part shade and moist soil.
H & s: 90cm/36in z: 4[4–9]

REHMANNIA
(Gesneriaceae)   China
R. elata (syn. *R. angulata*) is a long-blooming self-seeding perennial with strange hooded foxglove-like flowers of rose purple with spotted inner markings in early and midsummer. Useful in a border. Sun or shade and well-drained soil.
H: 60–90cm/24–36in s: 30–60cm/12–24in
z: 8[8–10]

RESEDA
(Resedaceae)   mignonette
R. odorata (northern Africa) is a hardy cottage-garden annual with honey-scented fluffy flower-spikes, greenish-yellow in the species but red-tinged in some named varieties. Plant in groups as a subtly toned front-of-border filler.
H: 30–60cm/12–24in s: 15–23cm/6–9in
ANNUAL

RHEUM
(Polygonaceae)   ornamental rhubarb   China
R. palmatum is one of the best foliage perennials for waterside with deeply toothed broad rough leaves, green tinged with purple in the type, while *R. p.* 'Atrosanguineum' (syn. *R. p.* 'Atropurpureum') has vivid red young foliage that turns deep wine-purple as it matures. Tall plumes of white, pink or red astilbe-like flowers are borne in summer. Sun or part shade and deep moist soil.
H & s: 1.8m/6ft z: 5[5–9]

RICINUS
(Euphorbiaceae)   castor oil plant
R. communis (tropical Africa) is a tender evergreen tree-like shrub of upright habit grown for its handsome palmate leaves. Grow as an annual from seed sown the previous summer, and overwintered free from frost, to make attractive textural contrast in border plantings. Red- or bronze-leaved forms are valuable too.
SMALL SHRUB H: 150cm/60in s: 90cm/36in
ANNUAL

RODGERSIA
(Saxifragaceae)
Deciduous perennials that flourish in moist soil, rodgersias spread quickly to make weedproof mats of handsome greeny-bronze leaves that contrast beautifully with light green or feathery foliage. Pink or cream plumes of flowers are a bonus in midsummer.
R. aesculifolia (China) has large crinkled bronze chestnut-leaves that set off clustered plumes of creamy-white flowers, and also harmonize with neighbouring pink-toned flowers.
H: 90–150cm/36–60in s: 60–75cm/24–30in
z: 4[4–9]
R. pinnata 'Superba' is a striking cultivar with very deep green bronze-flushed pinnate leaves and brilliant pink astilbe-like flowers.
H: 90–120cm/36–48in s: 60–75cm/24–30in
z: 4[4–9]
R. tabularis (now correctly *Astilboides tabularis*;

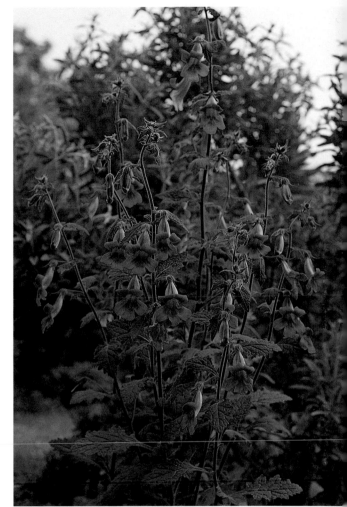

Rehmannia elata (syn. *R. angulata*)

from China, Korea) has smoother umbrella-shaped light green leaves like a small gunnera. Produces tall panicles of creamy-white flowers.
H & s: 90cm/36in z: 4[4–9]

ROMNEYA
(Papaveraceae)   California poppy, tree poppy California
R. coulteri is an herbaceous perennial with deeply lobed glaucous leaves. Huge papery-white poppy-flowers, yellow-centred and fragrant, appear in late summer and autumn. *R. c.* 'White Cloud' has even more splendid flowers. Slow to establish, but potentially invasive: grows into a substantial shrub in warm climates, where it flowers earlier. In colder zones is cut to the ground by frost. Well-drained deep soil, and sun and shelter in cold areas.
H & s: 1.2–1.8m/4–6ft z: 8[8–10]

Rosa 'Albertine'

Rosa 'Penelope'

ROSA

(Rosaceae)   rose

This summary concentrates on roses that combine gracefully in general plant compositions rather than those chosen for perfection of individual bloom, which usually demand privileged treatment in the garden. The list could be expanded infinitely: here are some examples.

Roses for mixed borders

Many roses merit 'key' status in borders, though some rank as companion plants.

Hybrid musks are valuable shrubs with a branching fan-like habit – good for combining with lower-growing herbaceous perennials – and huge trusses of flowers in midsummer, with a second flush in late summer if dead-headed. Colours vary from pure white to some bright pinks (*R.* 'Penelope' is a gentle pink) and the warm cream-bronze of *R.* 'Buff Beauty'.

Modern shrubs – many of which are the result of crosses between Hybrid Teas and various species roses – offer a wide range of shrubs, some displaying the elegant and thrifty habit characteristic of a species parent. A wide choice of flower colour is available, with main flowering in summer and some intermittent blooms later. Plants are robust and relatively disease- and trouble-free. Favourites are the gigantic *R.* 'Cerise Bouquet' and pale yellow *R.* 'Frühlingsgold'.

Bush roses are grown less for habit than for flower impact. This grouping includes highly developed Hybrid Teas, with shapely flowers best massed in formal settings in areas of the garden that can be bypassed in winter when the pruned bushes are unsightly. More suitable for border schemes are Floribundas, with informal clustered blooms, and their parent Polyanthas – compact bushes with small flowers in closely packed bunches.

Roses for informal planting

In less formal garden areas many of the species roses and their near hybrids contribute attractive foliage and subtly beautiful flowers in season. *R. pimpinellifolia* (Scotch or Burnet rose) forms a suckering thicket of fern-like leaves and has forms with pink or white double or single flowers in early summer followed by black hips. Flourishes in poor soil and shady beds. Where its root-run is contained, makes a charming hedge for the more formal flower garden.

Alba roses flower once, in early summer, and have soft grey leaves, an attractive shape and pretty pale pink or white double or semi-double fragrant clustered flowers. *R.* 'Alba Maxima' and *R.* 'Great Maiden's Blush' are favourites.

Rugosa forms have apple-green deeply veined wrinkled leaves and very thorny pale wood. Scented flowers from white to pink and deep wine-crimson are freely borne all summer, followed by globe-shaped red hips. Make attractive and impenetrable hedging. Rugosa roses are hardy, trouble-free and tolerant of salt-laden winds, and many Rugosa hybrids have inherited these useful qualities. *R.* 'Fru Dagmar Hastrup' has single pink flowers and good fruit, and does not grow too large.

Roses as backdrops

On a larger scale, roses curtain vertical surfaces or cascade over banks to add a third dimension of flowers to garden layouts. Perhaps the loveliest backdrops are created by species and cultivars with small or clustered flower-heads combining in massed colour effects.

Rambling and twining roses need the framework of a trellis or pergola for support. Many Ramblers have *wichuraiana* breeding: *R.* 'Albertine' has reddish-copper buds opening to strawberries-and-cream pink; *R.* 'Albéric Barbier' bears cream flowers and glossy green leaves. The more vigorous such as *R.* 'Bobbie James' may be allowed to clamber into trees. *R.* 'Paulii' has single white flowers and prickly branches that will flow down a wall or clothe a slope. Trailing *R.* × *jacksonii* 'Max Graf' produces gold-centred rose-pink flowers.

Climbing roses are for walls, and may be pruned spring into architectural shapes. Stronger-growing climbers usually have a main flush of flowers in early summer and then repeat on and off throughout the rest of the summer: choose deep reds or rich yellows to enhance specific colour schemes, or paler tones for a less eye-catching backdrop. A modest old-fashioned climber is *R.* × *odorata* 'Pallida' (syn. 'Old Blush China'), the rose with delicious semi-double pink flowers that appear in almost every month of the year.

ROSMARINUS

(Labiatae)   rosemary

R. officinalis (southern Europe, Asia Minor) is an evergreen shrub with greyish-green linear leaves and pale mauvish-blue flowers in spring. Deserves a place in every garden, sprawling informally or clipped into a low hedge. Improved forms offer brighter blue flowers and a choice of upright or more compact habit, but are often less hardy.
MEDIUM SHRUB H: 1.8–2.1m/6–7ft
s: 1.5–1.8m/5–6ft   z: 8[8–10]

RUDBECKIA

(Compositae)   coneflower   N. America

R. laciniata (cutleaf coneflower) makes a robust perennial clump of deeply cut leaves to provide late-summer colour at the back of a large-scale border. The species has large yellow flowers with drooping ray florets and greenish cones. *R.l.* 'Golden Glow' is a double form with brassy yellow flowers. May be invasive.

H: 1.8–2.1m/6–7ft   s: 0.6m/2ft   z: 3[3–10]

SALVIA
(Labiatae)   sage

Sages tend to have handsome textured leaves and spikes of tubular flowers ranging from subtle to showy. Hardy culinary sage is a useful foliage plant, while many of the more tender New World species are worth nurturing for their ornamental flowers in striking colours. Needs sun and good drainage.

S. argentea (eastern regions of Mediterranean) is grown principally for its rosette of large silver-white hairy leaves with crinkled and toothed edges. This biennial virtually becomes a perennial if the flower-buds are removed, in summer. (I personally like the low-key whitish-green flower-spires.)

H: 90cm/36in   s: 60cm/24in   z: 5[5–10]

S. farinacea 'Victoria', a cultivar of the tender mealy sage, is a perennial usually grown as an annual. Long-lasting flower-spikes of intense violet-blue appear in late summer on branching felted stems with grey-green foliage.

H: 45cm/18in   s: 30cm/12in   z: 9[9–10] or grow as ANNUAL

S. fulgens (cardinal sage from Mexico) has velvety flower-spikes of vivid scarlet, in late summer, above this evergreen sub-shrub.

H: 60–90cm/24–36in   s: 45cm/18in   z: 9[9–10]

S. guaranitica (S. America) is a semi-evergreen sub-shrub with rough dark green leaves. Intense royal-blue sage-flowers appear in late summer and autumn. Mulch well. Not reliably hardy: cuttings may be rooted in autumn.

H: 150cm/60in   s: 60–90cm/24–36in   z: 9[9–10] or grow as ANNUAL

S. leucantha (Mexico) is a tender evergreen sub-shrub with arching grey-white stems and textured leaves. In late summer and autumn slender sprays of little lavender-white flowers are produced in conspicuous felted violet-toned calyces.

H & s: 60–90cm/24–36in   z: 9[9–10]

S. microphylla neurepia (Mexico) is a tender evergreen shrub with fresh green leaves and a succession of little brilliant scarlet flowers from early summer to autumn.

SMALL SHRUB H: 120cm/48in   s: 90cm/36in z: 9[9–10]

S. officinalis (sage from southern Europe) and its

various forms make useful matt-textured foliage plants – low-growing bushy evergreen shrubs, with variegated or purplish leaves to tone with different colour schemes. Small spikes of violet-blue tubular flowers appear in summer.

SMALL SHRUB H: 60cm/24in   s: 45cm/18in z: 7[7–10]

S. patens (Mexico) is a compact leafy tuberous perennial that bears loose spikes of bright blue hooded flowers on branching stems in late summer and autumn. Is evergreen in a warm climate, becoming woody with age; sow seed each spring in colder areas.

H: 45–75cm/18–30in   s: 30–45cm/12–18in z: 9[9–10] or grow as ANNUAL

S. sclarea turkestanica (Turkestan) is a biennial or short-lived perennial with wrinkled leaves and sturdy stems carrying sage-flowers with conspicuous lavender-purple bracts in summer.

H: 90cm/36in   s: 45cm/18in   z: 8[8–10]

S. uliginosa (bog sage from S. America) is a perennial carrying loose spires of bright azure-blue flowers on tall arching stems in late summer. Not reliably hardy: protect from frosts, or root cuttings in autumn for overwintering. Relatively moist soil and warm site.

H: 150cm/60in   s: 45–60cm/18–24in z: 8[8–10] or grow as ANNUAL

S. viridis (syn. *S. horminum*; clary from southern Europe) has showy coloured bracts in different muted shades of purple-blue, soft rose-reds, pinks and white that tone together well and last from mid- to late summer.

H: 45cm/18in   s: 23cm/9in   ANNUAL

SANGUINARIA
(Papaveraceae)   bloodroot

S. canadensis 'Multiplex' (syn. *S.c.* 'Plena') is a rhizomatous perennial and double form of the wildflower of Canadian woodlands. Flower-heads of tightly packed creamy-white petals are freely carried in spring from folds of leaves. These later open out flat to display handsome grey-green lobes and provide ground cover until they die down in summer. Part shade and well-drained rich loamy acid soil.

H: 15–23cm/6–9in   s: 30cm/12in   z: 3[3–9]

SANTOLINA
(Compositae)   cotton lavender   southern Europe

Santolinas are useful small evergreen shrubs,

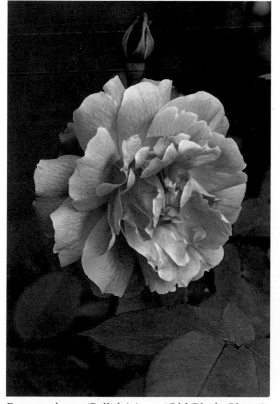

Rosa × odorata 'Pallida' (syn. 'Old Blush China')

Salvia viridis 'Rose Bouquet'

Selinum tenuifolium

hardy where full sun can ripen the wood and where roots are not waterlogged in winter. Vigorous spring pruning keeps the shape neat and prevents woodiness. Good for edging, low hedges and ground cover.
S. chamaecyparissus makes a dense rounded bush, greenish in spring but silvery later. Small yellow button-flowers in summer may be trimmed off where they vie with cool pastel schemes of mauves and pinks.
SMALL SHRUB H & S: 45–60cm/18–24in
z: 7[7–10]
S. rosmarinifolia rosmarinifolia (syn. *S. virens*) has narrow pale green leaves and attractive sulphur-yellow summer flowers. *S.r.* 'Primrose Gem' has paler yellow flowers.
SMALL SHRUB H: 60cm/24in   s: 90–120cm/
36–48in   z: 7[7–10]

SARCOCOCCA
(Buxaceae)   Christmas box, sweet box   Asia
These little glossy-leaved evergreen shrubs have tiny intensely fragrant flowers in midwinter, followed by coloured berries. Are handsome when

grouped to make ground cover in shade of taller golden-leaved shrubs.
S. hookeriana digyna and the slightly smaller *S. humilis* (which suckers) have black fruits.
SMALL SHRUB H & S: 38cm/15in   z: 7[7–9]

SAXIFRAGA
(Saxifragaceae)   saxifrage
Although many species are alpines and thrive in well-drained rocky sites, most adapt happily to ordinary border conditions.
S. cortusifolia fortunei 'Wada' is a semi-evergreen or herbaceous perennial with rosettes of glistening leathery rounded leaves, green above and carmine below. Sprays of starry white yellow-centred flowers appear on red stems in autumn. Good for a cool sheltered corner.
H & S: 30cm/12in   z: 7[7–9]
S. moschata (Pyrenees to Caucasus) is an ever-green perennial forming a moss-like cushion of deeply divided bright green leaves. Forms have pink or yellow saucer-shaped flowers in summer.
H: 7.5–15cm/3–6in   s: 30–45cm/12–18in
z: 5[5–9]

S. stolonifera (mother-of-thousands, strawberry begonia; from eastern Asia) has rounded or kidney-shaped leaves marked with silvery veining and with reddish undersides. Airy racemes of little white flowers appear in summer. This evergreen perennial colonizes by long overground runners ending in little plantlets. Tolerates shade and damp or dry soils.
H: 23–30cm/9–12in   s: 30cm/12in   z: 7[7–10]
S. × urbium (London pride) is an evergreen peren-nial. Makes a weed-smothering mat of fleshy apple-green leafy rosettes above which a haze of pink flowers is borne on wiry stalks in early summer.
H & S: 30cm/12in   z: 5[5–9]

SCILLA
(Liliaceae/Hyacinthaceae)   squill
Spring-flowering hardy bulbs that are at home in any well-worked soil.
S. bifolia (southern Europe and Asia Minor) has loose racemes of mauve-blue to blue flowers in early spring; there are also pink and white forms. Naturalizes in grass. Tolerates shade.
H: 5–10cm/2–4in   s: 10cm/4in   z: 5[5–10]
S. peruviana (Cuban lily from western regions of Mediterranean) has dense blue flower-heads rising above substantial clusters of strap-shaped leaves in early summer. Plant in a warm spot.
H: 23–30cm/9–12in   s: 20cm/8in   z: 8[8–10].
S. siberica (Siberian squill from central and south-ern Russia) has three or four stems each with a few brilliant blue bell-shaped flowers in early spring.
H: 5–10cm/2–6in   s: 10cm/4in   z: 4[4–9]

SEDUM
(Crassulaceae)   stonecrop
These herbaceous sedums make strong plants for open sunny borders, their fleshy glaucous leaves and flat heads of crowded starry flowers in late summer associating well with neighbours in sun and well-drained soil.
S. 'Herbstfreude' ('Autumn Joy') is a perennial with long-lasting large domed heads of rich pink that turn salmon-copper and rusty-red.
H & S: 60cm/2ft   z: 4[4–10]
S. spectabile (ice plant from eastern Asia) is an her-baceous perennial with pale green fleshy leaves that emerge in spring and grow slowly into a clump. Flowers at the end of summer, heavy flower-heads of cool dusty-pink often sprawling outwards. *S.s.* 'Brilliant' has flowers of stronger pink. Useful for the front of a border.
H & S: 30–45cm/12–18in   z: 4[4–10]

S. telephium 'Munstead Dark Red' is a perennial and has flat flowers, of sombre dusky-red, held on compact stems with darker green leaves.
H & S: 45–60cm/18–24in   z: 4[4–10]

SELINUM
(Umbelliferae)
S. tenuifolium (Himalayas) is a graceful cow-parsley-like perennial with finely cut ferny leaves and flat umbels of black-anthered white flowers in summer. Part shade; dislikes intense heat.
H: 90–150cm/36–60in   s: 60cm/24in
z: 4[4–8]

SENECIO
(Compositae)
S. 'Sunshine' (now correctly *Brachyglottis* 'Sunshine') is an evergreen shrub with grey felted leaves. Spring pruning and summer shaping encourages fresh leafy growth in place of bright yellow daisy flowers, which mar the plant's predominantly silver colour and compact habit. Flowers in early to midsummer. Good as a specimen, to frame corners of traditional borders, or massed in a group.
SMALL SHRUB H & S: 120cm/48in   z: 8[8–10]

SILENE
(Caryophyllaceae)   campion
S. uniflora 'Flore Pleno' forms a low perennial mat of grey-green leaves covered with white carnation-like flowers from mid- to late summer. Sun and well-drained soil.
H: 15cm/6in   s: 30cm/12in   z: 4[4–9]

SILYBUM
(Compositae)
S. marianum (milk thistle from Mediterranean regions) makes a rosette of dark glossy leaves, spined and lobed, with veins marked in white to give a marbled variegation. Branched stems of purple thistle-flowers appear in late summer and often self-seed in a sunny site. Overwinter seedlings in pots in cold climates.
H: 60–120cm/24–48in   s: 60cm/24in
ANNUAL/BIENNIAL

SISYRINCHIUM
(Iridaceae)
S. striatum (Andes) is a semi-evergreen perennial with grey iris-like leaves. Slender spikes of pale creamy-white star-shaped flowers appear in summer. Seeds prolifically once established. Sun and

well-drained humus-rich soil. *S.s.* 'Aunt May' has leaves boldly striped with creamy-yellow, is more tender and needs protection from intense sun.
H: 45–60cm/18–24in   s: 23–30cm/9–12in
z: 7[7–10]

SMILACINA
(Liliaceae/Convallariaceae)
S. racemosa (false Solomon's seal, false spikenard; from N. America) is a deciduous perennial woodlander. Arching stems bear pairs of pale veined leaves like those of Solomon's seal, with lemon-scented fluffy cream flower-plumes in spring. Part shade and deep rich soil.
H: 45–90cm/18–36in   s: 30–45cm/12–18in
z: 3[3–9]

SMYRNIUM
(Umbelliferae)
S. perfoliatum (southern Europe to Caucasus) has heart-shaped leaves clasping the stems and small heads of cow-parsley flowers in early summer. This short-lived perennial or biennial seeds freely once established. Allow to naturalize on the garden's edge in shrubberies or light woodland.
H & S: 45–60cm/18–24in   z: 5[5–9]

Smilacina racemosa

Smyrnium perfoliatum

SPARTINA

(Gramineae)   prairie cord grass
S. pectinata 'Aureomarginata' has graceful narrow arching leaves striped with yellow. Pendulous green flower-spikes are draped with purple stamens in season. Dry soil, to curb invasiveness of this rhizomatous perennial.
H: 1.8m/6ft   S: 0.9m/3ft   Z: 5[5–9]

SPHAERALCEA

(Malvaceae)   globe mallow
S. munroana (western N. America) has trailing stems bearing hairy lobed and cut leaves. Produces little mallow-like flowers in tones from red to apricot and pink all summer. Sun-loving and drought-tolerant deciduous sub-shrubs for poor well-drained soil.
H: 30–90cm/12–36in   S: 30–45cm/12–18in
Z: 8[8–10]

SPIRAEA

(Rosaceae)
Deciduous shrubs to mass in informal planting or for use as border plants between perennials. There are forms with spring, summer and late-summer flowers.

LEFT *Stipa gigantea*

S. 'Arguta' (bridal wreath, foam of May) carries white flowers all along its stems in spring.
MEDIUM SHRUB H & S: 1.8–2.4m/6–8ft   Z: 4[4–9]
S. thunbergii (China, Japan) has small narrow pale green leaves that turn yellow in autumn. White flower-clusters appear before leaves in spring.
MEDIUM SHRUB H: 1.5–1.8m/5–6ft
S: 1.8–2.4m/6–8ft   Z: 4[4–9]
S. veitchii (China) has long downy arching branches covered with dense flat corymbs of tiny white flowers in midsummer – a good foil to an arching shrub rose. Rich moist soil.
LARGE SHRUB H & S: 3m/10ft   Z: 6[6–9]

STACHYS

(Labiatae)
S. byzantina (lamb's ears from the Caucasus to Iran) is an evergreen perennial making attractive low clumps of felted silvery leaves. Woolly flower-spikes of mauvish-pink, borne by the type in summer, mar the smooth carpet effect and need trimming – unless seedlings are welcome. Opting for the sterile cultivar *S. b.* 'Silver Carpet' avoids these complications. Sun and well-drained soil.
H: 30–45cm/12–18in   S: 30cm/12in   Z: 4[4–10]
S. grandiflora (syn. *S. macrantha*; from the Caucasus) has distinctive green triangular leaves and deep purple lipped tubular flowers carried in

SOLANUM

(Solanaceae)   S. America
Semi-evergreen climbers for a sunny position.
S. crispum (Chilean potato tree) has slightly scented purple-blue potato-flowers with yellow centres from midsummer. *S. c.* 'Glasnevin' is a brighter blue and has a longer flowering season. Has a bushy scrambling habit: allow to clamber over stumps and sturdy shrubs or train on a wall.
CLIMBER H: 5–6m/15–20ft   Z: 8[8–10]
S. jasminoides 'Album' is more tender, but where it is suited bears an abundance of clustered bluish-white yellow-centred potato-flowers in summer and autumn. Allow to twine upwards or to tumble down a sunny bank.
CLIMBER H: 3–5m/10–15ft   Z: 9[9–10]

× SOLIDASTER

(Compositae)
× *S. luteus* has open heads of light canary-yellow daisy-flowers on wiry leafy stems in summer. Useful as a low-key border perennial.
H: 60–75cm/24–30in   S: 45–60cm/18–24in
Z: 4[4–10]

Symphytum × *uplandicum* 'Variegatum'

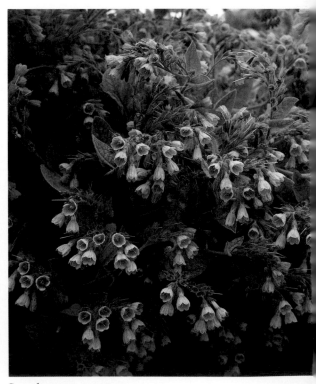

Symphytum caucasicum

whorls in early summer. Grow this perennial beside bare-stemmed shrub roses, perhaps selecting the pink or violet forms for harmonizing tones. Sun or part shade.
H: 30–60cm/12–24in   S: 30–45cm/12–18in
Z: 3[3–10]

STAUNTONIA
(Lardizabalaceae)
S. hexaphylla (north-eastern Asia) is a twining evergreen that bears exotically scented violet-tinged white flowers in spring. Grow over host trees and shrubs in a sunny sheltered spot.
CLIMBER H: 10m/30ft   S: 3m/10ft   Z: 8[8–10]

STEPHANANDRA
(Rosaceae)
S. tanakae (Japan) is a graceful deciduous shrub with arching red-brown stems and lobed leaves of a fresh green that show up well in shade or against dark evergreens. Autumn tints are muted orange tones. White star-shaped flowers are borne in summer.
MEDIUM SHRUB H & S: 1.5–2.1m/5–7ft
Z: 6[6–9]

STIPA
(Gramineae)   feather grass
S. gigantea (Spain) makes a dense perennial clump of grey-green almost evergreen foliage. In summer produces tall plumes of oat-like flower-heads, opening purple-tinged and becoming a shimmering tawny-yellow. Sun.
H: 90–180cm/36–72in   S: 60–90cm/24–36in
Z: 6[6–10]

SYMPHYTUM
(Boraginaceae)   comfrey
S. caucasicum (Caucasus) makes good coarse perennial ground cover in shade, but is invasive. Rough-textured greyish leaves turn green in summer. Loose sprays of forget-me-not blue tubular flowers glow in spring.
H & S: 60cm/24in   Z: 3[3–9]
S. × uplandicum 'Variegatum' is a handsome slow-growing perennial specimen plant with typical hairy borage-leaves, pale green margined with creamy-white. Pink-budded flowers open to pale violet-blue in late spring and early summer. Part shade and deep moisture-retentive soil.
H: 90cm/36in   S: 60cm/24in   Z: 4[4–9]

SYRINGA
(Oleaceae)   lilac
All the following small-leaved lilacs are useful in borders next to perennials or herbaceous plants.
S. meyeri 'Palibin' (Korean lilac) is deciduous and has lilac-pink flowers in early summer. Perfect for a small garden.
SMALL SHRUB H & S: 1.2m/4ft   Z: 5[5–9]
S. microphylla 'Superba' bears a flush of pretty scented rosy-pink flowers in early summer, and continues to flower intermittently until autumn. Leaves are small and deciduous.
SMALL SHRUB H & S: 1.2m/4ft   Z: 4[4–9]
S. × persica (Persian lilac from Iran to China) is deciduous and has a graceful habit. Abundant pale pink scented flowers appear in late spring. *S. × persica* 'Alba' is a white form.
MEDIUM SHRUB H: 1.8–2.4m/6–8ft   S: 1.8m/6ft
Z: 5[5–9]

TAGETES
(Compositae)   marigold
T. erecta (African marigold from Mexico) is grown for its glowing late-summer colour at the front of a border. Single or double flowers above deeply cut and scented glossy green leaves may be yellow, gold or orange: choose hybrids in the tone you prefer.
H: 60–90cm/24–36in   S: 30–45cm/12–18in
ANNUAL

TANACETUM
(Compositae)
T. haradjanii (Anatolia) is a superb evergreen sub-shrubby perennial carpeter, its little fern-like silvery leaves creeping to form a dense mat. Full sun and well-drained gritty soil.
H: 15cm/6in   S: 30–38cm/12–15in
Z: 8[8–10]

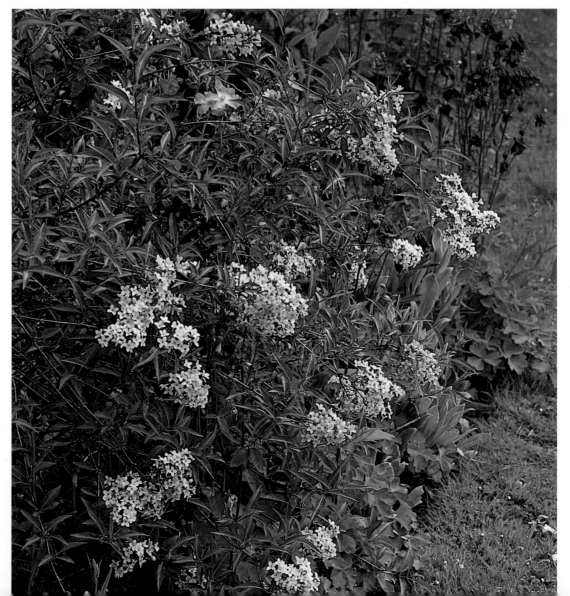

Syringa × persica

TEUCRIUM
(Labiatae) germander
T. chamaedrys (wall germander from Europe) is a shrubby perennial with neat dark green leaves and spikes of pale pink-lipped inconspicuous flowers in summer. Good for ground cover and hedging.
H: 25–30cm/10–12in   S: 30–45cm/12–18in
Z: 5[5–10]
T. fruticans (tree germander from southern Europe) has small simple aromatic leaves, green above and hairy below, giving this evergreen shrub an overall impression of silver-grey. Pale lavender flowers in summer continue into winter in a warm site. Grow in a mixed border or in dry soil against a wall.
SMALL SHRUB H: 120–150cm/48–60in
S: 90–120cm/36–48in   Z: 9[9–10]

THALICTRUM
(Ranunculaceae) meadow rue
Thalictrums are graceful perennials with elegant ferny leaves that make delicate masses of foliage to contrast with more sculptural neighbours in both formal borders and cottage-garden mixtures.
T. aquilegiifolium (Europe, northern Asia) has glaucous green leaves resembling those of aquilegia. Tall open panicles of fluffy flowers in early summer are usually mauve; *T. a.* 'Thundercloud' is deep purple. *T. a. album* is a most attractive white form with grey-green leaves.

H: 60–90cm/24–36in   S: 30–45cm/12–18in
Z: 5[5–10]
T. delavayi (western China) has daintier foliage, and the sprays of tiny pinkish-mauve flowers which appear in summer, are more open, with conspicuous yellow staments. *T. d.* 'Hewitt's Double' has long-lasting double mauve flowers without the touch of yellow.
H: 120–150cm/48–60in   S: 45–60cm/18–24in
Z: 5[5–10]
T. flavum glaucum (syn. *T. speciosissimum*; yellow meadow rue from Europe) has beautiful glaucous divided leaves and tall stems with fluffy yellow flowers in summer. From spring to autumn leaves associate well with other grey-green foliage. Stake firmly but unobtrusively.
H: 90–150cm/36–60in   S: 45–60cm/18–24in
Z: 6[6–10]
T. rochebrunnianum (Japan) creates an effect similar to that of *T. delavayi*. Its mass of elegant glaucous foliage is crowned by large loose panicles of pale purple flowers with light yellow stamens in summer.
H: 120–180cm/48–72in   S: 45–60cm/18–24in
Z: 5[5–10]

THYMUS
(Labiatae) thyme
Thymes boast an attractive combination of grey-green leaves and tiny pinky-mauve flowers in

summer. Plant creeping thymes where the foliage may be brushed or bruised to release the bonus of scent: in border edges and paving cracks, or carpeting lawns and seats. Sun and good drainage.
T. × citriodorus is an evergreen with forms offering coloured or variegated leaves as well as a lemon scent.
DWARF SHRUB H: 5–20cm/2–8in   S: 30cm/12in
Z: 4[4–10]

TIARELLA
(Saxifragaceae)
T. cordifolia (foam flower from N. America) makes attractive weed-suppressing perennial ground cover in shade between shrubs. The low evergreen mat of rich green lobed foliage is bronze-tinted in winter; creamy-white feathery spikes of flowers shimmer above the leaves in early summer.
H: 15–30cm/6–12in   S: 30–45cm/12–18in
Z: 3[3–9]

TOLMIEA
(Saxifragaceae)
T. menziesii (pig-a-back plant from western USA) is a perennial that is sometimes semi-evergreen. Produces an attractive mound of hairy maple-like mid-green leaves and spires of greenish or copper-tinted small flowers in early summer. Little plantlets form on old leaves and root easily to make new

ABOVE *Tiarella cordifolia*

RIGHT *Tricyrtis formosana*

Trachelospermum asiaticum

plants. Good for ground cover in shade or moderate sun. *T.m.* 'Taff's Gold; irregularly variegated with creamy-yellow, resembles dappled sunlight.
H: 15–30cm/6–12in   s: 30–38cm/12–15in
z: 8[8–10]

TRACHELOSPERMUM
(Apocynaceae)
These evergreen twining climbers have dark green glossy leaves that turn red and yellow in winter. Fragrant creamy-white jasmine-like flowers appear in summer. Tender: good for warm microclimates (or conservatory walls) in temperate zones.
T. asiaticum (Japan, Korea) is the hardier species with neat small leaves and a compact habit that will clothe a wall densely with foliage.
CLIMBER H: 5m/15ft   z: 8[8–10]
T. jasminoides (China) is vigorous, with longer glowing leaves and a more sprawling habit that may need some training into shape.
CLIMBER H: 6m/20ft   z: 9[9–10]

TRICYRTIS
(Liliaceae/Convallariaceae)   toad lily
Toad lilies have exotic flowers, like little upturned lilies, in late summer. Plant these perennials where the flower detail may be examined and enjoyed. Part shade and moist soil.

T. formosana (Taiwan) carries sprays of purple-speckled mauve flowers, with yellow throats, on branching stems clothed in glossy dark green leaves.
H: 60–90cm/24–36in   s: 45cm/18in   z: 5[5–9]
T. hirta (Japan) has upright unbranched stems and hairy leaves. Flowers are whitish, spotted with lilac, and greenish-white in the form *T.h. alba.*
H: 30–90cm/12–36in   s: 60cm/24in   z: 5[5–9]

TRILLIUM
(Liliaceae/Trilliaceae)   wake robin, wood lily
Woodland perennials that flower in spring, trilliums have leaves, sepals and petals in sets of three. Shade and acid rather moist loam. Good for borders.
T. grandiflorum (snow trillium, white wake robin; from eastern USA) has shining leaves with pronounced veins making a dome-shaped plant. Funnel-shaped pure white flowers have slightly reflexed petals.
H: 30–45cm/12–18in   s: 30cm/12in
z: 3[3–9]
T. sessile (toadshade from central USA) produces leaves marbled in grey-brown and deep green. Dark maroon stemless flowers are held upright.
H: 20–30cm/8–12in   s: 23–30cm/9–12in
z: 5[5–9]

TROLLIUS
(Ranunculaceae)   globe flower
Trollius make attractive clumps of dark green deeply cleft leaves all season, with shapely flowers in late spring and early summer. These herbaceous perennials prefer waterside sites, but also thrive in borders where soil is moisture-retentive.
T. × *cultorum* garden hybrids have big globe-shaped flowers resembling double buttercups. Colours include a range of yellows and oranges. *T.* 'Alabaster' is a delicate ivory-cream; *T.* 'Canary Bird' has clear pale yellow flowers.
H: 60–90cm/24–36in   s: 30–45cm/12–18in
z: 4[4–9]

TROPAEOLUM
(Tropaeolaceae)
T. peregrinum (canary creeper from Peru) is a vigorous short-lived deciduous perennial climber usually grown as an annual. Has light green lobed leaves and bright clear yellow flowers, with green spurs and fringed petals, in summer and autumn.
CLIMBER H: 4m/12ft   s: 0.9m/3ft   ANNUAL
T. speciosum (flame creeper, flame nasturtium, Scotch flame flower; from Chile) is a deciduous

perennial whose six-lobed leaves are as decorative as green flowers against a dark-leaved host. Small brilliant scarlet nasturtium-flowers are borne continuously in late summer. Cool acid soil.
CLIMBER H: 3–5m/10–15ft   s: 0.6–0.9m/2–3ft
z: 8[7–9] or grow as ANNUAL
T. tuberosum (Bolivia, Peru) is a more tender deciduous perennial climber, suitable for a sunny wall in temperate zones. The mass of slightly glaucous lobed leaves is lit up in late summer by spurred tubular flowers in tones of red and yellow, borne on red stems. *T.t.* 'Ken Aslet' is earlier flowering.
CLIMBER H: 3m/10ft   s: 0.9m/3ft   z: 9[8–10] or grow as ANNUAL

TULIPA
(Liliaceae)   tulip
A progression of different tulips provides flowers from mid-spring well into early summer. With their elegant sculptural flower-heads, the hybrids and cultivars of these bulbous perennials are for deploying in deliberately orchestrated colour schemes. Simpler forms of species tulips are for more informal groupings.

Tropaeolum tuberosum

Tulipa acuminata (syn. *T.* 'Cornuta')

Species

T. acuminata (syn. *T.* 'Cornuta'; horned tulip; actually an old cultivar), in late spring, bears red or yellow flowers whose slender petals each end in a twisting point.
H: 45–60cm/18–24in   s: 10–12cm/4–5in
z: 3[3–9]

T. clusiana (lady tulip from Iran to Kashmir) has narrow erect grey-green leaves. Slender white flowers flushed with crimson on the outside petals, creating a striped effect, appear in late spring.
H: 23–30cm/9–12in   s: 7.5cm/3in   z: 3[3–10]

T. kaufmanniana (waterlily tulip from Turkestan) bears short stems and slender creamy flowers that open wide into a star-shape in early spring. Petals are flushed red at the base and on the outside. Kaufmanniana hybrids are stockier plants, often with two-coloured flowers and attractively marked leaves.
H: 12–25cm/5–10in   s: 15cm/6in   z: 3[3–10]

T. sylvestris (Europe, western Asia, northern Africa) produces slender grey-green leaves and delicately fragrant pale yellow flowers in late spring. Plant in part shade under deciduous trees and shrubs.
H: 38cm/15in   s: 10cm/4in   z: 3[3–10]

Hybrids and garden cultivars

T. 'Golden Apeldoorn' (Darwin) has rich golden-yellow flowers with black bases in late spring.
H: 60cm/24in   s: 15cm/6in   z: 3[3–10]

T. praestans 'Fusilier' carries four to six brilliant orange-scarlet flowers on each stem in spring. Good on a rockery to complement dwarf azaleas.
H: 25cm/10in   s: 12cm/5in   z: 3[3–10]

T. 'Purissima' (Fosteriana) has large outer petals of milky-white to cream; grey-green leaves are attractive before flowers emerge in spring.
H: 50cm/20in   s: 15cm/6in   z: 3[3–10]

T. 'Queen of Night' (Single Late) produces large flowers of deep velvety-maroon in late spring.
H: 70cm/28in   s: 15–20cm/6–8in   z: 3[3–10]

T. 'White Triumphator' (Lily-flowered) is tall-stemmed, with beautiful creamy-white reflexing petals. Flowers over a long period in late spring and early summer.
H: 65cm/26in   s: 15cm/6in   z: 4[4–9]

VANCOUVERIA
(Berberidaceae)
V. hexandra (Vancouver fern from western USA) spreads in woodland conditions – even dry shade – to form perennial ground cover of dainty fresh green foliage, the lobed leaflets resembling little ivy leaves. Wiry stems hold loose panicles of little white flowers above the leaves in late spring or early summer.
H: 15–45cm/6–18in   s: 100cm/40in   z: 5[5–9]

VERATRUM
(Liliaceae/Melanthiaceae)   false hellebore
These perennials grow best in rich soil in part shade, or at least out of scorching sun.
V. nigrum (black false hellebore from Europe, Asia) is a remarkable foliage plant. Large leaves, folded and pleated like a fan, push through the soil in early spring to make arching mounds of fresh green (which slugs unfortunately find irresistible). Established plants produce imposing flower-stems, bearing brownish-maroon plumes composed of tiny stars, in late summer.
H: 90–150cm/36–60in   s: 60cm/24in   z: 3[3–9]
V. viride (Indian poke from N. America) has stems clothed in leaves. Dense panicles of starry light yellow-green flowers are borne in summer – a beautiful foil to the pleated foliage.
H: 1.2–2.1m/4–7ft   s: 0.6m/2ft   z: 3[3–9]

VERBASCUM
(Scrophulariaceae)   mullein
Verbascums have large basal leaves of leathery green or felted grey from which soar stout stems bearing flower-spikes in summer. Their architectural quality makes valuable accent plants in well-drained and sunny mixed borders.

V. chaixii (southern and central Europe) forms a handsome perennial clump of ground-covering grey leaves and slender spires tightly massed with small yellow flowers with purplish eyes.
H: 75–90cm/30–36in   s: 45cm/18in
z: 5[5–10]

V. olympicum (Turkey) is a biennial giant mullein with huge rosettes of felted silvery leaves and a woolly candelabra-stem bearing clustered yellow flowers. Sow seeds *in situ*, or select self-sown seedlings to flower the following year.
H: 1.8–2.4m/6–8ft   s: 0.9m/3ft   z: 6[6–10]

V. 'Vernale' is virtually a larger version of *V. chaixii* with branching flower-spikes of bright yellow flowers.
H: 1.8–2.4m/6–8ft   s: 0.9m/3ft   z: 6[6–10]

VERBENA
(Verbenaceae)
V. patagonica (syn. *V. bonariensis*; S. America) is an outstanding perennial grown as an annual in cool climates. Produces strange square stems and umbrella-like clusters of tiny lilac-purple scented flowers rising above neighbouring plants in mid-summer. Allow to seed between lower-growing silver- or grey-leaved plants such as lavender to make an airy network of scent and toning colour at midheight.
H: 90–150cm/36–60in   s: 60cm/24in
z: 9[8–10] or grow as ANNUAL

V. rigida (vervain from southern Brazil to Argentina) is often grown as an annual, but is perennial in mild areas. Leafy branching upright stems are topped by glowing violet-purple flower-heads in summer.
H: 30–60cm/12–24in   s: 30cm/12in
z: 9[8–10] or grow as ANNUAL

Garden hybrids
Half-hardy or tender perennial bedding verbenas are often grown as annuals from seed and may be propagated by cuttings for overwintering. Make cushions of attractive dark green deeply cut leaves, transformed in late summer into a mass of often vividly coloured flower-heads, many with a white eye. Good old cultivars propagated from cuttings, include: *V.* 'Hidcote Purple' (deep rich purple); *V.* 'Loveliness' (pink); *V.* 'Silver Anne' (soft pink and scented). *V.* 'Sissinghurst' is shrubby and unscented but a vivid eye-catching pink.
H & s: 50cm/20in   ANNUAL

VERONICA
(Scrophulariaceae) speedwell

Veronicas are easily grown perennials in sun.

V. austriaca teucrium (southern Europe, northern Asia) forms a loose mound of erect or sprawling stems and toothed oval leaves for the front of a border. Soft spikes of intensely blue flowers are borne in summer.

H & S: 30–45cm/12–18in   Z: 5[5–10]

V. gentianoides (gentian speedwell from Caucasus) is a front-of-border species forming a mat of glossy-leaved rosettes that produce spires of ice-blue flowers in early summer.

H: 30–60cm/12–24in   S: 45cm/18in   Z: 5[5–9]

V. virginica (correctly *Veronicastrum virginicum*; blackroot, bowman's root; from eastern N. America) is an elegant ethereal plant that contrasts well with neighbouring bushy shapes and domes. Erect stems bear horizontal whorls of slender mid-green leaves and terminate in delicate flower-spikes of palest blue, lilac-pink or white in late summer.

H: 120–180cm/48–72in   S: 45–60cm/18–24in
Z: 4[4–10]

VIBURNUM
(Caprifoliaceae)

This large genus has a vast number of excellent species and hybrids, offering interesting flowers, foliage, fruit and form in varying permutations.

V. × bodnantense is a deciduous shrub bearing clusters of sweetly scented pink tubular flowers on leafless branches from late autumn through most of winter. Young growth is bronze-flushed; autumn leaf colour is good too.

LARGE SHRUB H & S: 2.7–4m/9–12ft   Z: 7[7–10]

V. × burkwoodii (China) is one of the best hybrids, producing scented pink-tinted white flowers for many weeks from late spring. Undersides of the dark green leaves are grey-brown and felted. A good evergreen wall shrub in warmer zones: deciduous in zone 5. Hardy and unfussy about soil.

MEDIUM SHRUB H: 2.4m/8ft   S: 2.7–4m/9–12ft
Z: 5[5–9]

V. × carlcephalum is deciduous, with good autumn colour; large rounded heads of fragrant creamy-white flowers open from pink buds in late spring.

MEDIUM SHRUB H: 2.4m/8ft   S: 1.8–2.1m/6–7ft
Z: 5[5–9]

Verbena patagonica and *Anemone × hybrida*,
Nicotiana sylvestris, *Lablab purpureus* (syn.
Dolichos lablab) and *Macleaya*

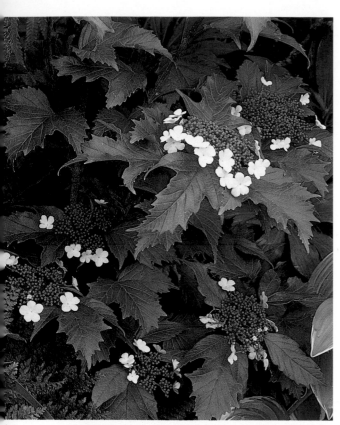

Viburnum sargentii 'Onondaga'

V. opulus 'Xanthocarpum' is deciduous and a garden form of the European guelder rose with clear golden-yellow fruits. Is good in early winter against glowing autumnal foliage.
LARGE SHRUB H & S: 4–5m/12–15ft
z: 3[3–8]
V. plicatum 'Mariesii' is deciduous and strongly architectural, with horizontally tabulated branches laden in early summer with white flowers as if with snow. Good for autumn colour.
MEDIUM SHRUB H: 2.4–3m/8–10ft
s: 3–5m/10–15ft z: 5[5–8]
V. sargentii 'Onondaga' is deciduous and has bronze-tinged young leaves that also colour well in autumn. 'Lacecap' panicles of white flowers opening from pink buds in early summer later turn into deep red berries.
MEDIUM SHRUB H & S: 1.5–2.1m/5–7ft
z: 3[3–9]
V. tinus 'Eve Price' forms a compact rounded evergreen bush with the dark healthy-looking leaves typical of laurustinus. Deep pink buds open to flat corymbs of pinkish-white flowers from late autumn to early spring, followed by blue-black fruits. Tolerates shade. Good for hedging.
SMALL SHRUB H & S: 90–120cm/36–48in
z: 8[8–10]

VINCA
(Apocynaceae) periwinkle
Vincas spread to make evergreen ground cover of handsome glossy dark green simple leaves, with flowers as a colour bonus. Although tolerant of shade and neglect, these perennials look and flower better if given an open site, rich feeding and an annual dead-heading and trim.
V. difformis (western regions of Mediterranean) carries beautiful pale blue flowers all through winter.
H: 30cm/12in s: 60cm/24in z: 9[9–10]
V. minor (lesser periwinkle from Europe) has rich blue, plum or white flowers, often double; those of *V.m. atropurpurea* are very deep purple, and of *V.m.* 'Azurea Flore Pleno' double and a clear blue. Flowers appear in spring and early summer, often continuing until the frosts.
H: 15cm/6in s: 60cm/24in z: 4[4–10]

VIOLA
(Violaceae) heart's ease violet, pansy
V. cornuta (horned violet, tufted pansy; from the Pyrenees) makes a spreading straggling perennial carpet of fresh green leaves topped with tall stems bearing lilac-blue flowers (white in *V.c. alba*) in summer. Dead-head or shear to encourage further flowering. Cool moist soil.

Viola riviana purpurea (formerly *V. labradorica purpurea*)

Viola cornuta

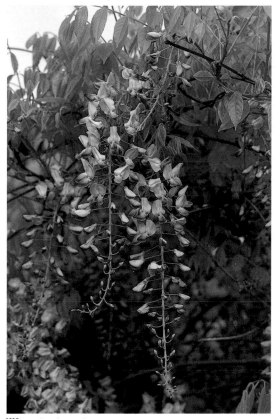

Wisteria sinensis

H: 15–30cm/6–12in   s: 30–38/12–15in
z: 6[6–10]
V. obliqua (syn. *V. cucullata*; from eastern N. America) is a rhizomatous perennial. Dainty violet-flowers in shades of lavender, with darker tracery on lower petals, appear in late spring and early summer.
H: 25–30cm/10–12in   s: 30cm/12in   z: 4[4–8]
V. riviniana purpurea (formerly known as *V. labradorica purpurea*) is a rhizomatous perennial with dark purple leaves and bright violet-blue flowers in early summer; leaves turn dark green by the end of summer. Grow next to grey foliage, beneath roses, or in formal bedding patterns: informality creeps in as plants self-seed readily.
H: 15cm/6in   s: 30–38cm/12–15in   z: 3[3–9]
Garden forms
Two old 'viola' or tufted pansy cultivars that flower from spring to autumn, and are evergreen perennials, are *V.* 'Irish Molly', with curiously attractive greenish-bronzy-yellow flowers, and *V.* 'Jackanapes', with rusty red-brown upper petals, bright yellow lower ones. Propagate from cuttings. *V.* 'Bowles' Black', another classic, seeds freely between plants in a blue border, making

deep shadow-tones. This short-lived perennial flowers from spring to autumn.
H: 10–15cm/4–6in   s: 23cm/9in   z: 6[6–8]

VITIS
(Vitaceae)   vine
Clinging vines can be trained to make shady curtains and canopies of leaves or can be allowed to ramp through suitably robust host trees and shrubs.
V. 'Brant' is deciduous and has leaves that turn a mysterious tone of deep bronzy-red in autumn, while the veins remain green. Bears red-purple grapes.
CLIMBER H: 6m/20ft   z: 6[6–10]
V. coignetiae (Japanese crimson glory vine) is a bold vigorous deciduous climber. Large broad heart-shaped leaves are smooth on top but felted with reddish hairs beneath. Autumn colour is dramatic, as the common name suggests.
CLIMBER H: to 27m/90ft   z: 5[5–10]
V. vinifera 'Purpurea' (claret vine, teinturier grape) is a cultivar of the common grapevine and deciduous. Purple-red leaves all summer darken to a deeper shade in autumn.
CLIMBER H: 6m/20ft   z: 6[6–10]

WISTERIA
(Leguminosae)
Nothing can be more beautiful than the early-summer festoons of long pendulous racemes of pea-flowers, in lilac, pale mauve or white, of these deciduous twiners, draping pergolas or arbours or growing into old trees.
W. floribunda 'Multijuga' (syn. *W.f.* 'Macrobotrys') is a form of Japanese wisteria with 90cm/36in long fragrant racemes, lilac tinged with violet-purple, and light green pinnate leaves.
CLIMBER H: to 9m/27ft   z: 5[5–10]
W. sinensis (China) is more vigorous, with scented 30cm/12in long racemes of mauve or deep lilac borne on leafless branches. *W.* 'Black Dragon' is a hybrid with dark purple double flowers.
CLIMBER H: to 18m/60ft   z: 5[5–10]

YUCCA
(Agavaceae)
Yuccas are statuesque and long-lived evergreens, useful all year for emphasis and for contrast with leafier neighbours. Magnificent flower-spikes add drama in late summer. Desert plants, they thrive in sun and poor sandy soil with minimal moisture.

Y. filamentosa (Adam's needle from south-eastern USA) is an evergreen shrub with fairly stiff glaucous green leaves edged with dangling filaments. *Y.f.* 'Variegata' has leaves striped and margined with cream, but may be less hardy. Carries erect panicles of creamy-white fragrant bell-flowers.
SMALL SHRUB H: 60–75cm/24–30in
s: 90–120cm/36–48in   z: 4[4–10]
Y. recurvifolia (south-eastern USA) has narrow arching evergreen leaves in huge elegant rosettes on a slow-growing trunk. Elegant flower-spikes of creamy-white.
SMALL SHRUB H & S: 90–180cm/3–6ft
z: 6[6–10]

ZANTEDESCHIA
(Araceae)
Z. aethiopica (arum lily, calla lily; from S. Africa) is a tuberous perennial usually grown in the hardy form *Z.a.* 'Crowborough', which tolerates drier border conditions (the species likes moisture, even waterlogging). Flowers in late spring; flaring pure white spathes surround a scented yellow spadix. Is also a handsome foliage plant, with broad spear-shaped glossy dark green leaves. Rich moist soil; protect from frost until established.
H: 90–120cm/36–48in   s: 30–60cm/12–24in
z: 9[8–10]

ZAUSCHNERIA
(Onagraceae)   California fuchsia
Z. californica latifolia (syn. *Epilobium canum latifolium*) is a sub-shrubby perennial making a mound of pale grey hairy leaves above which slender erect stems bear scarlet trumpet-flowers in late summer. Mass plants in a sunny site. Needs good drainage: useful for a rockery or raised bed.
H: 30–90cm/12–36in   s: 45cm/18in
z: 8[8–10]

ZINNIA
(Compositae)
Z. elegans garden cultivars, grown as half-hardy annuals, look best in bright sunlight but are often too startling to mass as front-of-border infills: showy flowers, in summer and early autumn, are often bi-coloured and sold as gaudy mixtures. Some are available in separate colours; others in harmonizing blends. Plants grow quickly from seed, and colours may be chosen for specific schemes when first flowers appear; or mixtures may be sown and undesirables rogued out.
H: 15–75cm/6–30in   s: 20–60cm/8–24in
ANNUAL

Zone chart

Approximate range of average annual minimum temperatures

1	below $-45°C/-50°F$
2	$-45°C/-50°F$ to $-40°C/-40°F$
3	$-40°C/-40°F$ to $-34°C/-30°F$
4	$-34°C/-30°F$ to $-29°C/-20°F$
5	$-29°C/-20°F$ to $-23°C/-10°F$
6	$-23°C/-10°F$ to $-18°C/0°F$
7	$-18°C/0°F$ to $-12°C/10°F$
8	$-12°C/10°F$ to $-7°C/20°F$
9	$-7°C/20°F$ to $-1°C/30°F$
10	$-1°C/30°F$ to $4°C/40°F$
11	above $4°C/40°F$

The hardiness zone ratings given for each plant – indicated in the text by the letter Z and the relevant number – suggest the approximate minimum temperature a plant will tolerate in winter. However, this can only be a rough guide. The hardiness of a plant depends on a great many factors, including the depth of its roots, its water content at the onset of frost, the duration of cold weather, the force of the wind, and the length and heat of the preceding summer.

ACKNOWLEDGMENTS

Author's Acknowledgments

I owe so much to Frances Lincoln and her team. I doubt if other authors are as fortunate. Frances herself is always involved from the very beginning, and so are Erica Hunningher, her editorial director, and Penny David, who has been my right hand in editing all my books. They are there to provide a total infrastructure, ready to criticize and cajole as well as to give inspiring advice at every moment of writing. Caroline Hillier and Louise Tucker have made the book beautiful using the pictures Anne Fraser, with untiring efforts to get the best and most appropriate for every page, has discovered. The photographers seem to become more and more skilful each year, capturing images of plants and gardens that are both inspirational and informative. Tony Lord has given invaluable help with the horticultural content, including identifying plants and their correct names. It would have been impossible to complete the book without all these links in the chain of production.

I would also like to thank the National Trust for allowing me and my husband John Malins to be guardians of Tintinhull. I could not have written about flower gardens without the inspiration which Tintinhull gives me and the lessons I learn from working here. But I could never have written this book at all without my husband John to help me. I am most grateful to him for all his patience.

Publishers' Acknowledgments

The publishers would like to thank the following people and organizations who kindly allowed us to photograph their gardens:
Richard Bisgrove; Beth Chatto; Helen Dillon; John and Mary Hawgood; John and Caryl Hubbard; Frank Lawley; The National Trust (Wallington); The National Trust for Scotland (Malleny House); Jim Reynolds.

The publishers are also grateful to the following individuals for their help in the production of this book:
Jo Chisholm, Serena Dilnot, Susan Kennedy and Sarah Mitchell for their editorial contribution; John Laing and Claudine Meissner for design work.

Horticultural Consultant   Tony Lord
Editor   Penny David
Art Editor   Louise Tucker
Picture Editor   Anne Fraser
Production   Adela Cory

Editorial Director   Erica Hunningher
Associate Art Directors   Tim Foster, Caroline Hillier
Production Director   Nicky Bowden

Photographic Acknowledgments

R=right   L=left   B=bottom   T=top   M=middle

Nic Barlow 52, 79
Deni Bown 168, 195
Boys Syndication/Jacqui Hurst 56
Geoff Dann 45 © FLL
John Fielding 159, 160, 166B, 170R, 172, 177R, 180R, 202T, 208T
Garden Picture Library: Stephen Robson 55; Marijke Heuff 173B, 187; David Russell 180L, 197
Giancarlo Gardin 94R, 104, 105
John Glover 194T
Nancy-Mary Goodall 69, 167T
Mick Hales 7, 54, 109, 110, 135B, 139, 140
Jerry Harpur 24 (designers: Oehme, van Sweden and Associates), 39B (designers: Oehme, van Sweden and Associates), 61L (designer: Arabella Lennox-Boyd), 73, 74 and 75 (designer: Edwina Von Gal), 91, 102, 103, 108, 128, 129, 133, 135T, 141T, 144L, 145, 146, 157, 207 (Peter Wooster)
Marijke Heuff 23 (Beeuwkes), 25, 26 (van Bennekom-Scheffer), 27 (Adriaanse), 32 (Greve), 37 (Great Dixter), 44T, 53T (Greve), 61BR (Goossenaert), 63L and 63BR (van Bennecom-Scheffer), 64L (Ton ter Linden), 64R and 65 (Greve), 67T (Ton ter Linden), 68 (Beth Chatto), 70B (Ton ter Linden), 83, 84L, 92, 94L, 98, 99, 100, 101, 117 (Greve), 123, 125, 137L (Greve), 142BR, 201R (Beth Chatto), 204R (Goossenaert)
Saxon Holt 30R, 33, 35B, 42, 43, 44B, 76R, 95, 96, 114, 121, 144R, 154, 155, 164L
Jacqui Hurst all © FLL: 34, 38, 49, 71T, 77 (reproduced by permission of The National Trust and the Knightshayes Garden Trust), 84R, 85, 87R
Michèle Lamontagne 147
Andrew Lawson 1, 2 (Powis), 10, 11, 12TL, TR and BL, 14, 15, 17, 18, 19, 20, 21T, 29, 30L, 31, 35T © FLL (Powis), 39T © FLL, 41, 47 (Marwood), 48, 58 © FLL (The Gables), 60 © FLL (Crathes), 62, 63TR, 66B (Kemerton), 67B (Kemerton), 112, 115, 118, 119 (Marwood), 120, 126 © FLL, 127 © FLL, 130, 131, 137R, 141B, 143 © FLL, 148, 149, 150, 151L, 158R, 161R, 163, 164R, 166T, 169B, 170L, 171, 173T, 174, 175, 176T, 179R, 181, 182, 183, 184, 185R, 188B, 189, 190, 191, 192, 193, 194B, 196L, 198, 199L, 201L, 202BL, 203, 204L, 205T, 206, 208BL and BR, 209
Georges Lévêque 36, 46, 80, 113T, 124, 134, 138, 152, 153
Tony Lord 51, 59, 61TR, 70T, 71B, 76L, 93B, 136R, 176B, 177L, 178, 188T
Marianne Majerus 13 © FLL, 53B, 88 © FLL, 93T, 113B © FLL, 122, 196R
S & O Mathews 111, 162, 165, 186L
Clive Nichols 57, 136L
Elizabeth Rodgers 97
Smith Collection 16, 158L, 161L, 169T, 177M, 179L, 185L and M, 186R, 199R, 200, 202BR
Rosemary Weller 9, 12BR
Elizabeth Whiting and Associates/Jerry Harpur 82 (Miriam Rothschild), 86, 89, 107
Peter Woloszynski 40
Steve Wooster all © FLL: 4, 21B (Beth Chatto), 28 (Beth Chatto), 50, 81, 87L, 116, 142T and BL, 151R, 205B (Beth Chatto)